Pragmatic Enterprise Architecture

Pragmatic Enterprise Architecture

Strategies to Transform Information Systems in the Era of Big Data

James V Luisi

ELSEVIER

AMSTERDAM • BOSTON • HEIDELBERG • LONDON
NEW YORK • OXFORD • PARIS • SAN DIEGO
SAN FRANCISCO • SINGAPORE • SYDNEY • TOKYO

Morgan Kaufmann is an imprint of Elsevier

Acquiring Editor: Steven Elliot
Editorial Project Manager: Kaitlin Herbert
Project Manager: Malathi Samayan
Designer: Matthew Limbert

Morgan Kaufmann is an imprint of Elsevier
225 Wyman Street, Waltham, MA 02451, USA

Library of Congress Cataloging-in-Publication Data
Luisi, James V.
  Pragmatic enterprise architecture: strategies to transform information systems in the era of big data/
James Luisi.
    pages cm
  Includes bibliographical references and index.
  ISBN 978-0-12-800205-6 (paperback)
1. Information storage and retrieval systems–Business. 2. Management information systems.
3. Business enterprises–Data processing. 4. Business enterprises–Information technology. 5. System
design. 6. Computer architecture. 7. Organizational change. I. Title.
  HF5548.2.L835 2014
  658.4'038011–dc23

                                                                                2014003632

British Library Cataloguing-in-Publication Data
A catalogue record for this book is available from the British Library

ISBN: 978-0-12-800205-6

Printed and bound in the United States of America
14   15   16   13   12   11   10 9 8 7 6 5 4 3 2 1

For information on all MK publications,
visit our website at www.mkp.com or www.elsevierdirect.com

Dedication

This book is dedicated to everyone interested in affecting beneficial change in large organizations by promoting constructive behavior and good outcomes; by clearly demonstrating modesty, interest in others, and a good work ethic; by showing a willingness to mentor and an eagerness to cooperate; and by making everyone eager to get back to work the next day.

Even more so, we salute the management style that contributes all good things to their teams and coworkers. It was Dwight Eisenhower who said, "Leadership consists of nothing but taking responsibility for everything that goes wrong and giving your subordinates credit for everything that goes well."

I have to give special thanks to Dr. Malcolm Chisholm for the invaluable advice he gave me for this book, and the repeated proofreading which rendered him more nights of unexpectedly deep and blissful slumber.

Most of all, I thank the loved ones in my life as that is what makes it all worthwhile, especially my wife and my daughter, whose life story or at least her first 30 years I will one day have to write.

Contents

Foreword

Enterprise Architecture (EA) units can be found in most major enterprises today. This is encouraging for a relatively new field which was only formally recognized in the 1980s. Indeed, there is now a widespread recognition that EA is a very important undertaking that can have far-reaching benefits for the organizations that embrace it.

This promise of EA, however, all too often clashes with a different reality when we examine just what EA units are doing in enterprises. Some of these units are simply "product pickers" who select technology for their IT departments. Perhaps that is a little harsh, since managing the technology portfolio is certainly necessary and arguably a core function of EA. But if technology selection is the only thing an EA unit does, then it is falling far short of the acknowledged goals of the overall discipline of EA.

In other organizations, EA units can be found that are theoretical "talking shops" staffed by individuals who constantly refer to EA theory and the inevitable arguments that exist within any body of theory that is still being worked out. Again, this judgment may be overly harsh, since theory is vital. Without theory, we do not know why we are doing, what we are doing, or what we should be doing. Yet, an almost total focus on theory blinds EA practitioners to the urgent and practical needs of the enterprises they work for. Such enterprises do not need EA to spend its time trying to optimize the way that EA works—they want EA to deliver something useful.

Another failing of EA units is an overly tight coupling with Information Technology (IT) organizations. Today, attitudes to IT in most large enterprises are increasingly negative. Fairly or unfairly, IT is seen as an expensive, self-referential, and incompetent cost center. Fifty plus years of organic growth in IT infrastructures have created increasingly unmanageable information management environments that now threaten the possibility of business change. This is one of the core problems that EA must solve, but it cannot be done if EA functions as subordinate to, or merely an extension of, IT. The IT mindset of needing to be told every requirement, of working in projects, and of being more aligned to the IT industry than the business of the enterprise in which IT finds itself, is fatal to EA. EA must engage with the business; in fact, it must break down the distinction between IT and the business. Regrettably, too many EA units cannot break out of the IT mindset.

It is against this background that Jim Luisi's *Pragmatic Enterprise Architecture* stands as a clear and comprehensive vision of how EA can be done and should be done.

Jim has taken his experience in EA and a variety of technical IT fields and synthesized an approach that can be implemented. A key concept that Jim has put forward is that EA is not a single discipline, but a constellation of many disciplines. It is fair to say that EA has traditionally been broken down into the four main areas of Information Architecture, Business Architecture, Technology Architecture, and Application Architecture. However, Jim goes far beyond this to show how EA is really many disciplines which EA brings together to make work in harmony, rather like the conductor of an orchestra.

Intuitively, this makes sense. After all, how can an individual who is an expert in data obfuscation fill the role of an expert in analyzing business capabilities? These architectural disciplines are also bound to come into being as overall information management advances, and disappear as old ways of doing things fall away. Thus, the role of an Enterprise Architect is to understand what disciplines need to be brought to bear on the enterprise, and to ensure that the disciplines relevant to an enterprise are staffed and functioning well.

Jim also points out the flaw in the opposite approach, whereby generalist enterprise architects try to address specific disciplines. In the first place, all generalists will carry with them a set of experience, which is likely to be concentrated in just a few areas. Second, the generalist may simply not recognize the depth of knowledge required for a particular discipline, perhaps even failing to recognize that such a discipline actually exists.

A further set of problems exist because technology and methodologies change over time. Long ago, when mainframes ruled in enterprises, data was thought of as an uninteresting by-product of automation. In those days, the automation of hitherto unautomated manual processes was the focus of IT. Today, automation is prevalent and packages for operational systems exist for an incredibly wide array of enterprise needs. By contrast, the role of data has become increasingly elevated to the point where today the value of data is almost universally recognized. Over this period, the ascent of data has been accompanied by new technologies, such as relational databases, and new methodologies such as data warehousing.

EA must therefore be careful to stay updated with the new architectural disciplines that are needed, and be prepared to de-prioritize disciplines that are declining in importance. It is therefore very important that Jim has included a number of sections on Big Data and its implications for EA. Already we see enterprises rushing into this area and willing to spend large sums on standing up technology. Yet without the understanding of the disciplines involved, there is likely to be a high failure rate, and anecdotes of this are already circulating. Jim's sections on Big Data are particularly welcome at this point in time, because they build on disciplines around data that are necessary to manage traditional relational data, but which again have often been poorly implemented in many enterprises.

Another major architectural challenge that many enterprises are struggling with today is complexity. Complexity is difficult to understand because it is very often the outcome of historical processes. As noted earlier, 50 years of organic growth have created complexity that is difficult to understand, let alone manage. Innumerable decisions made to get projects done in the short term have led to the gradual emergence of massive problems in the long term. This is outside the experience of many IT staff. Such professionals may have experienced working on many projects, all of which were deployed in time and met the requirements they were designed for. More likely, these professionals will have experienced many failed and suboptimal projects. Yet, even if a long series of projects has been successful as individual projects, they typically do not work well together for the enterprise. IT professionals fail to grasp how a set of "successful" projects can lead to a crisis of unmanageable complexity in an enterprise, leading to a situation that prevents business change and inhibits the adoption of new technology.

Again, Jim speaks to the issue of complexity. The role of EA in "doing the right thing" is emphasized throughout this book, and the architectural "big picture" is held up as a constant reference that informs the activities of all the varied different architectural disciplines.

Complexity is made more difficult to deal with today due to another outcome of another set of historical processes, by which enterprises have gradually lost the ability to abstract the business away from the technology. As Jim points out, long ago when processes were entirely manual, staff understood what the business was doing. Today, staff typically interact with automated systems; they understand how to work with these systems, but not necessarily the business goals the systems are trying to achieve. Further, staff cannot see how all the systems work together to make the overall enterprise work. Again, long ago, when everything was manual, staff could actually see how things were done and talk to the people who were doing them. Of all the challenges that Jim outlines, this one is the most worrying to me. Relatively few individuals now exist in enterprises who really can really think about the business independent of the technology that is supporting it. This problem seems to be getting worse as the years go by. One symptom is that when an application is replaced, the idiosyncrasies of the old system are perpetuated into the new system since nobody really understands why they are there, and are afraid to change them. Again, this is an issue that Jim tackles, but to find out more, you will have to read the book.

Malcolm Chisholm

Inside the Cover

When dealing with big challenges, success is elusive only until you bring the appropriate skills and personalities together.

J. Luisi

A lot of ideas expressed in this book, while not odd, are certainly new. As such, it may be appropriate to shift the conventional wisdom of what Enterprise Architecture means and what it should do to give us a better way to get where large organizations need to go.

As we shall see, the value of an idea can only be realized after it has been executed, and prior to that it is only an idea, whether or not a plan exists to achieve it. This book, therefore, explains this latest philosophy of what Enterprise Architecture is from a successful experiment in a large financial services company, one of the top 10 in size in the United States. The philosophy employed was evaluated by a reputable research company to be radically different than what has been seen previously, but most importantly, its success at meeting its business objectives was irrefutable.

While this book deals with most every important architecture concept, there is one nonarchitectural aspect that is best mentioned here that is also found in the book, *Good to Great: Why Some Companies Make the Leap*, by Jim Collins, which is the need for the right kind of like-minded individuals that can enable the successful implementation of any new strategy. The author, in his professional life, has spent endless hours identifying and recruiting personnel with the right attitude and skill set necessary to participate in the journey.

To borrow the analogy of the bus from Jim Collins, you need to get the right people on the bus and the wrong people off the bus before you decide where to take the bus. Specifically, the right people on the bus must have a sense of adventure, a good sense of humor, and more importantly, the people on the bus should want to be on the bus not because of where the bus is going as that can change, but instead each individual should want to be on the bus because of who else is on the bus.

Along this journey, the team had to overcome significant challenges from both business and IT, including radical budgetary swings and pressures, violent rip tides of internal politics, external interference from large vendors, and adversities from within. But once the right collection of individuals are assembled on the team, they automatically go out to accomplish what is best for their company, and the internal and external challenges become more like the weather for the bus to travel through.

Additional features of this journey included a sense of discovery as we learned new synergies among various architectural disciplines, as well as having attained a sense of accomplishment by making new ideas materialize. In the end, however, the journey itself is what everyone remembers most fondly, and the bonds of friendship that persist in its aftermath.

It is therefore no big surprise when Steve Jobs shared insights into his life explaining that his biggest reward was the experience of his personal journey. In kind, hopefully your journey through the pages of this book will be rewarding, as was the journey writing it.

Prologue

Whenever I learn something, I often wonder how I must have thought about things prior to knowing what I learned. I don't know if every reader ponders this, but if you do, try to drop me a note afterward to let me know the difference between your thoughts before and after reading this book.

To begin, I find that information has entropy in a manner similar to that of matter and energy in physics. As such, entropy in information is the randomness of information that occurs naturally. Information is random and becomes more random unless some force imposes order upon the information. Whether or not others realize the importance of doing so often determines whether we make advances in discovering new things. Prior to written language, the sciences moved at an awfully slow pace. Collecting information allows others to share it and to think about it more concretely, in a way, that is what this book is all about.

Few books have been written about enterprise architecture. This could be due to the fact that the few managers who are successful with it do not have sufficient time for the commitment necessary to write a book. As luck would have it, this author has had prior experience writing books and articles and, with a proclivity toward architecture, realized that various articles could be planned out over a number of years to help develop the framework of a useful book. That said, one thing for sure is that this author did not plan on having such an interesting story to write about when it finally came time to creating the book.

There are widely varying perspectives on what Enterprise Architecture is and what it should be, including where it should report into within large organizations, what the qualifications should be to run it, and what authority that individual should have without running the risk of further debilitating an already cumbersome IT organization. Further delaying delivery of software that business needs to either compete in the marketplace or survive the global winds of economic and regulatory change, or just being blamed for further delaying software delivery, is one of the fears that executives face.

This book will address reality by looking at the big picture that is reasonably common to a global company. Most conglomerates are global, and this includes various types of industries, such as financial, retail, manufacturing, energy, health care, or government, such as the U.S. government, which is a global conglomerate itself.

As we all know, some books move slowly, carefully developing and revealing their knowledge to the reader in minute detail, while others move at a rapid pace, thereby covering vast quantities of material within the confines of the front and rear cover. Since your time is valuable, this book is the latter. As such we attempt to provide a framework that encompasses the vast reaches of enterprise architecture, without belaboring the issue.

As for its usefulness, it is perhaps most like the film, "The Matrix," which is a relatively recent cultural reference where characters can download the ability to extend themselves into a new area or skill. After you read a chapter, you may not be able to fly a helicopter, but this book can get you going in a variety of architectural topics while preparing you with an ample supply of key concepts that are pertinent to the topic to allow someone with a moderate background in IT the ability to dive in and be effective in early conversations. As examples, if the topics were Big Data or Data Center Consolidation Life Cycle (DCCLC), after reading those sections the reader would be equipped to have an intelligent conversation about many of the issues.

Much of the story depicted in this book represents the experience from within a number of U.S. Fortune 50 financial conglomerates that will remain nameless, although the savvy individual would have no trouble deducing their probable identities. Most of these organizations employ an approach to IT that is commonly known as a federated model, where there is the concept of a federal government (corporate) that maintains responsibility for shared services in conjunction with a set of states (lines of business) that maintain responsibility for local services to rapidly meet the needs that are unique to the local business unit.

Within large organizations, there are always areas that most would agree should be centralized, such as the shared services associated with communications, procurement, and human resources, as well as some areas that have clear advantages to being decentralized back out to the lines of business, such as front office operations, distribution channel operations, back office operations, and operational business intelligence capabilities associated with specific areas that rely upon the in-depth knowledge of the business domain.

Similarly, there are also a collection of areas that must participate within the lines of business that must roll up to a counterpart at the corporate level, such as risk management, legal, compliance, audit, regulatory reporting, accounting, brand management, public relations, government relations, and customer relations.

As one will see, understanding the many parts of a large organization is essential for a potentially successful enterprise architecture practice. If this were not the case, then enterprise architecture should be renamed to "IT Architecture," or in a smaller scope, "Software Development Architecture," or in its smallest scope, "The Application and Technology Inventory Tracking Department."

The Main Characters

The main characters of this journey include a collection of individuals who are either on the IT or business side, as well as some that straddle both, such as the new hybrids of "technology savvy business people" and "business savvy IT people" that cross what is often that demilitarized zone that exists between pure business and pure IT.

Among them are characters within Enterprise Architecture for which proper names have not yet been established. We will identify these newly established characters as we address the need for architectural disciplines that must span the company horizontally across geographic locations and lines of business.

That said, there are also several characters that many of us are already familiar with, such as the Chief Information Officer (CIO), Chief Enterprise Architect (CEA), and the heads of Auditing, Legal, Legal Compliance, Regulatory Compliance, HR Compliance, and IT Compliance. A couple of recently emerging ones also include the Chief Data Officer (CDO), which has been created to confront the challenges such as navigating the approval process to source data from disparate lines of business, and the Chief Customer Officer (CCO), which has been established to focus on customer-related strategies, such as providing an overall better customer experience than does the competition.

It is also important to recognize the way that various stakeholders approach their roles.

As examples:

- CIOs tend to think and communicate in terms of expense areas providing automation services, application stacks that support business capabilities and lines of business, as well as strategic objectives and resource consumption relative to meeting those objectives,
- CEAs tend to think and communicate in terms of technology stacks and infrastructure, as well as application development team governance, standards, and data landscape complexity,
- CDOs tend to think and communicate in terms of business intelligence platforms and use cases, as well as data quality and master data management, and
- CCOs tend to think and communicate in terms of customer retention, emerging markets, designing the end-to-end customer experience, and understanding the cause of customer complaints and customer behaviors.

Culture

How these characters interact and how they relate to one another is largely a function of the approach of how management organizes reporting structures, but organizational culture is the dominant factor that determines whether and how an organization comes together to work toward greater effectiveness.

Perhaps the single most significant message that the CEA can convey to the executive management team is that enterprise architecture is actually the area that determines the epigenetics of the IT organization. As such, enterprise architecture is best positioned to make the IT organization responsive and efficient in reacting to the business direction of executive management and IT management.

This may appear at first to be a fine line to traverse, but let's explore the subject of epigenetics to better understand the distinction between the roles of the Chief Information Officer (CIO) and the Chief Enterprise Architect (CEA).

We will begin by making an unusual analogy, which is that the role of the CIO is more like the genes of an organism, and the CEA being more similar to epigenetics.

Epigenetics

Although many have not heard of epigenetics before, it is a cornerstone in science for understanding how designs are expressed for building living things. Unlike a single sheet of paper, called a blueprint, that can express how a house should be built, the way designs of living things are represented is somewhat more dynamic.

For a little background in the field of genetics, DNA carries the instructions for building proteins that are the key components of each living cell and body. Genes are long snippets or chunks of DNA that are the basic units of inheritance representing traits of living organisms that are passed on from parents to children. Genes determine how long a protein should be, how much to make, and when to make it. Genes also determine how to edit DNA strings to make different proteins. This is how the body can make about a million different proteins from merely 20,000 genes.

Just to complete our taxonomy, chromosomes are strands of DNA arranged in pairs wrapped around spherical proteins called histones. Each chromosome strand contains many genes. Humans, for example, have 46 chromosomes.

Genes provide all of the directions for how to build a body and the systems that keep that body healthy. In this sense, genes contain all of the commands for subordinate components to do everything that needs to be done to build and operate the body from an executive management perspective.

We know however that DNA alone does not determine the outcome for building an organism, any more than a general can control the outcome of a military operation by issuing commands to his commanders. The orders may be brilliant, but depending upon the preparedness of the troops, a variety of outcomes are always possible.

When it became obvious that DNA and their genes do not determine the outcome for building each cell of an organism, scientists had to look at more than just the genes. They eventually realized that while all of the genes were present on the DNA, it was the environment that determined which genes would be expressed and which genes would not.

Scientists learned that at the microscale each cell knew whether it should develop into a heart cell, brain cell, taste bud, or any other cell, while at a macroscale they learned that our environment determines what genes are expressed over our lifetime through a series of chemical mechanisms that influence gene expression as we grow up and age.

As a result, genes can be expressed to generate a healthy fully functioning individual or they can be expressed in some suboptimal way as a response to a variety of environmental factors such as stress or a lesser abundance of food or shelter.

Expectedly, when the environment is more conducive to a healthy way of life, genes are expressed differently, and in a better way than when the environment is unhealthy.

Similarly, an IT environment can be determined by the chance, which is what many organizations achieve as the outcome of their activities, or the IT environment itself can be influenced in a positive direction, ultimately improving the ability of the organization to express the commands of its executive management.

In that manner, enterprise architecture works behind the scenes to influence the greater environment of automation. As we will see in this book, over even a short period of time, this influence can help the organization be far more prepared to act effectively on commands from the CIO, and from the head of application development.

First, we will try to understand a little better how an influence over an organization can have such a profound effect.

Degrees of Civilization

Organizations express themselves in certain ways. As groups of individuals increase in size, a culture naturally develops from its individual members. For the most part, immediate families and extended families behave in certain ways. Similarly for the most part, small tribes, larger tribes, and collections of neighboring and perhaps related tribes also behave in certain ways. For example, a leader is usually chosen by each tribe.

Tribal culture can be rather sophisticated with many rules for getting along with other individuals and tribes. In tribal societies, sophisticated dispute resolution often evolves for trading pigs, cows, or women in an attempt to avoid escalating cycles of conflict. But in the end, it is quite different than the culture that results when compared to modern cultures that develop from there being the higher influence of a State. (*The World until Yesterday*, Jared Diamond, 2012, Penguin Group, ISBN 987-1-101-60600-1)

In short, the influence of a state is what makes it relatively safe for citizens within a society to deal with individuals whom they have never met and do not know. Strangers know that there are police, courts, and judges that exist as part of the state. Civilization as we know it is the product of a higher level influence upon our society.

This includes many quality of life advancements that are available within our society for reasons such as the fact that individuals can easily communicate and conduct commerce with others whom they have never met. In contrast, it is common in tribal societies to chase away or kill anyone not related to the tribe as a way to protect the resources and safety of the tribe.

In this book, we will see how a modest, effectively staffed, organized, and well-led enterprise architecture team can become a higher level influence across an organization. While they are not police, they so have a number of ways to influence the environment.

These include methods, such as:

- frameworks that act as accelerators to get the work that needs to be accomplished done with less effort,
- subject matter expertise to mentor IT staff across the organization at the moment that additional expertise is needed,
- standards that incorporate the interests of organizational stakeholders that otherwise could not monitor each and every application team across a large organization, and
- direction that has been thought through and approved by the CIO for making technology and application decisions.

In short, the role of the modern enterprise architecture organization is to develop the appropriate level of civilization across automation resources to ensure the preparedness of automation resources across the organization to rapidly act on the directions given by the CIO. Tribal methods must give way to a more advanced more cooperative and more intelligent way of reacting to the commands of executives.

In other words, scattering the bones of enterprise architects outside the offices of a tribal line of business or application team should no longer occur, except in only the most extreme circumstances.

Organizational Fitness

In simpler terms, enterprise architects become the fitness leaders of the organization to improve the health and effectiveness of the IT organization. Enterprise architecture shapes the automation personnel into a leaner more effective set of resources that have the right architectural disciplines at their disposal to get the job done. The role of enterprise architecture is to be prepared to meet the evolving needs of the IT organization, while significantly reducing the emergence of IT health-related issues and the overall cost of addressing those issues.

The role of enterprise architecture is surprisingly like that of a physical fitness leader. In fitness, the more difficult thing is to make the time and apply the effort to exercise and to eat properly. Exercising means work. Once one develops a culture that enjoys exercise, then it is not as difficult to get the motivation to exercise.

Eating properly means eating three meals a day and choosing the right things to eat. It may even mean eating more than before, but eating more healthy things to displace the urge and ability to choose unhealthy foods. The worse thing to do is to start skipping meals as a way to lose weight.

At first skipping meals seems to get results. The weight starts coming down and the waist begins to slim down; however, the true effects remain hidden for some time. Instead of improved health, the strategy of skipping meals leads to a cycle of poor health and damage to body structures and systems.

The hidden effects include:

■ decrease in bone density,
■ loss of muscle mass, and
■ damage to organs.

The ultimate logical conclusion of what enterprise architecture is can be best defined as the combination of three things.

They are that which creates the most appropriate:

■ environment across IT that will allow it to properly express the commands of executive management,
■ degree of civilization that facilitates rapid and effective cooperation across the organization, and
■ level of fitness that ensures the long-term health of the IT organization that will allow it the agility to meet the needs of the CIO.

It is the epigenetics of an organization that positively influences the health of the organization by fostering the appropriate enablers to express themselves by intelligently shifting the habits of the organization to exercise their minds and adopt healthy habits. Effective enterprise architecture staff members help automation personnel by mentoring them to get their work done in ways that have healthy long-term effects.

The alternative is an unresponsive bunch of tribes that have bad health habits.

Automation in Perspective

For the most part, while automation itself does not develop the strategies and business environment that make a company more successful as a business, when automation is inefficient and/or ineffective, it can certainly drag a company down. A healthy IT organization is even more important in highly regulated industries where new demands may be placed on IT to deliver information to regulators and/or calculate and adhere to new capital requirements from across a large number of countries and a much larger number of automation systems.

Toward that end, this book will show one way in which enterprise architecture can shape the development of automation services going forward such that it can deliver services and solutions at an entirely new level of quality and efficiency.

The key is that automation resources have the appropriate level of health that they can deliver, and then it sometimes helps if they actually chose to deliver.

Shortcuts

Many companies are simply reducing IT budgets and choosing to outsource their entire set of automation delivery capabilities; however, simply reducing the food supply to an organism or outsourcing the feeding of an organism will not facilitate its development into a healthy and responsive body. In fact, it only increases that organism's chances of expressing even less desirable traits and even failing.

Too often in today's economic environment, the board of directors of large public companies are selecting executive management who cut costs in automation that like the strategy of skipping meals, leaves the organization less healthy and less responsive. All too often the techniques used create the impression that the goal for many of these individuals in leadership roles is to simply cash out, whether that is the intent or not.

It comes down to the arrangements that the board of directors make with their executive management team. In the vast world of unintended consequences, it always comes down to the issue of always being wary of what one wishes for.

As an example, when one sees the number of large organizations that are borrowing money at low interest rates simply to have the organization buy back its own stock, one has to wonder what the business objective is.

While it is perfectly fine to buy back one's own stock out of profits, unless management is planning to take the firm private or defend it against a hostile takeover, borrowing to buy back one's stock does not enhance market share, improve efficiency, increase productivity, nor reduce its debt.

The motivation for leadership to borrow money to drive up the price of the stock is most likely to drive up the value of stock and stock options. Once this is accomplished, the company will naturally roll over its financing at low rates until such time as interest rates increase. Higher interest rates are generally a good deterrent for this kind of situation arising.

When interest rates eventually increase, which they will, the organization will struggle to survive. In the meantime, the previous leadership team will in all likelihood will have already cashed out, leaving new leadership and shareholders with the prospect of having to issue more stock and/or sell off parts of the company.

The flip side of this of course is that there are other insightful leadership teams that recognize the business opportunities created by poorly managed organizations. They recognize opportunities for positioning themselves to buy poorly managed organizations at bargain prices and for expanding their market share when less effectively managed companies are driven into financial difficulty.

Outsourcing is a common shortcut. Although outsourcing can be properly implemented as part of an intelligent business strategy, it is often the result of management not knowing what to do and having the desire to avoid doing a lot of work and assuming a great deal of risk while doing that work even if it is probably the right course of action.

In the end, outsourcing is not a substitute for creating an environment across IT that will allow it to better express the commands of executive management, it will not raise the degree of civilization that will facilitate rapid and effective cooperation across the organization, nor will it improve the level of fitness that can help ensure the long-term health of the IT organization that will allow it the agility to meet the needs of the CIO.

The problem is often so difficult that often the company that was outsourced to then outsources the automation to another company.

Rise and Fall of Organizations

It is not easy to retain a company's greatness. Just look at the list of the top companies in the Fortune 500 every 10 years over the past century. However, as numerous organizations decline, others rise. The issue becomes understanding the factors that contribute to making companies rise. (*Good to Great*, Jim Collins, 2001, Harper Business, ISBN 978-0066620992)

It comes down to good management and creating a culture that is conducive to being a strong competitor, and then building that into the culture so that it survives the executive management team that established it.

How does a good idea take hold?

The ability to spread good ideas and practices to other areas of an organization determines the effectiveness of a company in the marketplace. Good ideas and practices can emerge within any department where talent is able to thrive, such as enterprise architecture, solution architecture, a particular application development team, or a CTO organization over potentially prolonged periods of time.

The ability to make good things persist across an organization has much to do with the incentives to identify and champion good ideas. On the other hand, it is frequently staggering how many times individuals and teams have come together and developed great ideas, concepts, and work, only to have them disappear into the randomness of information.

Part of our mission here is to find ways to institutionalize the right kind of environment, the necessary degree of civilization, and the habits that retain a healthy level of fitness. Limiting oneself to eight weeks of fitness will not achieve anything worthwhile.

How to Read This Book

To a large extent, his book was meant to be read sequentially due to the way it introduces and builds upon concepts. To a large extent, this book is intended to depict the scope of enterprise architecture and as such, many sections are quite small, sometimes just a paragraph to lend a sense of the topic. For example, the section on artificial intelligence is only a page, whereas the previous book I wrote is only about the subject of artificial intelligence. Likewise, every section in this book can be an entire book on its own and I only expand into several pages when it is critical to do so. You will also find that many sections can be viewed as subsections of prior sections. Please don't let that disturb you.

For the most part, it is the industry understanding of the many topics of this book and how they relate to one another that this book is addressing. The scope of enterprise architecture I would assert has been previously misrepresented.

If you are an architect and have a specific near term need, then jumping to that chapter is a good idea. That said, it is best to come back and read up to those areas sequentially when you have the time.

One additional point worth pointing out is that this book is about enterprise architecture in the era of Big Data and quantum computing. While we will discuss these two topics more than most, they are individually large topics each worthy of their own book.

Part I

Introduction

1.1 General Background

Regardless of the type of architecture, architecture itself is an organized accumulation of knowledge within a particular domain. While we generally conceive of its representation as a set of diagrams, containing specific notations and taxonomies of symbols and glossary terms, an architecture may actually be represented using anything that can be arranged in a pattern to record information.

The earliest forms of architecture relate to architecting buildings, monuments, military disciplines, organized religion, music, storytelling, and various other forms within the arts. These early forms of architecture of course predate computer-related architectures by thousands of years. That said, it is worth noting that there are a number of common elements among architectures irrespective of their relative age, such as forms of standardization, reusable structures, the accumulation of knowledge, and providing a context for understanding something.

Needless to say, anyone can be an architect in a topic in which they have a deep understanding and appreciation of. While one obvious difference among architects is the amount and variety of pertinent experience, the less obvious difference is the degree to which an architect recognizes the potential forms of standardization, reusable structures, accumulation of knowledge, relationships among the components, and use of architecture as an accelerator to more rapidly understand the context and scope of a particular topic or to rapidly convey it to another.

Architectures as a result must be easy to understand. This should not be misconstrued to mean that architectures must be simple. In fact, an architecture that communicates a vast amount of knowledge may be quite intricate and detailed so that it can successful at conveying a large accumulation of knowledge, the context of that knowledge, and key interrelationships among that knowledge. That said, the notation, taxonomy, symbology, and glossary should be easy to grasp so that the wealth of knowledge contained therein can be rapidly assimilated in layers that begin at a high level.

1.1.1 How Did We Get Here

If asked how many senses we have as a human, many of us would still say five, and we would be able to cite the five senses listed by Aristotle (e.g., sight, hearing, smell, taste, and touch). Later, if we were paying attention of course, we would learn that there are at least nine.

These would include:

- thermoception—the sense of heat or absence of heat against the organ named skin,
- equilibrioception—the sense of balance as determined by the inner ear,
- nociception—the sense of pain from various locations in the body equipped with pain receptors, and
- proprioception—the sense that tells us where our body parts are without being able to see or feel them with our hands.

Some neurologists also include the sense of hunger and thirst, and then some people can detect electric fields, while others can detect changes in barometric pressure in their sinuses detecting weather fronts, and so on.

The basic point, however, is that we get a sense of many more things as we experience life, and although we may share many of the same senses, what senses we are conscious of and what each of us learn will differ depending upon the particular journey we travel.

While still a teenager, in the 1970s, I was given a tour of the Loeb Rhoades & Company offices in downtown Manhattan, which was one of the last big brokerage firms that still operated without automation. Upon exiting the elevator I was escorted into a large smoke-filled room of desks by my girlfriend's dad, who incidentally smokes cigars—they still allowed smoking indoors within offices at that time, arranged in rows and columns without any partitions, where people answered classic rotary telephones to accept telephone orders from customers. There was no e-mail or texting, no Facebook, and no Twitter.

Orders were handwritten on paper tickets that had sheets of carbon paper inserted between them so that there would be copies on individual pages, which were manually collected from desktop baskets by a clerk and taken to the next large room for collation and distribution where they were written into journals before being batched and bundled together for delivery to the floor of the exchange.

A decade later upon graduating from CUNY Brooklyn College and getting a job on Wall Street, I found users who, instead of writing on pads with carbon paper, typed on bulky green monitors that provided access into an early version of CICS applications on IBM mainframes. By this time, when business users explained the business, it was now expressed in terms of what information was being entered into fields on the display screen that scrolled up and down and across using arrow keys, followed by pressing the enter key. When you asked them what happened after they press the enter key, they simply tell you that they do the next one.

Other than the few old-timers that were nearing retirement, business users had little awareness of what happened after they entered data, other than the reports that they could run on a dot matrix printer. Recalling these things makes me feel old. However, I am encouraged by the fact that my doctor tells me that I am amazing healthy, and that I at least have a few good hours left in me.

What was important to me back at the time was the realization that I had witnessed a rare glimpse into history, where a decade earlier I had viewed the last business users that manually processed the business as a routine part of their day-to-day activities. If only I had known at that time, I would have hurriedly interviewed them, posed for group pictures, and chronicled their activities among the flow of paper and ledger entries.

Another decade later, the growth of midrange computers caused data to spread out of the master files of IBM mainframes into minicomputers of various brands, shapes, sizes, and colors, significantly expanding the computing landscape and its associated data footprint, data designs, and internal representations.

Shortly after that bulky personal computers began emerging under or on top of desks, but luckily their limited disk space capacity relegated them to mostly composing correspondence. This however was to turn into a story something like "The Trojan Horse" as disk capacity grew to house countless business files and databases redundantly and in many ways.

Complexity was on the rise with business users now originating data on mainframes and across a myriad of midrange computers to support their need for information. Similar to data, business rules were being buried in multiple applications across the midrange computer landscape. Soon business users quietly began developing their own shadow IT organizations using desktop tools such as Lotus Notes, MS Access, and Microsoft Excel to manage data that made them more productive.

Increasingly, the number of disparate computer platforms, databases, data files, data formats, data type codes, data aging, and data quality issues launched automation complexity through the roof. Thousands of software products, technologies, and tools poured into businesses and thousands of applications were developed, purchased, and modified.

Another decade passed and the "Y2K scare" did not cause the end of the world. Instead, laptops rapidly replaced bulky personal computers under and over the desk. The last of the business old-timers were gone and production data spread out across millions of Lotus Notes, MS Access, and Microsoft Excel applications on Windows servers and laptops. The shadow IT organization within the business had no source code control, no testing procedures, often no backups, and operated away from production equipment without disaster recovery protections. These were exciting times.

Another decade later, we arrive to the present. Laptops are being replaced by virtual thin client desktop architectures, and the use of smartphones and smart tablets have appeared everywhere and are being connected to the network. Smart eyeglass wear has emerged to become the highly mobile eyes and ears of the Internet traveling everywhere we go, hearing what we hear, seeing everything we see, and detecting everything that catches the movement of our eye, a far cry from the world of carbon paper in less than half a lifetime, with no sign of it slowing down anytime soon.

There is software around us in our daily lives, including in our:

- cars,
- cable boxes,
- telephones,
- watches, and
- CD-DVD players.

The number of automation products is amazing. To begin, there are over 50 database management systems, 40 accounting products, 30 Web browsers, and 35 word processing products.

There are thousands of software products for mainframes, midrange, personal computers, smartphones, and tablets across a variety of areas of automation, such as:

- data center operations
- production support
- job scheduling
- system administration
- utilities
- security
- networks
- operating systems
- workflow
- content management
- collaboration
- data management
- metadata management
- software development
- software testing
- software deployment
- business applications

- publishing
- reporting
- desktop tools

With all of this going on around us, one of the roles of an enterprise architect is to develop strategies that keep all of this from getting more complex than it has to be.

1.1.2 UNDERSTANDING BUSINESS

While it may seem obvious that a good understanding of the business is essential for the success of enterprise architecture (EA), all too often EA retreats into a self-referential technical shell. In some cases, this leads to EA actively avoiding the business. Many problems flow from this attitude, including the inability for EA to properly influence the enterprise. After all, business people are unlikely to listen to an organizational unit they never interact with, and whose value they are unsure of. Even the concept of the divide between IT and the business is hurtful to EA's mission. If anyone thinks this divide truly corresponds to reality, then since EA is not part of the business, it must be part of IT. IT is generally poorly thought of by business people. It is seen as populated by individuals who are more oriented to the IT industry than the enterprise they work for, and who ultimately have less of a stake in the success of the enterprise than the business has. Clearly, EA will be diminished if the business thinks of it in the same way as it thinks of IT.

To properly gain an understanding about business, the best approach is for EA to first gain an understanding of business people. Generally speaking, a business-minded person has a clear focus, which involves weighing the numerous considerations to increase profitability, survivability, and market dominance (or to meet other business goals if the enterprise is a nonprofit). A business-minded person eagerly overcomes obstacles to achieve their goals. They are driven to learn what they need to know to succeed, who they need to succeed, and they view capital, manpower, and automation as tools for achieving each milestone on the path toward meeting their goals. Without business-minded people, the enterprise will fail.

If an organization places an obstacle in the path of a business-minded person, the business-minded person will either overcome the obstacle or leave for an environment that presents fewer such obstacles. A business-minded person sees their success as tied to the achievement of the goals they have set.

Unlike individuals in IT, there are usually readily identifiable metrics that can measure the productivity of individuals in business. In for-profit enterprises, the business-minded individual is primarily driven by the profit or loss on bottom line after accrued expenses, liabilities, capital outlays, and exposures to risk. It is also our experience that most business-minded individuals do not concern themselves with compliance and regulatory issues unless it they are to be held personally responsible in some real and meaningful way.

1.1.2.1 Direction of the Business

Strange as it may sound, IT may be engaged on initiatives and projects that may not support the direction that the business desires to go. This situation is all too common in large organizations, where few individuals understand what the business direction is for the enterprise as a whole, or for any individual line of business. Yet, it all begins with the business strategy as the most important element that an enterprise architect should grasp before making recommendations that may change direction or divert resources to any initiative.

The role of EA, first and foremost, is to develop various frameworks for automation that align business vision and strategy with IT delivery.

1.1.2.2 Pain Points

While supporting business direction is the highest priority, a close second is remediating business pain points. The important thing to recognize is that there are hundreds if not thousands of business pain points that will be present in any sizable company.

As such, finding pain points is not a difficult task; however, identifying the more important ones takes a good deal of effort, albeit effort that is critical to ensure that resources are not squandered on pain points less valuable to the business, leaving the ones that would be the most valuable for profitability undiscovered.

Business has no problem understanding the notion that all pain points cannot be remediated, and that all points will never be remediated. Like pet projects, individuals will always have their favorite pain points that they want remediated. Once pain points and pet projects are inventoried, along with their projected cost, schedule, personnel resources, ROI and business benefit, and associated business sponsor, then they may be evaluated and prioritized among competing pain points and pet projects for anyone to openly view. Giving the potential list the light of day is the best way to get the less beneficial projects withdrawn and quickly forgotten about.

Companies that shift to such approaches including complete transparency often experience significant decreases in the number of pain point projects, pet projects, change requests, and new automation requests, leaving more resources available for the activities that optimally enhance business profitability.

1.1.2.3 Business Problems Common to Large Organizations

A *sailboat* surges forward more rapidly, the better the wind fills its sails. In any race, a subtle adjustment of a rope and/or the rudder simply cannot be made by committee.

Whether it is to meet competitive pressures or simply a desire to control one's own destiny, the motivation to make decisions as locally as possible will always be necessary. At the same time, in a place far away from the front lines of the business, centralized areas will yearn to control many of the same decisions to orchestrate an overall strategy.

That said, both sides are right, and both sides are wrong; however, once the appropriate principles have been identified, the answer is simple.

Big companies can grow through a variety of methods. Depending upon their available capital, they may expand their business internally by establishing additional branch offices, sales staff, third-party distribution channels, and products. Depending upon legal restrictions, a company may expand by leveraging the capital and energy of others by franchising, through arrangements such as a license, joint venture, partnership, dealership, and distributorship. The most common method of expansion used by the biggest companies is merger and acquisition, and rapidly emerging is expansion by distributing products and services using the marketplace of the future, the Internet.

The large public sector or other not-for-profit enterprises grow through expansion of the scope of their mission or mandate. Consolidation, including mergers of enterprises, can happen here too, and the emergence of the Internet is also a force for expansion.

The most egregious architectural challenges faced by large enterprises stem from business and IT expansion from mergers and acquisitions, and the complexities that ensue such as developing a massive patchwork of Internet applications that offer thousands of products and services globally. Some conglomerates resolve their architectural challenges by investing in the elimination of complexity that resulted from their most recent acquisition by rapidly consolidating their business and processing into either the previously existing or acquired set of business and IT operations (or combination thereof), hence retiring the acquired business and IT operations.

Some conglomerates cannot choose to combine their acquisitions into their existing operations or cannot combine their acquisitions into the existing operations because they do not have a comparable business and IT operation to consolidate them into.

The list of business problems most common to large companies is still much longer, and of these, there are a few that reoccur frequently such that they should be seriously considered as a means to significantly reduce operating cost and enhance business agility.

Some of the less obvious problems that remain hidden within the organization until expressly searched for include the emergence of shadow IT organizations, inconsistent processes and procedures, a lack of frameworks, and the lack or inability to identify and capture reliable metrics.

Some of the more obvious problems that reveal themselves over and over again include the challenges of integrating systems because of the fact that there is such a poor understanding of the data landscape within ones' own automation systems, while poorly understood differences in functional capabilities between ones' own and acquired automation systems provide another source of difficulty in integrating automation systems.

1.1.2.4   Shadow IT Organizations

One problem common to large organizations is the so-called Shadow IT Environment. It is a serious problem for the entire enterprise. Shadow IT environments are information processing environments that have been developed from within business departments without involvement or guidance from IT. These environments often utilize desktop tools, such as Microsoft Excel, Microsoft Access, E-mail, instant messaging, file formats, and anything else the business can use without getting IT involved.

The occasional use of technology by business is one thing, but once motivated to avoid IT to meet their needs, business staff can go further and faster than most any IT department. They can organize the technology they are working with to capture Production data and mold it to become increasingly competitive. In doing so, they begin to create a "Shadow IT Organization," by hiring dedicated resources that deal with their automation needs directly—either to administer them or even to develop small solutions with them. This trend can be pushed even further until something resembling a full-blown IT organization existing within business departments, but are entirely independent of enterprise IT, their standards, and protection. Naturally, in this model, EA is also excluded by the business as EA would certainly have to report the situation to IT management.

Environments with enterprise IT and EA involvement incorporate many disciplines that Shadow IT lacks. A small list gives some idea of the scope of what is missing, such as standards that pertain to application architecture, information architecture, data in motion architecture (e.g., ETL, ESB), directory services architecture, job scheduling architecture, infrastructure architecture, source code control, data management, testing levels, management approvals, production backups, data security, production controls, system access controls, controlled backups, disaster recovery, business continuity planning, application portfolio management, and production support, to name some. Very rarely can one find these present in a Shadow IT Organization.

A Shadow IT Environment deliberately avoids the skills and disciplines provided by IT, as these add additional costs and delays. Often the business doesn't understand why standards and procedures are necessary for something that they could simply create themselves. In fact, many IT resources don't understand why standards and procedures are necessary either. For these characters in our play, their focus is on meeting ad hoc business needs in a few days or weeks, as opposed to months or years. At first this is easy, but eventually a Shadow IT Organization will find itself in difficult situation.

Problems include:

- As time passes, technology changes and the Shadow IT Environment personnel find that it uses tools in a way that prevents them from being upgraded. They have to retain old versions, or obsolete technologies just to keep the environment functioning.
- Tools and techniques are selected in isolation for each business need. As the Shadow IT Environment grows, so does the complexity of it, and so does the need for resources to administer it. Eventually, no further resources can be allocated for continued growth.
- Solutions in the Shadow IT Environments are heavily connected to particular contributors. The lack of maturity in the development of these solutions means that individual contributors are essentially part of these solutions. If the individual contributors leave, the solution becomes unmaintainable. Strangely, the individual contributors are often praised for their hard work and ingenuity, rather than recognized as creating risks, which can vary. On the low end, a developer may simply act as lone developer that inadvertently makes the business dependent upon the individual developer. On the high end, a developer may plan to coerce the enterprise by placing "time bombs" in an application, whereby a computer program that has been written so that it will stop functioning after a predetermined date has been reached. If the developer no longer works at the enterprise when this happens, he or she will likely be recalled by the enterprise to fix the problem. Does this really happen? Yes, and unfortunately we can write an entire book on just this topic.

1.1.2.5   The Benefits, Costs, and Risks of Shadow IT

Shadow IT organizations emerge when the enterprise IT organization fails to support business at the pace required by the business. Initially, Shadow IT organizations meet pent-up demand within the business and appear to save the business significant time and money (e.g., to get much needed reports to facilitate business decision making). Although this may be the situation initially, a Shadow IT organization can rapidly grow to represent a significant waste of budget and resources.

The notion that Shadow IT organizations save money stems from the fact that the business can achieve somewhat instant gratification by creating their own mini IT departments. In contrast, the costs of Shadow IT organizations are high, but typically only appear later in time. These costs often come from the creation of a staggering degree of redundancy of reports, applications, and duplication of development personnel who are redundant with the IT organization as well as redundant across all other Shadow IT organizations across the business. Shadow IT also creates a staggering amount of data duplication, as well as a myriad of data quality issues. To be fair, IT application development teams are not blameless in this respect either.

Closely related to data duplication is another significant risk—the origination of data outside any true, IT-administered production environment. Sometimes these data many never find its way into a true production environment and hence are never available to any of the other appropriate stakeholders across the company. In other cases, it does get into production environments, but no one can easily identify where it originated from and when.

Many additional risks exist in Shadow IT and stem from the lack of IT standards and architectures. Some of these risks have immediate cost impact, while others many not be manifested in terms of unnecessary cost for years. Such risks include the application complexity, data landscape complexity, not testing, not having source code control, not being compliant with regulatory agencies or legislation, not having the ability to properly restore an application or database from a backup, and not submitting a job on time because it was run manually and not under the control of a job scheduler.

There are ways to prevent Shadow IT organizations from emerging and growing, but the best way is to provide a clear incentive to the business to get their needs met in a manner that is better, cheaper, and easier than creating a Shadow IT organization. We will discuss this further in the section that addresses the new philosophy of enterprise architecture.

In the end, what the enterprise must do is to get control of the IT organization to make it responsive to the needs of the business. This is a key role for the modern EA practice, as is the next challenge of inconsistent processes, which occur in business departments as well as IT.

1.1.2.6 Nonstandard Processes

Another business problem common to large organizations is that of nonstandard or inconsistent processes, which can occur in any department across the company, including among supporting vendors and service providers, and representatives of your company. This includes external distribution channels, outsourced service providers, remote call centers, external data center hosting providers, and personnel working from home offices.

Nonstandard processes are manual processes or procedures that can vary individual by individual as they perform what should be the same task. Whether the customer is an internal customer or an external paying customer, the level of service that each individual delivers should not vary randomly. Essentially, every customer should expect to consistently receive the same great service every time and they should expect to receive the same great service as every other customer regardless of who provides that service. If companies or departments decide to provide a premium service to its premier customers, then the same rule holds; customers receiving premium service should receive great and consistent premium service regardless of who provides that service, and customers receiving the nonpremium service should receive great and consistent nonpremium service regardless of who provides that service

To best understand the value of a consistent process, let's imagine how businesses that have tight profit margins, such as printing businesses and fast food chains, regiment and tune their manual processes to be as efficient as possible.

When a competitive business with tight profit margins standardizes their manual processes, they must carefully determine the most cost-effective process possible to perform each service they provide including each of the tasks that are necessary to invoke to deliver that service. They must then train their staff to perform the process with exacting detail. If one of these businesses fails to operate as a well-oiled machine, its profitability, and possibility its viability, will assuredly decline.

Every department within a big company renders a particular set of business capabilities that complement the enterprise in some important way, which are performed as activities by the individuals within that department either manually or with the aid of automation. To be more precise, each type of business request, such as "a request to generate a particular pamphlet," may have to leverage one or more business capabilities.

In a nonstandardized environment, the most experienced members of the department will use an approach that is superior to junior members of the department. This superiority may manifest itself in a number of different forms, such as producing outcomes that may be less error prone, less time consuming, less effort, or provide a better customer experience. Depending upon the company and department, it may be important for management to determine their objectives and then design the most appropriate process that should be adopted to deliver each type of request, and then ensure that their staff members receive the training or tooling to ensure that the desired process is consistently performed.

With few exceptions, nearly all departments within nearly every enterprise operate using nonstandard processes. This creates a number of business problems, the first being that objective measures are generally not present under these circumstances, and as a result, there is usually no clear path to achieve verifiable process improvement to control, never mind outcomes that are simply consistent and predictable.

1.1.2.7   Lack of Useful Frameworks

Similar to nonstandard processes, inconsistency among applications reduces chances of software component reuse and increases complexity causing individuals more effort to understand how something works ultimately leading to longer and more costly maintenance. The cause of inconsistent IT components is the lack of useful frameworks that would cause software developers and infrastructure support staff to use a common approach within each architectural discipline.

Interestingly, this is one of the least recognized business problems, costing manpower to be wasted and misdirected over prolonged periods of time. The reason it is the least recognized is that unlike a business problem that is tangible in the sense that everyone can see, this manpower expense manifests itself by something that is absent. That said, what is it exactly and why is it so important?

If we go back to the early days of automation, there were no IT departments. Early automation often consisted of a big machine the size of a small automobile placed in the middle of the mail room. These machines sorted 80 column cards in accordance to the pattern of large, color-coded cables plugged into a square board that had a grid of holes that the plugs fit into that slid upright in and out of one end of the machine.

The concept of programming at this time was the ability to customize the sort columns and sort order by rearranging which holes the cables were plugged into, which was determined depending upon what the particular business needs were, such as sorting by zip code to find contributors within a particular district to raise campaign funds. This was communicated by a business manager telling someone in the mail room who was trained to rearrange the cables to make it sort differently.

Not until the emergence of the first mainframes, where there were cooling requirements, was there, typically a room dedicated to automation called the "computer room," with specialized personnel to support the computer room, such as a systems manager, systems programmer, a few computer operators, application programmers, and a roomful of card punch operators.

As computers became more advanced, the process of programming the machine by arranging wires that plugged into a board was replaced by software. The machines still used punch cards, but now the business capabilities being automated were the core business capabilities in accounting, consisting of a single customer master, product master, and transaction master, which generated the journal entries that were accumulated to populate the general ledger.

Instead of one big machine sitting in the middle of the mail room, now the entire automation landscape consisted of a single separate computer room with large air conditioners, a mainframe computer with a card reader and a main console. Cabinets that housed the punch cards of each master file were typically just outside the computer room, where a handful of application development and systems staff had their desks where they could look through big windows into the computer room. The budgets associated with IT were now a few million dollars for a major department.

Fast forward a few decades later and we find that the typical automation landscape of a large organization consists of multiple data centers spread across the globe, tens of thousands of computers that range in size from mainframes and super computers to personal computers, smart phones and tablets, hundreds of thousands of files, thousands of databases, millions of lines of application code spread across repositories around the world, thousands of IT staff, and a budget in the billions.

As existing applications evolve and new ones developed, they employ several dozens of different types of technologies. There are various types of networks, operating systems, job schedulers, security systems, database management systems, change management tools, hardware platforms, reporting tools, and so on, in use across the same enterprise, requiring people who have been trained in each flavor of each type of technology, all doing things differently. While executives can see a lot of people in IT, they do not see the lack of useful frameworks for each type of technology. While some executives may detect one or two areas where commonality would help, they generally lack familiarity across the many types of technologies to see the true impact of many people using many technologies across many types of technologies in different ways.

The sheer volume of existing automation components across large enterprises today contributes to a level of complexity that no one individual, or few individuals, can comprehend, and as if the challenge wasn't big enough, there is no shortage of new types of technologies emerging all of the time.

To provide an example within the limited technology space of Big Data open source software, there are new workload optimization technologies, such as Zoo-Keeper, Oozie, Jaql, HCatalog (aka HCat), Lucene, Pig, and Hive, new integration technologies, such as Flume and Sqoop, new file systems, such as HDFS and GPFS, and new analytic engines, such as R language (aka R). Additionally, there are the countless non-open source technologies in the Big Data space.

The way to manage these technologies and organize the data that they contain in an approach that does not result in an upsurge of complexity where each individual reinvents their own wheel is to have useful standards and frameworks.

However, standards and frameworks themselves must be carefully envisioned and developed to address the challenges of the business. If standards and frameworks are out of date or poorly formed, such as being overly abstract, largely undefined, ambiguous, or inconsistently depicted, then one will have incurred costs for having standards and frameworks without the benefits.

In addition, it is often important for architectural frameworks to integrate with one another, such as involving data governance and information architecture. As one might expect to find, architectural frameworks of a large enterprise are rarely coordinated with one another as they are often developed under different organizations, which also means that these frameworks are not usually integrated with one another.

Like the various disciplines within IT, what would happen if each discipline of the military were to draw up plans independently? The most likely result would be a general unavailability of equipment, fuel, food, munitions, manpower, and surveillance support when needed, as well as the unintended consequence of potentially falling under friendly fire.

1.1.2.8 Lack of Metrics

When I was young my first car was a 1968 Buick Special. I used to tune the engine with just a timing light, although after a while I could do it by simply listening carefully to how the engine sounded. Either way, whether I used the timing light or judged by the sound of the engine, I was using a form of metrics. If I adjust the timing screw in the wrong direction, I could see the strobe light move further from the mark and I could hear the engine running less smoothly. If I did not have either a timing light or the sound of the engine to go by, we could be fairly certain that my car's engine would be worse off than if I had just left it alone.

Similarly, a challenge to management is to have the need to improve business operations without useful metrics on hand to show how well things were running before adjustments are made and then useful metrics to show how well they are running after adjustments have been made. The simple timing light is no longer sufficient to tune the organization. Tuning a modern automobile needs computer-driven diagnostic tools that are information driven, and tuning modern organizations need computer-driven diagnostic tools that are information driven.

Metrics, however, cannot be a measure of just anything. Unless specifically measuring the opinions of your customers, such as their degree of satisfaction or sentiments, metrics should not be reliant upon the opinions of others. For example, to measure customer satisfaction or sentiment objectively one should be measuring the revenue per customer visit, customer referrals, and customer loyalty. In short, metrics must be measuring the right things in the right ways. Hence, the first trait that metrics should have is that they should be "strategic," which encompasses being correlated and relevant to intended outcomes, and it must be reliable, as in originating from a reliable or trustworthy source, which cannot be circumvented by individuals looking for loopholes.

Another essential trait of useful metrics is that they should be easy understand by everyone involved across all areas levels of the organization so that individuals can get on board with them and then consciously or unconsciously move toward achieving the strategic objectives associated with the metric. Hence, another required trait of useful metrics is "simplicity."

An additional trait that is important is that the metric must be available in a short enough time frame to still be useful. Having metrics originate from the end of an assembly line or from year-end earnings reports is sometimes too late to be useful. Hence, the next trait of useful metrics is that it must be "timely."

The uses for metrics go beyond tuning a business or IT operation. When considering the largest enterprises that are reliably successful at incorporating acquisitions into their business and IT operations, the most important success factor is their ability to collect reliable and meaningful metrics on almost everything they do.

Customer experience metrics provide an ability to improve retention and growth, particularly for strategic customers within emerging markets. Business and IT operational metrics can provide operational radar into the efficiency of business capabilities within each department of the company, whether the department is a business department or IT department, and whether the business or IT capability is off shore or outsourced.

Metrics that are gathered through automation have advantages over metrics gathered manually, as automated metrics collection provide the only consistent and reliable source of objective information about what is happening inside your business. In the absence of operational metrics, it is difficult at best to reliably determine which staff members achieve the best results, whether it regards their productivity, the fact that they generate fewer defects or assist others more frequently, or create a greater level of customer retention. Without metrics, it is generally not possible to reliably determine whether changes to organizational structure, personnel, roles, or operational procedures are having an overall beneficial or detrimental impact.

1.1.2.9 *The Pain of not Understanding Ones' Data*

First, there are a number of causes for not understanding ones' data. Although it can be as simple as not understanding the business area associated with the data, the causes typically go far beyond a lack of business knowledge. However, even if one knows the business thoroughly, the sheer number of potential data points and their particular taxonomy tends to form an immense barrier to being able to comprehend ones' data.

One essential step toward addressing this challenge is having the benefit of leveraging a business data glossary. A business glossary acts as a sort of business dictionary that has the business name of the data point with the synonyms that are used across the industry and other departments. It should also include a definition of the data point including how it is used, as well as some other business information, such as whether it feeds into the general ledger and whether the data point is governed by privacy rules based upon legislation and regulation, or simply as the result of promises that were made to the customer or other parties. Even though a good business data glossary is an essential foundational step toward understanding ones' data, there are a myriad of other causes that still create a formidable barrier to comprehension.

Common barriers that are formidable are surprisingly numerous. One of the most difficult to address is complex database designs. Complex database designs are particularly common among purchased software products, where the ability to interpret the data requires the complex logic that was built into the application software. However, the data from complex databases and applications that are developed within ones' enterprise can be just as difficult to interpret.

That said there are additional barriers that are also formidable. If we first assume that we have an excellent business data glossary, and a solid understanding of the database designs as to which physical database fields correspond to which business data glossary items, the next barrier is called "data quality."

When dealing with data quality we may find that the formats of our data may be inconsistent, such as dates not all being in a consistent format of a four-digit year, followed by a two-digit month, followed by a two-digit day, but besides that we may find that the actual values of the dates make no sense, such as birth dates in the future, and death dates that precede the invention of electricity, or simply missing data values where the fields are simply empty.

There are additional causes for not understanding ones' data, but these few give the reader an idea as to how easy it is to have a severe problem comprehending ones' data, so that now we are ready to understand the pain this causes an enterprise.

The impact that is first and foremost for not understanding ones' data is the high cost in time, money, and manpower associated with developing reports, data analytics, data mining, data integration, data virtualization, developing and maintaining applications, and the inability to establish business self-service for ad hoc reporting. In terms of business value to executives, this means that informed decision making is generally not possible unless there is a great deal of lead time available.

When put into perspective as a percent of IT budget, the statistics to look for are the ratio between the total IT budget to the budget used to generate reports and analytics, and the IT work months required to support a typical ad hoc report request. Optimally, the number of IT work months should be zero because the business user was able to find the existing ad hoc report in a few minutes or because they could create the ad hoc report themselves in less than an hour.

1.1.2.10   The Pains of not Understanding Ones' Business Capabilities

To those among most industries, the notion of not understanding ones' business capabilities is going to sound rather strange. In a mortgage bank, for example, the business capabilities involved in creating a mortgage are relatively well understood, at least by the individuals who work in those departments. The challenge is that the individuals outside those departments, unless they previously worked in those departments, generally have little understanding of the business capabilities that are supported within those other departments, particularly if we are talking about individuals within an IT department understanding the business capabilities of a business department, or vice versa.

In addition, as we had mentioned earlier, another major challenge is that even individuals within a given department often do not know much, if anything, about what happens within the automation systems that they use, even though they may use them on a regular basis. When developed in-house, knowledge of these automation systems resides with the IT team that maintains the application. When the automation system is acquired externally, then knowledge of its business capabilities resides within the vendor.

The impact of not understanding ones' business capabilities is multifaceted. Perhaps most significant is that business capabilities that are not well understood can become regularly encrusted with new additional layers of business capabilities that attempt to deliver new or augmented business capabilities. One major bank encountered had so many layers of business capabilities added on to one of their business operations that in the end no one could definitively understand the accounting. As a result, interpretation of the accounting was performed by a team of individuals who poured over the figures and then prepared a summary of their beliefs to the CEO.

Another impact of not understanding ones' business capabilities is the difficulties that arise when attempting to set up disaster recovery capabilities. Companies frequently find that they have to engage specialists to go in and inventory what business capabilities each department performs, what automation systems they use to support these business capabilities, and what databases and infrastructure are required to support these automation systems.

The merger and acquisition process is also impacted by not understanding ones' business capabilities. If your own business capabilities are not well understood, then there is a much greater likelihood that acquired business processes and automation systems will have to sit side by side with your already existing business processes and automation systems, adding to the complexity, and of course the myriad of costs, associated with conducting business.

That said, perhaps one of the most important pain points of not understanding ones' business capabilities is the inability to align organizations to strategic intent, and to accelerate and improve the quality of results.

As such, these represent a respectable sampling of some of the more common business challenges that are faced by many large enterprises, and how we generally got there. Now let's understand IT.

1.1.3 UNDERSTANDING IT

The first thing to understand about IT is that it is an outgrowth of business, which traveled through the premechanical age culminating with number systems and written language, then through the mechanical age which developed manually operated machines to perform mathematical calculation, then through the electromechanical age that harnessed electricity to represent and transmit information as analog electrical signals, and then to our present digital electronic age where information is encoded digitally as bits to be stored and transmitted over networks.

Just as business used automation to optimize the profitability of manual tasks for the production of goods, business used information technologies (IT) to optimize the profitability of mental activities for the processing, storage, retrieval, and analysis of information.

It is true that automation can be used for scientific research (e.g., supercomputers) or entertainment (e.g., computer game platforms), but for the vast majority of enterprises in which enterprise architects work, the primary goal is still to increase the top line (generate more revenue) or increase the bottom line (be more profitable).

From the next highest level perspective, the way to understand IT is to understand the high-level architectural disciplines that exist within IT, even if these are not always formally recognized. While it is not important for an enterprise architect to be an expert in all architectural disciplines, it is critical to know what the disciplines are, how they are defined, their scope, and the handful of fundamental principles that illustrate their proper management.

After understanding the various architecture disciplines, the next highest level perspective way to understand IT is to understand the mindset of engineers, which varies depending upon the degree of separation that they typically have from business.

However, there is another perspective that needs to be understood in order to fully appreciate the functioning of IT, and this is the difference between control systems and information systems. Different disciplines pertain to each of these families of automation system. Enterprise architects need to understand the differences between the two families and which architectural disciplines apply to each.

1.1.3.1 Varieties of Automation Systems

"Control systems" operate in the tangible world of physical objects. They may be measuring instruments, e.g., thermometers, anemometers, and steam engine governors. They may operate mechanical equipment, such as a soda machine that accepts money, determines denomination, authenticates currency, facilitates a product selection, routes product for delivery, and makes change. A "control system" may also be as complicated as a B-2 bomber, which is far too complicated for any human pilot to control without a computer.

In contrast to control systems, "information systems" strictly process information, such as the activities involved in the disciplines of bookkeeping and accounting, which crosses into the world of intangible ideas and concepts (e.g., journals, accounts, fees, and taxes).

One additional area of software system includes software for certain types of games that in some sense obey the laws of physics and operate within a virtual world of physical objects. These are an advanced type of "control system" which I call "virtual world control systems." A "virtual world control system" is a hybrid comprising a "virtual world system" and "virtual control system." The "virtual world system" replaces the tangible world and the "virtual control system" operates within the "virtual world system" allowing one or more participants (i.e., human or automated) to interact within the "virtual world system" through some sort of user interface.

There are some candidates for other families of automation systems. Artificial Intelligence (AI) is one. Yet, AI is more of one or the other, rather than a different family. AI applications can sometimes be classified as a control system because they operate machinery. Sometimes, they can be classified as information systems because they perform functions that are analogous to thought, such as making a decision on whether to extend credit. Perhaps the most accurate way to view AI is that there are components that are control systems, such as the body of an artificially intelligent device, and other components that are information systems, such as the brain of the artificially intelligent system.

It could also be argued that simulations and games are yet another family of automation system. However, they are comprised of a combination of control and information systems. Games are a variant of control systems in that they operate within and among objects of an imaginary world. Yet they are also a variant of information systems in that they track intangible ideas and concepts.

Although control and information systems can use many of the same tools, languages, and techniques, there are differences between them. Such differences include analysis, design, implementation, testing, deployment, and support principles. To illustrate just a few of the differences in their paradigms, we will discuss error handling, data handling, testing, and, most importantly, financials.

1.1.3.1.1   Differences in Error Handling
Although there are many differences, perhaps one of the most interesting differences in the programming of control systems versus information systems is the way in which they perform error handling.

Imagine the flight software of a B2 stealth bomber encountering a program error, say a zero divide, during a mission. The last thing the pilot would want is for the software that is flying the aircraft to suspend its activities so that it could take a program dump—which is what an information system would do to allow the programmers to find the error.

When a control system encounters an error, the software goes to great lengths to rapidly work around the problem so that flight may continue. In contrast, when an information system encounters an error, it automatically terminates its activities and produces a diagnostic dump to better facilitate discovery of the root cause of the error. With an information system, the primary concern is to protect data integrity and the quality of the information, and stopping its processing is a minor price to pay to protect information, particularly when it involves financial data.

Error handling is an illustration that control system analysis and design are dominated by a process-oriented focus, with an emphasis on control modeling to properly operate a piece of machinery.

1.1.3.1.2 Differences in Data and Testing

Information systems typically deal with a large breadth of information, while control systems deal with a comparatively narrow breadth of information. As a result, information systems have a variety of features emphasizing the criticality of data integrity that control systems almost never have, such as database backups and restores, forward recovery from backup, transaction rollback, distributed computing, and distributed data.

In contrast, control systems are typically physically centralized as opposed to distributed, they are more response time critical, and they are more likely to employ a variety of sensory I/O devices with few data points being received often at a high frequency (e.g., anemometer).

When implementing an information system, one of the decisions typically involves the selection of a commercially available operating system. In contrast, when implementing a control system, the task is often how to design the custom operating system and develop the custom I/O drivers.

As a result of having such a customized environment, the control system has a unique set of test issues. Unlike establishing the various testing levels for an information system, such as unit test, integration test, user acceptance, production, and disaster recovery, the control system has a variety of program-specific integration and test environments, such as host-based test beds, real-time closed loop test beds, real-time open loop test beds, operational test beds, and production units.

Regarding control systems, host-based tests depend upon a host platform that facilitate testing of the control system application; real-time closed loop test beds are test environments that provide feedback into the control system application; real-time pen loop test beds are test environments that do not provide any feedback to the control system application; operational test beds test the control system in operation; and production involves deployment of the operational control system.

While generating test data is not a trivial task with information systems, control systems, or virtual world control systems, the types of data that are involved and the support of differing types of test beds require a wholly distinct set of disciplines.

1.1.3.1.3 Financial Differences

The primary costs associated with an information system involve the development life cycle, deployment, ongoing production support, and subsequent maintenance.

Due to the enhanced custom nature of control systems, the primary costs also involve a significant manufacturing component, including product-specific hardware, operating system SDLC, firmware development life cycle, test bed development, various types of system tests, operational testing, assembly line development, manufacturing of production units, deployment of production units, and maintenance of production units.

Similarly, the profit areas for information systems are typically sales and licensing copies of software, as well as the associated maintenance of the software.

In comparison, the primary control system profit area is in hardware unit production and sometimes in maintenance and support agreements.

1.1.3.1.4 Varieties of Automated Systems Conclusion

Probably, the vast majority of enterprise architects will deal exclusively with information systems and may never see a control system in their professional careers. Yet, in order to fully understand the nature of IT, it is necessary to appreciate the variations in automation systems that exist.

The contrast between control systems and information systems will at a minimum allow an enterprise architect to articulate why a discipline that is popularized in the world of control systems may not necessarily apply to the world of information systems. There are many such misconceptions among the general public, who tend to associate computerized systems with the military and space exploration, rather than with the financial services industry or pharmaceutical sector. Unfortunately, this may also extend to senior executives in large enterprises who may have difficulty understanding the role of EA—or may misconceive it completely. Realizing the differences between control systems and information systems can help EA properly articulate its role in the enterprise.

1.1.3.2 Automation as a Cost Center

Understanding the mindsets of others is the first important step toward relating to them. There are mindsets rooted in gender, generation, ethnicity, language, local culture, nationality, politics, religiosity, sexual orientation, sociability, athleticism, education, professional vocation, and income levels. These mindsets form the value systems, motivations, and the fabric of social interactions.

The primary focus of business users is directly tied to the mission of the enterprise, commonly which is realized by applying capital to produce sales of products and services at a profit, it could be to protect the citizens of a nation from those who might threaten harm, or it could be achieving a humanitarian mission in some particular part of the world.

From the perspective of business users, however, IT is often viewed as just a cost center that has lots of technically minded people that are stereotypically hard to talk to. It is thought that business users are not able to understand them, and of course, vice versa. The way business frequently sees it, IT continues to move further away from thinking like the business the deeper into IT areas of specialties that one goes.

It is true that some IT disciplines are complex, just as are many other disciplines, such as medical, pharmaceutical, and military intelligence. What business must understand is that competence in these areas of specialization is not measured in terms of the mission of the enterprise, but instead is in terms of the number and type of educational degrees and licenses earned over their lifetime.

From the perspective of business, its customers are viewed as those whom the enterprise provides goods and services to. From the perspective of IT, its customers are viewed as the business users, or if business users are not visible to them, its customers are the IT management that they do have visibility and awareness of.

In a healthy organization, the role of enterprise architecture is to understand the perspective of business and IT, as well as their respective needs and pain points so that business can understand and participate in prioritizing the use of capital and IT resources.

1.1.3.3 Our Need to Reduce Degrees of Separation

One important factor to help one understand IT is to establish an appreciation for the mindset of engineers. Many are familiar with the stereotype of IT engineer, such as being better in mathematics, science, logic, and puzzles than in dance, music, sports, public speaking, written communication, and people skills.

While generalizations can prove extremely misleading when evaluating any individual from a population, it is fair to observe that for the most part, engineers are natural problem solvers who strive to learn the inner workings of things so that they can better maintain them.

While any given area of technology is not overly difficult to understand, many areas are associated with a large amount of information, such that individuals who specialize cannot specialize in large numbers of them, as it simply becomes impossible to keep up with the volume of change regarding the related products and technologies. This volume of information together with the predilection of engineers being technology focused leads to typically being out of touch with the things that other individuals must focus on.

We must remember that IT was not always this way. In its early days, all IT resources sat with the business user. The number of specialty disciplines in IT back then was few. One of the points of this book is to get a sense of how many disciplines in IT there typically are in a large enterprise.

As a result of the number and depth of these disciplines, the degrees of separation from business will become apparent. One of our goals as enterprise architects is to demonstrate ways to reduce those degrees of separation in an efficient and effective manner.

1.1.3.4 Enterprise Architecture: Centralized vs. Decentralized

A theme that we encounter from time to time in large organizations is whether enterprise architecture should be decentralized and its resources distributed out to lines of business. When global organizations consider the advantages and disadvantages of centralizing their architecture capabilities, the arguments that are raised against centralization do not vary much from company to company. As a means to present this classic debate in one of its most native forms, we shall create a hypothetical situation with a number of actors, two of whom engage in the arena of an e-mail encounter.

A global conglomerate, which is based in the EU, Finansiella LTD, this week announced the consolidation of all country-level Chief Information Officer (CIO) and Chief Enterprise Architect (CEA) positions into a global CIO and CEA position, respectively. All former CIO and CEA positions will be renamed to Relationship Directors and Solution Architect Directors, respectively, with all architects moving into the organization of the CEA, which itself is now within the organization of the CIO.

Vladimir, formerly a country CIO, is now a Relationship Director, a title that he does not find appealing. As one would expect, he is a "Type A" personality, a temperament marked by excessive competitiveness and ambition, an obsession with accomplishing tasks quickly, and a strong desire to control as much as possible around him. Rather displeased with the announcement of the organizational change, Vladimir fires off a lengthy e-mail to Jean-Claude the new global CIO, and copies Antoinette the new global CEA, as well as all former CIOs and CEAs.

With the press of a button, the e-mail arena, complete with players and spectators, has now been formed. This e-mail exchange will explain and illustrate many of the arguments of centralization and decentralization for enterprise architecture.

To: Jean-Claude@finansiella.com
From: Vladimir@finansiella.com
CC: Antoinette, CIO MGT TEAM
Subject: architecture consolidation/concerns

First I should note that I may be more sensitive to this topic more than some as I come from a country where centralized planning replaced the ability of individuals to perform at their best, stifling innovation, and resulting in an inefficient and unresponsive bureaucracy. As such, the consolidation of architecture resources requires careful consideration, as it poses considerable risk to budgets, schedules, software quality, integration, deployment, and maintainability of our business automation.

More specifically, my initiatives are too large and complex, with aggressive schedules to suggest that we shift operating models in mid-stream. I apologize in advance for the length of detail that I supply below, but at its conclusion, I offer some suggestions that I would like to offer as possible alternatives for your consideration.

To begin, I concur that consolidation of architecture can be beneficial for a number of situations.

1. A consolidated architecture group best facilitates knowledge sharing across initiatives.
2. An inventory of architectural skills can be better managed from a consolidated architecture group.
3. Awareness of cross architectural disciplines can also be better facilitated from a consolidated architecture group.
4. Synergies between architectural disciplines can be better detected and pursued.
5. When initiatives are small or medium in size and scope, it is extremely effective at rendering critical architectural resources in and out as needed, as the costs of maintaining a standing team of the various specialists required are certainly prohibitive for a small or medium initiative. The resources come in, resolve the specific issues, and then move onto the next assignment.
6. There are times that architecture support simply requires answering a simple question, pointing the developer in a particular direction, or supplying the appropriate document or example, not requiring in-depth familiarity with the initiative, acting as an architectural help desk. This would also be true in the situation where the architectural direction is routine and repetitive across a large number of initiatives around the globe.

That said, it is not apparent that a consolidated approach works best for large, complex, long running initiatives, such as the initiatives currently underway in this area of the organization aligned with my area of expertise for the following reasons:

1. On large initiatives, it is significantly more critical that the architects become intimately familiar with the system and the business problem, which is simply not possible when using shared resources. The costs are naturally higher because the resources being deployed must spend time getting familiar with the initiative before they can be reliably effective, not to mention the additional time needed that is needed to get familiar with the various challenges facing the initiative.

   This assumes that the appropriate resources are even available when needed. It also assumes that these resources have outstanding soft skills to quickly blend into the personnel of my team.
2. To maintain a stable team of personnel, I ensure that the members of the team develop a bond that motivates them to remain working with the team more like a family. They conduct SCRUMs, work together, lunch together, and socialize outside of the workplace. As a result, we have an atmosphere where they are more inclined to help one another by putting in the extra effort to not let the rest of the team down in achieving the milestones of the initiative.
3. When the same individuals dedicate large amounts of their time and effort on developing something, they develop a sense of pride and ownership. The team in Apple that developed the iPhone did it because they were emotionally bound

to their team and their mission, as well as the opportunity to be successful for such a historic visionary as the legendary Steve Jobs.

4. It becomes possible to establish a shared vision among a team when the members of the team are not rolled in and out as needed.

5. Familiarity with an initiative can help foster innovation instead of hampering the creativity of individuals by allowing them the opportunity to amass the level of knowledge necessary for innovations to occur.

6. A consolidated architecture team requires a complex matrix organization with architects reporting to the central architecture organization as well as to the management of each initiative they support.

7. Having multiple masters creates confusion and reduces an individual's focus on the priorities of each manager.

8. Practice groups or centers of excellence provide a better alternative to a consolidated architecture group.

9. Attaining consensus on a team with staff rotating in and out is more time consuming, which would be highly detrimental to an initiative with an aggressive schedule to meet business needs.

10. Splitting responsibility and authority between a centralized architecture group and initiative management causes the initiative manager to have responsibility for schedules and budgets without authority to drive the team to achieve the objectives of the initiative. Likewise, centralized architecture has authority over architects, but lacks control over schedules and budgets.

11. Priorities may cause pooled architecture resources to be applied elsewhere in the organization, impacting my initiative.

12. If it were truly intended to give enterprise architecture real authority, then we should probably consider giving enterprise architecture direct responsibilities for enterprise projects upon which it could apply its own standards.

In summary, I would like to suggest that the few initiatives that are large, complex, aggressive in schedule, and business critical, particularly the ones that are in midstream, be permitted to continue without disruption to secure the greatest probability of success.

Best regards,

Vladimir, Relationship Director

As soon as this e-mail is received by former CIO and CEA staff members, the organization is abuzz with backchannel discussions speculating on the possible reaction by the new global CIO, Jean-Claude.

After Jean-Claude reads Vladimir's e-mail, he phones Antoinette, his new global CEA on her mobile phone and tells her to develop an appropriate response for Vladimir copying the same audience.

Antoinette reviews each of the points that Vladimir presented in his communication to the management team, collects her thoughts, notes to herself that this is an opportunity to demonstrate her abilities in her new position, and develops her first e-mail to the newly reorganized management team at the request of her new manager. Just before sending the e-mail, Antoinette sees the opportunity for a constructive mentoring opportunity and gives Vladimir the courtesy of conferring with him to discuss her pending reply before she sends it, thereby allowing him to experience how he might have better handled the matter.

To: Vladimir@finansiella.com

From: Antoinette@finansiella.com

CC: CIO MGT TEAM, Jean-Claude@finansiella.com

Subject: Fw: architecture consolidation/concerns

As we discussed, I appreciate your efforts in placing considerable thought with regard to this important issue. It is only through a rigorous intellectual process that we can arrive at the best model for moving forward to facilitate our competitive position. Please find my comments addressing your concerns in italics, and at your convenience I will be happy to discuss them in greater detail.

First, please know that complex projects such as yours will have dedicated resources as well as resources that are required on demand as appropriate to meet the priorities of the business, with a dotted line for reporting into you and/or your project management personnel.

1. On large initiatives, it is significantly more critical that the architects become intimately familiar with the system and the business problem, which is simply not possible when using shared resources. The costs are naturally higher because the resources being deployed must spend time getting familiar with the initiative before they can be reliably effective, not to mention the additional time needed that is needed to get familiar with the various challenges facing the initiative.

This assumes that the appropriate resources are even available when needed. It also assumes that these resources have outstanding soft skills to quickly blend into the personnel of the team.

The ramp-up of time of resources is a valid concern that I share, and is one that I intend to help you better resolve.

If we look at the big picture for a moment before addressing the specific points you raise, one of the first challenges we face within any initiative is the time consuming and labor intensive process of identifying and interviewing candidates, determining which candidates possess the appropriate level of expertise within the architectural disciplines that are needed, onboarding them, training them in our standards and processes, not to mention then acquainting them with of our business automation systems and operational support systems. Our consolidated model for architecture removes this overhead from your concern and streamlines the process of assigning a qualified resource when they are needed.

To address the valid concerns you raise, the biggest weakness of the model that embeds architects within specific initiatives is that for non-complex projects embedded architects have idle time with no easy way to utilize their expertise for other activities. This often leads initiative managers to assign them other work that could otherwise be performed by a less expensive resource. For large complex projects, embedded architects become a single point of failure.

Consider the following; in the situation where the ramp-up time is low, consolidation is certainly the best option as it allows architects to adapt to priorities as needed, thereby avoiding embedded architects and the issue of idle time. However, in the situation where the initiative is large and complex, the consolidated architecture model still allows for dedicated architects who work with the team, but with the additional advantage of being able to draw upon the resources of peers and train secondary and tertiary backups.

This approach increases overall flexibility for an initiative when either *the workload increases or decreases, while eliminating single points of failure. As a result of cross training, I believe that we will find that the ramp-up time actually decreases each time you require the expertise of any particular architectural discipline.*

2. To maintain a stable team of personnel, I ensure that the members of the team develop a bond that motivates them to remain working with the team more like a family. They conduct SCRUMs, work together, lunch together, and socialize outside the workplace. As a result, they are more inclined to help one another by putting in the extra effort to not let the rest of the team down in achieving the milestones of the initiative.

I too have worked in the past with consolidated resources who participated in SCRUM calls with the team members of initiatives on which they participated; the two are not mutually exclusive. An architect can be dedicated or not dedicated to a particular initiative and still be part of the team, befriending team members in and out of the office. An additional advantage for an architect to have when belonging to a consolidated architecture group is that they then feel that they have support of the architecture community, and that are now able to more readily leverage the knowledge and work of their teammates so as not to risk the possibility of reinventing the wheel.

3. When the same individuals dedicate large amounts of their time and effort on developing something, they develop a sense of pride and ownership. The team in Apple that developed the iPhone did it because they were emotionally bound to their team and the initiative, as well as the opportunity to be successful for such a historic visionary as the legendary Steve Jobs.

Good point, though I believe Apple has centralized enterprise architecture.

In the now famous story* when the iPhone was six weeks from deployment, Steve Jobs placed his iPhone in his pocket and realized that the screens were easily scratched by keys. Apple had to scramble to identify a superior material for their screens and then they had to pay to have nearly a million phones refitted, reentering and disrupting a step of the manufacturing process.

To continue your analogy, Apple does show that having a project focus works well, after all, they did build the iPhone. However, they could have greatly benefitted from better internal standards and governance to prevent the tunnel vision of dedicated teams such as the one that selected the initial glass component.

4. It becomes possible to establish a shared vision among a team when the members of the team are not rolled in and out as needed.

The manager can indeed help both dedicated and non-dedicated team members receive the vision of the manager; we would expect them to take their vision from the team they are participating in. That said, I would point out that the Enterprise vision is just as important here, and I expect architects to take that vision to each initiative they participate in. We would not want someone building a work of art that is in conflict with the vision of the initiative or not compliant with Enterprise standards.

5. Familiarity with an initiative can help foster innovation instead of hampering the creativity of individuals by allowing them the opportunity to amass the level of knowledge necessary for innovations to occur.

Familiarity with just one initiative versus multiple initiatives and architectural disciplines would appear to give the advantage to the latter. Also, the potential for innovations that are global in nature would probably deliver greater competitive value.

6. A consolidated architecture team requires a complex matrix organization with architects reporting to the central architecture organization as well as to the management of each initiative they support.

The matrix organization model has been used extensively throughout several industries, including our own. As such, I am not certain of the conflict you foresee.

Let's imagine a homeowner is installing a solar array in their backyard to generate their power requirements. They remain attached to the grid so that you can bank the excess power you generate during the day, which they may draw upon at night, thereby netting their electric bill to zero. However, when the first neighborhood blackout occurs during the day they realize that the installer designed the solar

---

*(Business Insider, Tech, "Steve Jobs Freaked Out a Month Before First iPhone Was Released and Demanded a New Screen", Henry Blodget, January 22, 2012).

system to automatically shut down when the power grid was down. However, the homeowner prefers to have the solar array power their home even when the grid is down. Although the installer who works for the homeowner can make the change, it violates the building codes of the state and local building department.

Since the licensed electrician refuses to violate the building code, let's say the homeowner then hires an unlicensed electrician to do the work. At some point in the future the grid goes down and unbeknownst to anyone else, the home now has uninterrupted power from the solar array. This appears quite advantageous for the homeowner.

At some point the electric company sends out a repair crew to fix the lines that were downed due to a fallen tree. The repairman knows that the power company has the power shutdown from their side, however the power company's repairman receives injuries from the power traveling from the opposite direction because someone's solar array was connected to the grid and did not shutdown automatically as required. As a result, the repairman loses income, the power company faces increased insurance premiums, the healthcare provider of the repairman faces costs associated with delivering medical services, the homeowner faces fines and civil penalties, and the unlicensed electrician faces civil and criminal charges.

Analogously, architectural standards are developed with the objective of controlling costs across the enterprise. Each initiative will be receiving the equivalent of "licensed" architects who will be responsible for enterprise architecture standards compliance, with a process in place to request exceptions. If an exception does not violate the interests of another stakeholder, and is clearly advantageous cost-wise over the potential life of the design, then simply put, the exception will be eagerly approved.

7. Having multiple masters creates confusion and reduces an individual's focus on the priorities of each manager.

The use of the matrix organization model has been around for so long, that those who are senior enough to be enterprise architects have been there and done that.

8. Practice groups or centers of excellence provide a better alternative to a consolidated architecture group.

Practice groups are better than nothing, but not the same as having a centralized group where cross training and collaboration across architectural disciplines is the norm rather than the exception. More importantly, practice groups do not actively ensure that initiatives do not inadvertently violate the interests of another stakeholder.

9. Attaining consensus on a team with staff rotating in and out is more time consuming, which would be highly detrimental to an initiative with an aggressive schedule to meet business needs.

My priority is to provide business value. To go back to your iPhone analogy, Steve Jobs wanted that iPhone built quickly. But it wouldn't do anyone any good if the iPhone was delivered to consumers and didn't comply with FCC regulations, the US power grid, or had a screen that was easily scratched.

Likewise, our architecture team must be able to respond quickly to changing events in order to incorporate changing business priorities, rapidly evolving technologies, and improved frameworks that could provide us a competitive advantage.

10. Splitting responsibility and authority between a centralized architecture group and initiative management causes the initiative manager to have responsibility for schedules and budgets without authority to drive the team to achieve the objectives of the initiative. Likewise, centralized architecture has authority over architects, but lacks control over schedules and budgets.

Various stakeholders exist across the organization. It is part of our job is to keep our stakeholders informed and to follow their standards The engineer that complains about serving multiple masters must recognize that our efforts are only useful if we operate while protecting the interests of our corporate stakeholders. This means while protecting the company's brand and reputation, while conforming to legal requirements, such as for records information management (RIM) and legal holds, complying with legislative and regulatory bodies at various jurisdictions ranging from global to local, adhering to customer centric directives as determined by our Chief Customer Officer, and while keeping within their schedule and budget as determined by the initiative manager.

11. Priorities may cause pooled architecture resources to be applied elsewhere in the organization, impacting my initiative.

This is an important point you raise, as when other enterprise objectives receive a higher priority than a particular initiative the impact can be high. That said, if a particular initiative is being starved of resources due to its relative priority then the most appropriate course of action is to address it via the management chain. At the end of the day it is the business's money we are spending, which our executive management directs us how best to do.

12. If it were intended to give enterprise architecture real authority, then we should probably consider giving it direct responsibilities for enterprise projects upon which it could apply its own standards.

Enterprise architecture does require implementation capabilities for a variety of tactical and strategic activities. This can be accomplished either by having its own tactical application development team or by being aligned with a global application development team that additionally support enterprise architecture.

In addition to the responses to your issues mentioned above, it is important to note that often the best talent within an organization tends to leave due to its being restricted to the scope of one initiative. In contrast, by being part of a team of their peers these individuals are offered a healthy learning curve developing and sharing knowledge, and it becomes more likely for them to stay abreast of industry innovations and frameworks, thereby not requiring them to seek alternate employment to grow.

To briefly summarize our thoughts, a building contractor retains the responsibility and authority from a budgeting and scheduling perspective to build a building. He still has to go to the zoning board for the various permits to ensure that he is compliant with the various stakeholders of the various jurisdictions. Otherwise, you end up driving in Shanghai or Mumbai.

Similarly, a product manager retains the responsibility and authority from a budgeting and scheduling perspective to deliver an initiative. He still has to go to the architecture review board to ensure that he is compliant with the various stakeholders of the various jurisdictions. Otherwise, you end up working at Lehman or a part of AIG that is now owned by MetLife.

In closing, this has been a thought provoking conversation, and I appreciate that you put yourself out there to engage. That said, I should also point out that the rumor that I offered Vladimir a Starbucks gift certificate to ask these specific questions are wholly untrue, although I am certain that we could all agree that he deserves one for putting his thoughts out there.

Thank you and if you have additional concerns I look forward to the pleasure of discussing this further at your convenience.

With warm regards,

Antoinette, Chief Enterprise Architect

Finansiella LTD

Antoinette presses the send button, and moments after, she receives a telephone call on her cell phone from her boss, Jean-Claude, the CIO. Jean-Claude tells her that her response was outstanding, which is a clear indicator of how smart he is for hiring her.

While this author does not take sides in this exchange, it is fair to say that the management style of the new leadership team is such that it would appear Finansiella LTD is becoming an attractive professional environment within which to work.

1.1.3.4.1 Enterprise Architects

It is interesting to contrast the attitudes of enterprise architects who started their career in the 1970s versus the 1980s versus the 1990s and ones who will be starting their careers today. We have observed that these attitudes manifest themselves in the decisions made by the architects that come from these different periods in time. This requires some explanation, since if the problems of EA have optimal solutions, we would expect many enterprise architects to arrive at the same conclusion, irrespective of when they learned their craft. Furthermore, a few decades is not really a significant amount of time.

The generalization does need some qualification. Some of today's architects do recognize and embrace the fluidity of the technology landscape, economic climate, and marketplace and have been extremely successful. Others, however, do not keep up with change and fail to adapt—sticking to old beliefs and ultimately hurting the enterprises that employ them. This problem can get a lot worse if there is an abundance of like-minded, inflexible personnel—promoting their outdated decisions as well as the ideas of their like-minded colleagues, thereby marginalizing and eliminating those enterprise architects that have embraced change.

The advent of the cloud, social networking, online collaboration, smart phones, and tablets has opened up a world of business opportunities. Cheaper, faster, and more efficient vendors now have a fighting chance against the entrenched IT vendors. Enterprise architects who recognize the benefits of these new technologies can easily outpace their outdated counterparts if they can provide their firms a competitive advantage by maintaining the same level or better level of service at a lower cost.

This is not meant to indicate that the long-established "blue-chip" IT firms do not offer solutions that meet enterprise needs anymore. What it alludes to, however, is that the impediments to the new breed of enterprise architects have taken their toll on the larger IT organizations contributing to their stagnation preventing them from moving away from any of the high price solutions that they acquired prior to more competitive actors entering the marketplace.

While it is true that IT should be making decisions related to technology working as a partner with the business, it is also true that every one of these decisions should provide tangible business benefit. If a technology decision cannot demonstrate a clear benefit to the business, it is certainly a decision that needs further investigation. This link, however, between technology decision making and business benefits is something that has been lost as some IT departments are more guided by the momentum of the past, while in all fairness others are sometimes more guided by the latest unproven solutions that are still in their early stages of hype.

1.1.3.4.2 Role of Enterprise Architecture

The role of enterprise architecture is to develop various frameworks for IT that both facilitate the direction of the business and address major pain points of the business, including representing interests of business stakeholders across the enterprise, such as the legal, compliance, and auditing departments, as well as profit centers and producers, thereby aligning business vision and strategy with IT delivery.

Although rarely stated as such, the mission of enterprise architecture within an organization is to develop the skills, business principles, standards, and frameworks for each architectural discipline necessary to prepare the IT resources of the organization to act effectively to achieve the direction set by the executive leadership team (e.g., CEO, CIO, and Head of Development). The degree of preparedness offsets the cost associated with uncoordinated efforts that have not considered the most effective combination of IT technologies and approach for the use of those technologies.

As such, one of the early and ongoing activities of enterprise architecture is to identify the IT technology areas that are of the greatest importance to the organization at present and in the near future.

Each area is then evaluated to identify:

- which architectural disciplines would be necessary to establish competency in the particular area of technology,
- what the costs would be to establish a reasonable level of competency, and
- an estimation of the immediate, near and long term costs for not managing the particular area of technology.

Due to the low cost structures, typical of enterprise architecture departments, enterprise architecture works behind the scenes in a rather opportunistic manner, to influence the greater environment of automation. Maintaining the preparedness of resources is much like a fitness regimen. One cannot exercise for a number of months and then expect to remain fit for a lifetime.

Although this is an accurate depiction of the intended role, EA in general has a long way to go to get there.

EA had humble beginnings, starting by organizing an inventory of technology products that had been purchased by the enterprise over the years, and by organizing an inventory of application systems that were home grown in-house, home grown but acquired through mergers or acquisitions, purchased and then customized, purchased and left as-is, or licensed as an outsourced service. These inventories, and the methods used to manage them, are referred to as technology portfolio management and application portfolio management, respectively.

Shortly thereafter, senior programmer analysts changed their names to solution architects or application architects, and data modelers changed their names to data or information architects. As we shall soon come to understand, the target state for an enterprise architecture practice that achieves its stated role is quite different in philosophy, taxonomy, organization, and skills. As such, let's briefly talk philosophy.

1.1.3.4.3 The Hedgehog and the Fox

Philosophy teaches us that there are many ways to view things. The way we think about something right now is certainly not the only way to view that topic.

"The Hedgehog and the Fox" was an essay written by an English philosopher named Isaiah Berlin in 1953, which is based on a fragment originally found written by an ancient Greek poet, Archilochus, circa 650 BC, around 2500 years earlier, which stated, "πόλλ' ο☐δ' ☐λώπηξ, ☐λλ' ☐χ☐νος ☐ν μέγα" ("the fox knows many things, but the hedgehog knows one big thing").

To paraphrase the story:

The hedgehog is an animal that goes about his business of keeping up his house and dealing with his chores to forage for food. Each day he leaves the safety of his den, chooses the path that will allow him to achieve what he wants to accomplish today, and then returns home. The fox, on the other hand, leaves the comfort of his den and, with a clever mind, searches for opportunities to get his next meal.

The fox knows many things and comes up with clever ideas for how to achieve his goals. When the fox encounters the scent of the hedgehog, he cleverly tracks it back to the den of the hedgehog and plans on following him the next day to make himself a lovely meal.

As planned, the next day the fox sits downwind of the hedgehog's den waiting, and then right on schedule, watches the hedgehog emerge from the safety of his den, and walks away along one of his favorite paths. The fox follows the hedgehog quietly circling him to be further down the path where the hedgehog must walk through a clearing, where the fox quietly waits anticipating his meal.

When the hedgehog walks deep into the clearing far from cover of foliage the fox charges forward at him. The hedgehog sees the fox and thinks, here he comes again, that silly fox. As the fox rapidly approaches, the hedgehog rolls up into a ball with his quills sticking out all directions around him. The fox quickly screeches to a halt and breaks off the attack, and the hedgehog goes back to his chores.

The End.

This story has been analyzed many times by many great writers and thinkers, and from this story, we learn many things.

First, foxes move on many levels, they are clever and quick, but they never integrate their thinking into a unified vision. The hedgehog, on the other hand, is very smart as well but instead reduces a complex world into simple ideas because they see patterns of what is essential and ignores the rest.

Using this story, we learn the "Hedgehog Concept," which we will refer to from this point on as we discuss the philosophical differentiators of the new breed of enterprise architecture.

1.1.3.4.4 Philosophical Differentiators

1.1.3.4.4.1 Business Focus The first philosophical differentiator of modern enterprise architecture is that it starts by integrating strong business knowledge into the enterprise architecture team. A small number of business industry experts render in-depth business knowledge to the group and to the business users they interact with.

With few exceptions of line managers running operational business areas, detailed business knowledge of processes is scarce across the business community. Business users that once knew the business have been replaced by business users who now only understand what information to capture and how. With barely enough time to manage their business operations during the day, the few line managers that know the business have no time for IT, unless of course they desperately need something from them, where the noteworthy word is "desperate."

Line managers today are among the few that have a need and the interest to read the pertinent business books and legislation. It should also be noted that it would be prohibitively expensive to repopulate the business community with experts in their respective areas of the business.

1.1.3.4.4.2 Development Capabilities The second philosophical differentiator of the modern enterprise architecture organization is the recognition that it requires access to a development arm, usually either its own adaptive application development team or access to an application development team that supports global initiatives. Without active support from a dynamic application development team, enterprise architecture would be adrift within the organization with no ability to take any action.

1.1.3.4.4.3 Agile Staffing True for many organizations, the third philosophical differentiator of the true enterprise architecture organization is to maximize flexibility in staffing and taking it to the extreme. Instead of hiring a large staff of full-time employees, staffing is accomplished with temporary consultants that are industry experts within their architectural discipline.

It is critical to establish an expert staff of architects in the pertinent areas with the most immediate needs, such as in BPM technology, workflow automation, information architecture, data obfuscation, data warehousing, content management, and technology portfolio and application portfolio management disciplines. These individuals help build a strong foundation of policies and frameworks that guide the IT and business community. They can always be converted to full-time employees once they have proved themselves, or they can mentor their eventual replacements in the principles, standards, and frameworks that they helped develop.

1.1.3.4.4.4 Synergistic Multipurpose Personnel The fourth philosophical differentiator of the true EA organization is to adopt the approach with the most modest footprint of staff, such as the use of data stewards within the discipline of data governance. Instead of hiring staff members to support each business department, where possible, select a business knowledgeable individual with interest in enterprise architecture. Training programs must be established to maintain some disciplines anyway, and it is a good practice to engage business users where it can make sense to do so.

1.1.3.4.4.5 Operations Architecture The fifth philosophical differentiator of the modern enterprise architecture organization is to recognize the distinction between the architectural disciplines associated with information systems architecture and the architectural disciplines that are associated with data center operations. As we shall see, the disciplines associated with operations are quite distinct from those of application and information architecture and are equally necessary.

For example, data center operations include infrastructure architecture, including servers, networks, CITRIX, and thin client architecture; disaster recovery architecture; and data center job scheduling technologies.

1.1.3.4.4.6 Advanced Business Users The sixth philosophical differentiator of the modern enterprise architecture organization is to recognize that many of today's business users are tech-savvy, thereby able to form strong opinions on the use of specific tools and technologies. As such, it is imperative that their opinions be respected as well as appropriately challenged. Management on both fronts (IT and Business) must respect dissenting opinions and evaluate solutions strictly on merit and architectural feasibility within a given environment as opposed to considerations of territorial responsibilities.

1.1.3.4.4.7 Self-service Is an Accelerator The seventh philosophical differentiator of modern enterprise architecture is that business should have as much self-service as possible. Business should not have to fund an ever-increasing inventory of IT staff to generate reports on demand. The new model is for IT to empower the business to be more competitive by encouraging the notion that IT get out of the way of the business, and that the business should take back control of those capabilities that will enhance their competitiveness in the marketplace.

Once business is properly empowered, both sides provide the appropriate checks and balances for the other to act beneficially to the overall enterprise. Business project managers will partner with IT to leverage their architectural knowledge and technology capabilities. Importantly, IT should not be expending resources on initiatives that the business does not understand or agree with as meeting their business objectives.

Part of this is to avoid unrealistic claims of self-service. One of the earliest self-service attempts was the language COBOL. This was designed to consist of terms that were similar to natural languages so that programmers would no longer be needed. Managers and business people could simply write what they needed and when. The result was that by the end of the 1980s, more professional programmers coded in COBOL than in any other language.

1.1.3.4.4.8 Stakeholders Frequently Palaver The eighth philosophical differentiator of the true enterprise architecture organization is that both business and IT must have representation on the executive leadership team. While business should have representation from finance, business origination, business servicing, business risk management, and compliance, IT should have representation from architecture (enterprise and operations architecture), IT operations, and application services (development and maintenance services).

Using this model, it is important to create and maintain the perception that IT and business are inseparable partners with a shared awareness of business direction and priorities.

1.1.3.4.4.9 Real Transparency not Virtual The ninth philosophical differentiator of the true EA organization is the presence of a new breed of enterprise architect who recognizes the criticality of IT expense transparency to the business, as well as business expense transparency to IT. Transparency fosters a trusting and cooperative relationship between business and IT and helps ensure that the limited resources of the business are being properly deployed. Transparency also provides insight into the ways that automation can assist the overall enterprise more competitive, and helps keep expenses in check for the activities in both IT and business.

The notion that IT is a financial black hole is about as counterproductive as the notion of business having a shadow IT organization hiding IT resources from IT so that it can get its needs met.

To accomplish expense transparency, business and IT must clearly define each and every initiative in a consistent manner for presentation to a combination of business and IT management for financial and architectural approval.

1.1.3.4.4.10 Business First, Business Second, Business Third The 10th philosophical differentiator of the true EA organization is that the newest breed of enterprise architect openly confronts the attitude of "entitlement" within IT, trying to position "IT" as resources hired to empower and service "business," as opposed to "business" being there to simply fund "IT" to fulfill the lifelong dreams of those in IT.

In this new competitive age, IT staff must forge a completely new type of relationship with the business, and IT initiatives must be flexible to address the ability to gain effective and actionable advantage in the competitive marketplace. Including business expertise is not sufficient, as attitudes in IT toward business must change sufficiently to alter relationships. In almost every company, IT doesn't drive; instead, it enables by making it possible to do more work faster, cheaper, more consistently.

1.1.3.4.4.11 Participators not Spectators The 11th philosophical differentiator of the true EA organization is that EA can no longer sit back and simply write standards documents and draw pictures that become shelf-ware. EA organizations must now become an integral part of solutions transforming the organization to its desired future state. They must roll up their sleeves and have a handful of strategic projects as a means to directly test their standards and frameworks.

In summary, the new philosophy of enterprise architecture demands a highly dynamic and adaptive team of modern enterprise architects that specialize in the architectural disciplines needed to address the challenges of the business today. The new EA must effectively communicate and educate individuals in both business and IT with strategies and frameworks that focus on the most prominent needs of the business.

In addition, each subject matter expert must have a hedgehog concept that encapsulates the primary mission of each architectural discipline. This hedgehog concept must be simple and easy to remember. We will discuss how to do this in more detail as we get into each architectural discipline.

Every enterprise has access to the same vast selection of technologies and products. That said, it is the new philosophy of EA that will ultimately determine how each enterprise views and coordinates technology to achieve a competitive advantage and meet its goals.

1.1.3.4.5 Taxonomy and Organization of Enterprise Architecture

Today, there are over 50 frameworks that are labeled enterprise architecture frameworks, including those that are openly available at no cost and those that are proprietary for a fee. Depending upon what one uses as a clear sign of when enterprise architecture began, we can say that as a practice it has been around at least with the introduction of The Open Group Architecture Framework (TOGAF) in 1995. To set its origins much earlier one would have to use Zachman as the first sign of enterprise architecture. That said, no matter how much we like Zachman, it has always been a system architecture framework, even though its contents unchanged were later relabeled or rebranded for marketing purposes as an enterprise architecture framework when EA as a term came into fashion.

Enterprise architecture is no longer your predecessor's view of enterprise architecture, which is a good thing as that prior view did little to change the industry over the past 15 years. A medical analogy may be useful. In bygone days, the majority of medical practitioners were general practitioners, pharmacists, and so on. Today, we have far more specializations than previously, in areas such as immunology, anesthesiology, dermatology, and more depending upon the size and type of hospital in which these personnel work. Similarly, EA must specialize to meet the challenges of the modern world.

To organize EA into its distinct architectural disciplines, there are six major areas that comprise the specific architectural disciplines, which technically include their governance so that there is a way to ensure that they achieve their objectives in an efficient and measurable way. These are:

- "business" architecture,
- "information systems" architecture,
- "information" architecture,
- "control systems" architecture,
- "operations" architecture, and
- "cross architecture disciplines."

We should reiterate that there is sufficient material for any of the topics within these five major areas of enterprise architecture to warrant their own book. However, it is only our intent to communicate the complete architectural framework of modern EA for enterprises with enough detail to understand what it does, why it is important, and to imply what the cost to the enterprise may be if it elected to leave a particular architectural discipline unmanaged.

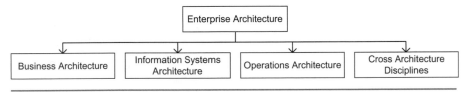

Diagram   Enterprise architecture overview.

Business Architecture

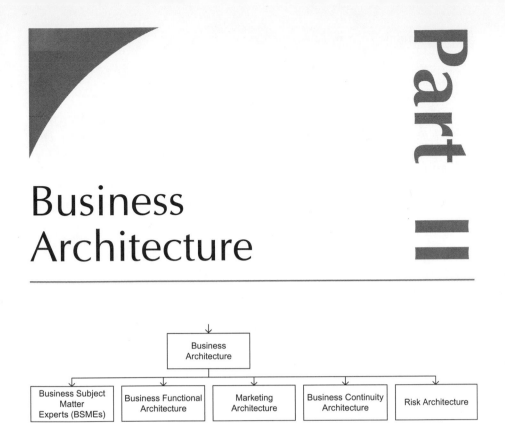

Part II

Diagram Business architecture overview.

▮ 2.1 Business Architecture and Governance Summary

The number of architectural disciplines with business architecture can fluctuate significantly depending upon a number of factors, such as the number of lines of business, mergers, acquisitions, divestitures, outsourcing and insourcing initiatives, number of IT development initiatives, number of information systems architects requiring business support, and degree of corporate restructuring that may be underway.

If the reader takes one hedgehog principle away from the section about business architecture, it is the flexibility that business architecture has in supplying business subject matter expertise to the parts of the organization that need it most at the right periods of time to properly align activities across the enterprise with the hedgehog principle of the business, including its strategic direction, and priority pain points.

2.1.1   BUSINESS SUBJECT MATTER EXPERTS

A young man who lives in Manhattan takes his new expensive sports car for a drive through the hills and farmlands of New Jersey. While driving he sees a sheep farm and on the side of the road he sees the farmer mending the fence. Being a talkative fellow the young man pulls off the road to chat with the farmer.

The young man says to the farmer, "I bet you one of your sheep that I can tell you exactly how many sheep you have across these hills." The farmer somewhat surprised exclaims to the young man that that would be a good trick, and agrees.

The young man with his fingers forming a triangle scans the hills spotted with sheep, and after a moment he concludes that there are eight hundred and thirty two sheep.

The farmer says, "That's amazing! That's right, and it looks like you've won yourself a sheep."

The young man then picks up an animal and puts it into the trunk of his car.

The farmer then says to the young man, "I bet I can tell you what you do for a living."

The young man, surprised, knowing that there is nothing visible on his clothes or in his car that could reveal his profession agrees.

The farmer then tells the young man that he is an enterprise architect by profession.

The young man startled, says, "That's right! How did you know?"

And the farmer says, "Because that's my dog you put in your trunk."

The point of this story is simple. A common theme that you see in large organizations is that no matter how smart IT is, they don't impress business users when they demonstrate that they don't really know the business.

Make no mistake about it, business people are the prerequisite for any company's success. The best business people will command the resources of a company to make it thrive, mediocre business people will generally keep a company afloat as long as there is no stiff competition, and poor business people will cause a company to bleed its capital and market share until it sells the assets of the company to another or is forced to do so in bankruptcy court. The point here is that without good knowledgeable business people, a company does not have long-term survival prospects.

At the same time, we must consider that to better compete, many aspects of the business have been automated with their associated business rules buried within computer programs, allowing companies to hire fewer and less knowledgeable business people. These factors permit companies to handle more business transactions, faster, more consistently, and at a reduced cost.

The challenges that today's companies face, however, are that the IT people are not business people, to a significant degree they are not business minded, and the further away they are from the revenue producing activities they are, the harder it is for them to quickly relate to the interests of the business. Instead of relating to the business, IT people think of ways of improving their lives with technology, desiring more financial resources to purchase or build additional software and faster hardware that naturally address their own direction and pain points.

That said, spending the resources of business in ways that do not coincide with the direction of the enterprise, or does not address a critical business pain point only serves to squander the limited resources of the business that could have been available to business to better carry out its mission.

In light of these facts, the business sensibilities that are most critical to infuse within the frameworks and guidelines of enterprise architecture are the sensibilities that are not well represented among most architecture teams and less so in most other areas of IT. As a result, it is important that each business subject matter expert (BSME) be just that, an expert in business to convey the hedgehog concept for each area of the business as a steady beat of the drum for each individual to follow.

As such, BSMEs must be extremely knowledgeable about their particular line of business, including awareness of which stakeholders, internally and externally, have interests that must also be taken into consideration. Ideally, it is best to find a BSME that previously owned and operated a small company in the particular line of business, as that would have caused them to be extremely knowledgeable in most aspect of that business.

With this in mind, the next factor is to determine in which business areas there would be an appropriate return on investment for a BSME. If the expenditures and activities of IT to support a particular line of business exceed 10 million dollars annually, which is typically the situation for any line of business in a large enterprise, then a BSME is likely to prove invaluable in either preventing expenditures that were not in alignment with business interests or influencing the activities to achieve a suitably realistic return on investment.

2.1.2 BUSINESS FUNCTIONAL ARCHITECTURE

Companies have numerous business capabilities. Some of them are basic business capabilities that most every company has, such as corporate actions, personnel, finance, accounting, vendor management, procurement, employee communications, IT services, and sales and marketing. The additional business capabilities that would be present are those that are specific to the particular lines of business that the company engages in, and among those there will be core business capabilities.

Core business capabilities are the business capabilities that differentiate your business in its present lines of business. They are not necessarily what your enterprise can do best given its talent and market conditions, but they are the main strengths that support your business that you would not be able to outsource to compete effectively as they may be the reason that customers come to you. In contrast, existing business capabilities that are not core business capabilities have the potential of being outsourced to someone that may do them better.

Business capabilities that do represent what the talent of your enterprise can do best given the market conditions are your true hedgehog capabilities that you can discover and foster as your ideal core business capabilities. These ideal business capabilities is what should drive corporate restructures that would align the assets and interests of the enterprise into what the enterprise can best excel at. If the restructuring is ultimately successful, it will be declared that you have successfully found your hedgehog concept and bravely steered in its direction.

For example, in the credit card industry, the core capability could be limited solely to the assessment of credit worthiness of an applicant. In this situation, the company may perform this business capability better and faster than any of its competition, without possessing an advantage in any other major step within that business such as supporting purchases, billing, or payment processing. In such an example, it can be worth considering the outsourcing the business capabilities that complete the business process but that do not provide a competitive advantage to the enterprise.

When outsourcing business capabilities to an external vendor, organizations must be careful not to also outsource their data. Whether a need for the data is perceived up front or not, organizations must always arrange for the transfer of data back to the enterprise as near real time as is possible within the necessary cost constraints.

Core business capabilities, also commonly referred to as "core competencies," are initially acquired from the company founders. Core competencies can be developed from within, and they may also be acquired through acquisition:

1. The first objective of business functional architecture should be to recognize existing and potential core competencies, and whether they are opportunities for consolidation or yet unrealized potential core competencies, they should be presented to the enterprise business review board (EBRB) for consideration by executive management.

For example, most large enterprises have large amounts of data that if cleansed of personally identifiable information and proprietary information, may prove to be a source of revenue in the data reseller market:

2. The second objective of business functional architecture should be to recognize a common capability that is redundantly distributed across many applications. In one of the largest educational testing and assessment organizations, common capabilities were found across hundreds of test administration systems. It is

the role of the business functional architect to understand the business and how it has been automated across the enterprise, and then present it to the EBRB for consideration by executive management as a potential long-term infrastructure investment.

Simplification by building out a core business capability that can replace disparate versions of redundant automation can be deployed various ways; a core competency may be automated from a global perspective and be shared and centrally deployed, or the code base of the core competency can be shared and then deployed regionally or locally.

Redundant automation systems, however, cannot be completely consolidated until every one of their major capabilities has been taken over by a shared business capability that both supports its business needs and integrates into the business operation. Hence, the management of the enterprise must have interest in considering the long view.

However, architecting a core capability across multiple silo applications, not to mention hundreds or thousands of them, is anything but trivial. As such, the role of business functional architect requires exactly the right combination of experience, a mature enterprise architecture organization comprised the right architectural disciplines, and a mature global application development capability.

For example, a core capability in an organization that makes payments from hundreds of applications to individuals and organizations around the world may be an individual well versed in "global payments processing."

2.1.3 Marketing Architecture

When this author was a teenager, everyone watched the same few programs on the same few television stations. With the advent of cable television, satellite television, and Internet, choices for media content began to multiply, and today, there is no end in sight to the number of specialty channels that can exist to address the many interests of viewers around the world. My parents listened to radio programs when they were teenagers, and advertisers had what seem like quaint commercials today interspersed within various radio programs, such as "The Shadow."

It wasn't that people have recently splintered into having many different interests that can now choose from a large selection of possibilities. It is actually that people have always had many interests and now there are outlets that are satisfying those interests.

Marketing, therefore, had to adapt to the rapid increase of media outlets, ever evolving in an attempt to get our attention. The difference today is that advertising is evolving at the speed of the technologies that we use every day, across our many interests, across the many media.

Today, scientific breakthroughs in understanding the brain are driving marketing techniques over the Internet. Our behaviors and interests are being collected for companies to purchase to predict our preferences for products and services, including when we will want them.

Traditional mass marketing outlets are rapidly falling out of favor as new outlets continue to emerge, attracting our attention to more specialized media outlets that better match our interests. What were once near monopolies, like newspapers and magazines, and nationwide network television and radio networks, are losing subscribers and advertisers by the droves and going out of business.

While global businesses are able to take advantage of the new world of marketing to drive customers to them from across the country and the world, local businesses are finding ways of using the same technologies to attract local customers.

Direct marketing via the US Postal System has mail delivery into a sorting ritual next to the waste paper basket or supply of kindling for the fireplace. The telemarketing industry has popularized telephone caller ID and screening techniques.

Today, marketing must deal with Web site design for computers as well as for smart phones and tablets, and ways to keep them rapidly synchronized with one another.

They must have knowledge of the various techniques for advertising on the Internet, including on search engines, professional networking platforms, encyclopedias, dictionaries, online language translation, and news and social sites. They must have awareness of click stream analysis, real-time feeds that are available from Twitter and Facebook, especially to search for conversations that may be tarnishing your brand with messages that spread geometrically in hours or minutes.

Given the media and information explosion, the growth in high-technology marketing options and emerging sources of information, companies have been creating a Chief Customer Officer (CCO) position with global oversight and direct access to the CEO.

In support of the CCO, marketing architecture is intended to develop standards and frameworks to accelerate implementation of the CCO's strategy, and to address the myriad of technology issues that must be woven into their global marketing strategy.

In its mature state, marketing architecture is a discipline of business architecture that develops and maintains an overall automation strategy with principles, standards, and frameworks that guide and coordinate social media marketing, Web-based marketing, and the new forms of direct marketing and mass marketing by considering the combination of the latest information available from the behavioral sciences and technology to adapt to the rapid population fragmentation that is occurring across media outlets today.

Advertisements are no longer placed for the greatest number of impressions. Instead, customized messages are strategically placed with the appropriate niche content at the appropriate niche location to get the attention of the precise population that marketing business users wish to target, when, where, and how using proven techniques for getting the attention of the target audience in coordination with marketing activities in various other venues.

Introductory offers for products and services are now more frequently free during introductory periods. Customer experiences are carefully designed by business executives to be carried out across business operational areas and automation across the company. Marketers must use technologies such as "wordtracker.com" to determine the most appropriate words and terms to associate with their Web pages.

As such, the role of a marketing architect requires a broad combination of knowledge and experience in social marketing, Web-based marketing, direct marketing and mass marketing with knowledge of all common electronic communities and numerous electronic communities that are pertinent to the industry, and products and services of their enterprise. They must also have the ability to determine where their competitors place their ads, links, banners, and content.

2.1.4   BUSINESS CONTINUITY ARCHITECTURE

Not long ago any planning for the advent of a major business disruption was an afterthought and was even thought of as a luxury. While many responsible companies recognized early on that a significant business disruption, although unlikely, represented a potential means of going out of business, many of them also realized that even a moderate disruption could cause them reputational damage with their customers that could potentially put them out of business as well.

In the post-9-11 period, more companies have been threatened by terrorism, further raising the risk of business disruption, not to mention the possibilities of loss of life and property damage. This has led to higher insurance premiums for business as well as for federal regulatory oversight to reduce risk to the economy in the event that business centers were attacked.

As a result, minimum standards and frameworks have been established legislatively to facilitate a reasonable rate of recovery of commerce across entire industries. This is particularly true of businesses that have been incorporated under a banking charter as they are regulated and supervised by the Office of the Comptroller of the Currency (OCC) within the Department of the US Treasury. The supervision is such that milestones for meeting minimum standards are negotiated with the Compliance Officer of companies, including the scheduling of business continuity tests with representatives from the OCC present to verify that the company has met each milestone. Noncompliance through neglect, mismanagement, or contempt can lead to fines and even a business shutdown.

In addition to ensuring that companies implement specific capabilities within their business operations and data centers, companies are also required to verify that the vendors that they outsource business capabilities also meet similar criteria. However, business continuity has evolved to include a few basics that companies need to know.

In the recent past, it was common to find business users and the automation systems that supported them housed within a data center that was colocated in the same building. Although convenient for the network engineers, this provided an easy way to lose the company's automation capabilities, business users, and often data in a single event.

As a result, it is now common to separate the location of business users from the location of the data center, as well as to separate business users to multiple locations and have the additional data center strategically distant from the first. This generally translates to the second business office and second data center having to be on a different power grid, on a different coast, and away from the same storm track, flood zone, geologic fault line, volcanic hot spot, and military and political hot spot.

However, having an alternate data center that is safe is just the beginning. Even after IT ensures that there is a high-speed communication link between the remaining data centers and the remaining business offices, the equipment and configuration information must also be present, as well as up-to-date data to allow a disaster recovery process to begin. Probably most important, business continuity must have a well thought through plan.

When considering the variety and complexity of applications that support the automation needs of a particular line of business, the number of applications involved is almost never limited to a single system. In fact, the number of applications involved to support a single line of business end to end is often dozens of all types, shapes, and sizes.

One of the most challenging components of a good plan is the realization that recovering some applications while not others often leaves that particular line of business unable to operate. As such, the sooner that a complete suite of applications are recovered that are used to support a line of business, the sooner that particular business line will be back in action.

Ensuring this level of preparedness requires detail planning, which is planning that we have seen a number of Fortune 100 companies fail to do. The consequence of improper planning the sequence of automations systems within each line of business and their relative priority is that when applications are recovered randomly, effectively no line of business is able to be back in business until nearly all applications have been recovered. Given the resources available to recover applications and the rate at which they can recover applications when a disaster has not occurred, the recovery of all applications in a true disaster scenario can be an unusually long time.

It is like having flat tires on an entire fleet of fully loaded 18 wheeler trucks, and then randomly repairing the tires across all of the trucks, instead of focusing on a particular truck first, perhaps the one with the most perishable cargo. If one were to address all of the tires on the particular truck with the most important loads first, those trucks would be back in service to deliver their cargo with little delay. The alternative is to have trucks and their drivers lingering for a prolonged period of time until the trucks with the most perishable cargo just happened to have all of their tires repaired through a slow random process.

Believing that the necessary equipment and plan are in place is one thing, but testing them to prove it is quite another. The most important reason for frequent testing of business continuity plans is that even great plans are subject to a constant disruption due to the unrelenting onslaught of change.

Change comes in many forms and sizes, and each must be carefully provided for. The smallest change that gets lost can prevent a line of business from being unable to operate. There is the flow of steady change of all types. There are changes in business personnel, IT personnel, and vendor personnel, including their associated access rights to systems and infrastructure. There are changes in facilities, business facilities, IT facilities, and vendor facilities. The only thing that doesn't change is the steady flow of change.

Automation systems themselves are constantly changing at various levels of their infrastructure, such as their compiled instructions, their interpreted procedural statements, and rules within their rules engines. There are patches to database management system components, operating system components, communications software, and changes to configuration parameters for each. There are updates to drivers, new versions of software, as well as changes within the network infrastructure, security infrastructure, and performance monitoring infrastructure. In addition, there can also be changes in business volume, resulting in changes to data volume and resulting in changes to system load and total available system capacity.

As a result, business continuity planning must regularly test alternate work sites to ensure that business personnel have access to telephone services, Web-based services, communications links to data centers, access to application systems, communications links to vendors that participate in their business process, and access to third-party application systems with the appropriate bandwidth from the appropriate locations.

Each location must have personnel that possess the appropriate instructions and technical expertise to troubleshoot when those instructions fail, not to mention the business personnel to operate these capabilities. Also present at each alternate site must be a reasonable set of spare parts and equipment to troubleshoot and operate the needed capabilities.

As such, the role of a business continuity architect requires a broad combination of knowledge and cumulative experience about the business operation. They must be intimately familiar with the change control process for each type of operational component that can change, which they need to audit periodically between tests.

The business continuity architect in business architecture must work closely with the disaster recovery architect in operations architecture to identify the production assets that support each inventoried infrastructural capability and business application, including databases, networks, operating environments, and the servers associated with them.

In collaboration with the disaster recovery architect, the business continuity architect must ensure the most orderly and coordinated process possible so that business operation recovery occurs in a corresponding recovery of the correctly prioritized IT automation systems and infrastructure. The business value of bringing a line of business back online sooner to serve customers can make a big difference to the reputation of a given enterprise.

2.1.5 Risk Architecture

Risk architecture, also referred to as risk data aggregation (RDA) in the banking industry, is a means of defining, gathering, and processing risk-related data to facilitate measurement between company performance against the levels of tolerance the company has toward each category of risk.

One of the most significant lessons relearned in each global financial crisis is that the scope of information under consideration was inadequate to establish appropriate preparedness. Each time, organizations lacked the ability to aggregate risk exposures and identify concentrations quickly and accurately at the enterprise level, within lines of business and between legal entities. Some organizations were unable to manage their risks properly because of weak RDA capabilities and risk reporting practices. This had severe consequences to these organizations and to the stability of the global financial system.

Every enterprise has a particular tolerance for risk and strategy for managing it, although few enterprises have a global view of the risks that influence their economic condition. The role of risk architecture is to develop and maintain a framework of the various categories of risk that can affect an enterprise from the perspective of a global economy, national economies, market economies, industry sectors, and individual companies, including creditors, insurers, customers, vendors, and suppliers.

The role of a risk architect within business architecture is to maintain such a framework and track the various tools, techniques, and vendors that offer risk measuring and tracking techniques.

2.1.5.1 Routine Risk Categories

The areas of risk that are commonly addressed by an enterprise involve financial, political, and legal risks.

Financial risks are usually measured by analyzing investments and credit markets, often using insurance to help mitigate those risks. A moderately more advanced enterprise may evaluate their global exposure to customers and insurers, while a relatively advanced enterprise will monitor the effect of contagions across the various financial markets with a good degree of preparedness to react to recognizable events.

2.1.5.2 Financial Contagions

A contagion is generally understood as a price movement in a market that is the result of a price movement in another market, where the secondary price movement exceeds the threshold that would be considered a comparable price adjustment when based upon an accurate understanding of the underlying fundamentals. Market knowledge and understanding, particularly knowledge about a specific industry or company, is highly asymmetric. Some individuals simply know more or their background allows them to intuit more information than what was communicated publicly.

The types of contagions relate to the ways that they can be initiated, such as significant informational changes about sector or company fundamentals, significant changes in the credit market or market liquidity, a significant unrelated market opportunity, or a simple portfolio adjustment involving large positions involving specific securities.

The market participants usually include informed traders/investors, uninformed traders/investors, portfolio managers, and liquidity traders including program trading automation. The degree of contagion is determined by various market pressures and the buildup of anticipated changes in market direction, but also informational asymmetries and the reaction across less sophisticated emerging markets exacerbate contagion. This is not to say that contagions only represent downward trends, as contagions can also represent an upward movement that attracts mass appeal.

For example, the life cycle of a contagion related to a change in information is often described as new information reaches informed traders/investors whereby then uninformed traders/investors react to the adjustment, thereby amplifying the price movement and volatility. Similarly, liquidity traders, who trade irrespective of fundamentals, can inadvertently trigger uninformed traders and investors to incorrectly attribute price fluctuations as having been initiated by informed traders/investors.

2.1.5.3 Comprehensive Risk Framework

The most advanced enterprises monitor the cascade effect of contagions from the global economy, national economies, market economies, industry sectors, and individual companies to their enterprise, while monitoring a wider array of risk categories, subcategories, and then approximately 200 distinct subject areas of risk depending on the particular lines of business and industries their enterprise operates within.

Some of the risk categories that these risk subject areas belong to include:

- financial risks,
- political,
- environmental,
- energy,
- infrastructure,
- legal,
- informational,
- psychological,
- technological, and
- business.

As an example, the infrastructure category can contain subcategories, such as:

- transportation,
- power, and
- communications.

As an example, the power subcategory can contain distinct subject areas of risk, such as:

- long distance power grid,
- metropolitan power grid, and
- local power grid, power substations and lines.

The value of a risk framework is that it gives the enterprise the ability to consciously determine which categories and subcategories it wishes to monitor, measure, and prepare for.

2.1.5.4 Risk Model Steps

An example of the steps that can be used to approach a comprehensive risk framework includes:

- Identification of stakeholders for the following areas
  - **i.** Enterprise risk management (e.g., financial risk, cyber security, operational risk, hazard risk, strategic risk, and reputational risk)
  - **ii.** Investment risk management (e.g., portfolio management)
  - **iii.** Compliance risk management (e.g., treaty zone, national, and subordinate jurisdictions)
  - **iv.** Legal risk (e.g., legal holds by category by jurisdiction)
  - **v.** Regulatory risk (e.g., RIM and regulatory reporting by jurisdiction)
  - **vi.** Business risk management (e.g., M&A, product development, economic risk, insurance risk, vendor risk, and customer exposure)
- Review of risk framework
  - **i.** Identify which risk areas in which each stakeholder perceives value
  - **ii.** Determine unambiguous scope and definition
  - **iii.** Present an information architecture (IA)-driven framework for assessing them
  - **iv.** Identify indicators of those risks
  - **v.** Identify sample sources (real time, near real time, and batch)
  - **vi.** Propose a scoring framework
- Present opportunities for developing a customized IA-driven model
  - **i.** Propose a process with which to evolve
    1. source discovery
    2. source evaluation
    3. source integration
    4. scoring
    5. analytics
    6. forecasting
  - **ii.** Identify services that can be offered enterprise-wide
  - **iii.** Identify services that can be offered externally
  - **iv.** Identify where analytics and forecasting models can be used enterprise-wide
  - **v.** Propose a change control refresh process for redeployment of forecasting models
- Technology framework
  - **i.** Forecast model technologies
  - **ii.** Reporting technologies
  - **iii.** Data mining technologies
  - **iv.** Mashup technologies
- Data persistence technologies

RISK INFORMATION ARCHITECTURE SAMPLE 200

GLOBAL ECONOMY	NATIONAL ECONOMY	MARKET	SECTOR	COMPANY

FINANCIAL (55)

CONTAGION
- GLOBAL FINANCIAL CONTAGION
- DOMESTIC FINANCIAL CONTAGION
- MARKET FINANCIAL CONTAGION
- SECTOR FINANCIAL CONTAGION

INSURANCE
- UNINSURED LOSS
- UNINSURABLE

CURRENCY
- RESERVE CURRENCY
- FOREIGN EXCHANGE ECONOMIC
- NON-RESERVE CURRENCY
- INFLATION/DEFLATION
- FOREIGN EXCHANGE TRANSLATION
- FOREIGN EXCHANGE TRANSACTION
- FOREIGN EXCHANGE CONTINGENT

ECONOMIC
- GLOBAL ECONOMIC
- EMPLOYMENT
- NATIONAL ECONOMIC
- CENTRAL BANK POLICY

FIXED INTANGIBLE ASSET
- TRADE ASSET
- PATENT
- GOODWILL

ORDERLY MARKET
- MARKET VOLATILITY
- MARKET LIQUIDITY

CREDIT
- SOVERIGN CREDIT RATING
- INTEREST RATE
- REINVESTMENT RATE
- FINANCIAL DEFAULT
- SOVERIGN DEFAULT
- CREDIT AVAILABILITY
- SECTOR CREDIT AVAILABILITY
- COMPANY CREDIT RATING

- CUSTOMER DEFAULT
- COMPANY DEFAULT
- INSOLVENCY
- BANKRUPTCY

FIXED ASSET
- REAL ESTATE
- COMMODITIES

INVESTMENT
- REAL VALUE DIVERGENCE
- NOMINAL VALUE DIVERGENCE
- REAL NOMINAL VALUE DIVERGENCE

BUBBLE
- REAL ESTATE
- EQUITY
- CURRENCY
- SECTOR
- COMMODITY

- BUILDINGS
- EQUIPMENT

- FAILED INVESTMENT

CONCENTRATION RISK
- SECTOR CONCENTRATION
- PRODUCT CONCENTRATION
- INVESTMENT CONCENTRATION
- CUSTOMER CONCENTRATION
- REGIONAL CONCENTRATION
- VENDOR CONCENTRATION
- SUPPLIER CONCENTRATION

POLITICAL (24)

REGULATORY
- TREATY ZONE REGULATORY
- NATIONAL REGULATORY
- MARKET REGULATORY
- SECTOR REGULATORY

LEGISLATIVE
- FEDERAL LEGISLATION
- STATE LEGISLATION
- FEDERAL TAX DEDUCTIBILITY
- CAPITAL GAIN
- NATIONALIZATION
- PRIVATIZATION
- STATE TAX AND FEE
- STATE TAX DEDUCTIBILITY
- LOCAL TAX AND FEE

EXECUTIVE ORDER
- TREATY ZONE EXECUTIVE ORDER
- NATIONAL EXECUTIVE ORDER

EXTREMISM
- CIVIL UNREST
- LOCAL VIOLENCE

TERRORISM
- TRADE ROUTE DISRUPTION
- COUNTRY-SPECIFIC TERRORISM
- MARKET-SPECIFIC TERRORISM
- SECTOR-SPECIFIC TERRORISM
- COMPANY-SPECIFIC TERRORISM

ENVIRONMENTAL (12)

NATURAL DISASTER
- MAJOR NATURAL DISASTER
- LOCAL NATURAL DISASTER
- CLIMATE CHANGE
- RESOURCE AVAILABILITY
- WATER / FOOD SUPPLY
- PANDEMIC

MAN-MADE DISASTER
- SPACE DEBRIS

- INDUSTRIAL DISASTER
- ENGINEERING FAILURE
- TRANSPORTATION FAILURE

LEGAL (20)

LITIGATION
- PRODUCT CATEGORY LITIGATION
- MATERIAL RELATED LITIGATION

- CONTRACT LITIGATION
- PRODUCT LITIGATION
- TORTIOUS LITIGATION
- SECURITIES LITIGATION
- EMPLOYEE LITIGATION
- ANTITRUST LITIGATION
- CRIMINAL LITIGATION

FRAUD VICTIM
- FINANCIAL FRAUD
- CURRENCY COUNTERFEITING
- INDUSTRY COLLUSION

- INTERNAL COLLUSION
- ESPIONAGE
- MONEY LAUNDERING
- GIFT AND ENTERTAINMENT ABUSE
- VENDOR FRAUD
- CUSTOMER FRAUD
- EMPLOYEE FRAUD

ENERGY (4)

FOSSIL FUEL
- FOSSIL FUEL SUPPLY
- LOCAL FOSSIL FUEL SUPPLY

NUCLEAR FUEL
- NUCLEAR FUEL SUPPLY
- LOCAL NUCLEAR FUEL SUPPLY

INFRASTRUCTURE (9)

TRANSPORTATION
- PEOPLE TRANSPORTATION
- MATERIEL TRANSPORTATION
- LOCAL PEOPLE TRANSPORTATION
- LOCAL MATERIEL TRANSPORTATION

POWER
- LONG DISTANCE POWER GRID
- LOCAL POWER GRID

COMMUNICATIONS
- SATELLITE COMMUNICATION
- COMMAND AND CONTROL COMMUNICATION LINES

Diagram Risk architecture (sample).

2.1.6 BUSINESS ARCHITECTURE AND GOVERNANCE

Traditionally, the role of business architecture has been to develop business process models, product hierarchies, and business capability models, all with their corresponding taxonomies and business definitions:

- *Business process models* are diagrams that illustrate the flow of steps that are performed. At a high level, they may depict the sequence of departments that support a line of business, or at a low level, they may depict the steps that are performed within a particular business capability found within a particular department. Business process models should also depict a consistent taxonomy.
- *Product hierarchies* are taxonomies, usually shown in diagrams that illustrate the various ways that products and services are rolled up into subtypes and types of products and services by the different constituents of the enterprise. In a large enterprise, there is sometimes a different product hierarchy for marketing, versus sales, versus accounting, and versus legal.
- *Business capability models* have been illustrated in various ways, but we prefer the forms that most represent a hierarchy of business capabilities that are most similar to a functional decomposition that starts at the top. This method establishes a taxonomy starting with the overall industry, or industries, of the enterprise (e.g., insurance and banking) and then decomposing them into increasingly smaller more numerous business capabilities (e.g., property and casualty, health, life, retail banking, wholesale banking, and dealer banking) eventually down to individual services that support the business capabilities of the enterprise.

While this has its uses in facilitating communication using a shared set of terms and concepts, when limited to these activities, business architecture does not realize its full potential. In the modern enterprise architecture, business architecture must also help the organization adapt to the evolving marketplace, address the needs and expectations of existing and future customers, counter the activities of existing and emerging competition, look to adopt innovations in technology that can transform business, and comply with the evolving regulatory landscape.

To best manage the extended capabilities of business architecture, it can be useful to create an EBRB to facilitate discovery and recommendations regarding a coordinated global business strategy. The enterprise architecture review board would address the following needs:

- determine the most appropriate team of BSMEs necessary to support the business topics that are of great strategic importance to the enterprise or line of business, staffing periods, staffing levels, funding levels, and staff selection;

- assess the efficacy of BSMEs supporting the other areas (e.g., information systems architecture, operations architecture, global application development, and local application development teams)

Staffing of BSMEs also works well as part of and within information systems architecture, as we have done because we did not have official control of business architecture within our area which encompassed the banking lines of business. However, as a coordinated effort across the enterprise, it could better focus on the hedgehog concepts that best define the enterprise and each line of business.

As with the other disciplines of enterprise architecture, the disciplines of business architecture must have readily identifiable metrics that can measure the productivity of each architectural discipline and each individual within business architecture. Together, metrics and planning will provide the necessary lead time in preparing management when to increase, decrease, or replace resources.

Information Systems

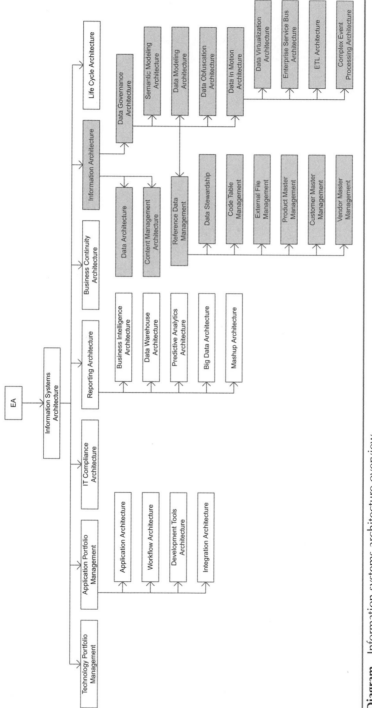

Diagram Information systems architecture overview.

3.1   "Information Systems" Architecture and Governance

The global operating model for information systems architecture is one where there are various distinct architectural disciplines that require architectural standards, frameworks, and services to deliver the following:

- align the many technical disciplines across IT with the strategic direction of the business,
- provide representation of stakeholder interests across a large number of application development teams,
- identify opportunities to executive management,
- manage complexity across the IT landscape,
- exploit the synergies across the various architectural disciplines of enterprise architecture,
- optimize the return of business investment into automation,
- act as an accelerator to the automation activities across each life cycle of the enterprise,
- continually illustrate architecture's return on investment.

Traditionally, information systems architecture has been simply referred to as enterprise architecture, without acknowledgment of there being a distinct set of architectural disciplines that belong to business architecture and operations architecture, or the distinction between information systems architecture and control systems architecture, or realization that there are a number of cross-discipline capabilities that span the aforementioned.

One may wonder why so many categories of architectural disciplines are valuable. After all, there are plenty of solution architects that are already assigned to application teams around the country and/or globe.

To understand this question more thoroughly, it is first important to look at the skill sets of solution architects and what their focus has been throughout their career, and what it is now.

Before the name "solution architect" came into fashion, solution architects would have been recognized the best and brightest programmer analysts and developers that implemented many of the applications within a large enterprise. Since solution architects are among the few that understand the majority of the critical application systems across the enterprise, they are valuable resources that cannot be readily replaced. In fact, it can take years to replace a typical solution architect as their accumulated knowledge of application systems is usually not documented to the extent that would be necessary to guide a substitute in a reasonable time frame.

Of the various roles across IT, solution architects have general to intermediate knowledge of many topics within technology. In fact, a typical solution architect can provide a fairly informative perspective on the widest variety of technologies of any type of resource across most any organization. So why not leverage solution architects to fill the role of enterprise architects? The answer can best be conveyed through a simple story.

> *A new management regime is introduced into a large enterprise. They reasonably set new business principles to leverage the economies of scale in negotiating with vendors for software licenses. They become aware of the fact that there are hundreds of different tools that are used for reporting and business intelligence (BI) purposes. However, they notice that none of these tools support the new Big Data space of technology.*
>
> *A team of the top dozen solution architects from across the company are assembled, as well as two members from enterprise architecture that are subject matter experts (SMEs) in information architecture, itself an immensely vast architectural discipline.*
>
> *Management proposes that a list of several Big Data technologies should be assembled for consideration to determine the best technology choice for the enterprise as a global standard.*
>
> *[Rather than picking on specific vendors and products, as this is certainly not the intention of this book, we will give fictitious product names, although we will try to associate a few characteristics to them that are realistic from a high-level perspective where they are necessary to serve the purposes of this discussion.]*
>
> *The team of solution architects schedule length daily meetings across a period of several months. The two enterprise architects divide their time so that only one of them has to be present for each given meeting, and they dial into the meetings when their schedule permits. It is also fair to state that the goal of the two enterprise architects is to have a good collaborative series of meetings with their architectural brethren.*
>
> *Unlike the well-facilitated meetings, these meetings were loosely facilitated, often driven by who could call out the loudest. The two enterprise architects stated the importance of getting requirements from the various stakeholders, although no requirements were ever collected from any of the lines of business. To obfuscate the fact that requirements were not available, the team adopted a resolution to state to management specific phrases like, "What we are hearing from the business is that they want, or would like, to be able to do deep analytics." After many hours of meetings, the team elected the path that they wanted to take. It is a path that many architecture review boards commonly take, and if it is good enough for architecture review boards that make technology decisions every time they convene, then it must be an industry best practice. This is the approach where a team of generalists decide to leverage the feature list of every major product from its marketing materials, and capture it in a spreadsheet to be used as the master set of evaluation criteria.*

Quite the feature list was assembled from scouring the marketing materials of the major Big Data products. In a number of cases, the features seemed to conflict with one another, particularly because some of the products had vastly different architectures, but why quibble over details. The weeks flew by.

Now that the feature list, which was being loosely used as business requirements, was assembled, the team proceeded to the next step of matching the candidate products to the master feature list to determine which products had more features than other products. However, not all products matched up to features on the basis of a clear yes or no. Some products partially had some of the features, and it had to be determined how much to award each product. More weeks flew by.

Finally, all of the products were mapped to the master feature list, with their varying degrees noted in the scoring system. However, a simple count of features that a given product had seemed somewhat unfair. Certainly, some features in this long list were more important than others, so now it had to be determined how much weight to assign each feature. More weeks flew by.

Eventually, the team had a new weighted score for each of the products. It should be noted that the weightings did not alter the relative ranking of the products, although it did bring some of them closer together in total score. Now many months later, the solution architects were quite pleased with their accomplishment, which selected the most expensive product from among the candidate products. But what did the enterprise architects think of it?

In fact, the enterprise architects could have saved 9 months off the process and countless man hours of effort because it was obvious to them that the outcome had to be the biggest, most mature, most expensive product of the bunch. It should always make sense that the most expensive product would have the most features and would have been the one that had been around the longest to build up those features. Newer products generally have to be less expensive to get market share, and they take years to accumulate a litany of features. But was the most expensive product the right choice from the perspective of a SME in information architecture?

The best choice from the perspective of the information architecture SMEs was actually the least expensive product, which ironically did not even make the top three in any of the scorings performed by the solution architects, and was summarily dismissed. However, it was less expensive by a factor of nearly 20 to 1 over a 5-year period ($5MM versus $100MM).

In fact, from a software internals perspective, it had the most efficient architecture, least complicated to install, setup and use, required less expensive personnel to manage, administer, and utilize it, with a significantly shorter time to deployment. It was also more suitable to be distributed across the many countries, many of which had medium to small data centers, and small budgets.

In all fairness to the solution architects, they played by the rules they were given. The actual recommendation from the two enterprise architects was to select two products. What we had found from being on conference calls with reference clients of the various products was that the least expensive product accomplished the job better than the most expensive one about 95% of the time. There were, however, 5% that needed some feature of the most expensive product. Clients indicated that the technology footprint for the most expensive product was therefore limited to the few areas that required those features, and that represented significant savings.

It is also fair to say that this author was very lucky to have been familiar with much of the internal design of the various products. However, it was that subject matter expertise that made it obvious early on as to which product a SME in the architectural discipline of database technology would select.

The point we make is a simple one. There is a benefit to having an SME in any of the architectural disciplines that represent areas of technology that are either already in use or will be in use across the IT landscape. Enterprise architects are SMEs in one or more particular areas of technology, as compared to a solution architect who is an expert in one or more applications and a generalist in the many technologies that those applications use.

Still another area of benefit has to do with the various corporate stakeholders from across the organization. These include the heads of departments such as Legal, Compliance, Auditing, and Chief Customer Officer, as well as external stakeholders such as outsourcing partners, customers, investors and regulators.

Since it is unrealistic to expect each stakeholder to interact with many solution architects, not to mention the fact that they may all have different interpretations of the various stakeholder interests, it is up to the few enterprise architects to incorporate the interests of the various stakeholders into the standards and frameworks of the architectural discipline in which they are an SME.

Equally as important, there are valuable synergies among architectural disciplines that offer opportunities of incorporating improved standards and frameworks that materialize simply from having enterprise architects who are SMEs in their respective discipline explain their disciplines to and collaborate with one another. This leads to added data security and data privacy benefits, such as easy and automatic data masking for ad hoc reporting.

Therefore, in the modern information systems architecture, technology challenges are addressed by instantiating the architectural disciplines that correspond to the areas of technology in use, or are planned to be in use, around the globe. Although the number of pertinent architectural disciplines for any company will vary, approximately 30 disciplines form a basic set that we discuss below. In addition, the specific architectural disciplines that may need to be instantiated at a given point in time can vary depending upon the technologies in use and the activities that are in progress or soon to start across the enterprise.

The operating model for information systems architecture is one where the expert defines the scope of their architectural discipline, and then identifies the hedgehog principle that drives the particular discipline, and a small number of additional metrics-driven principles that provide the ability to measure efficacy of the architectural discipline across the IT landscape.

Each SME must also determine the current state, future state, and a transition plan to get from the current state to the future state. Each SME must also present their discipline to their peers of SMEs for the other architectural disciplines. Each SME would identify the standards and frameworks that they propose and why, develop and refine these artifacts, and then mentor local governance boards, solution architects, and application development teams across the IT community.

Although this will be addressed in more detail later, local governance boards, solution architects, and application development teams should jointly participate in a process that determines whether designs and implementations are in compliance with the standards and frameworks, and to request exceptions, as well as a process to escalate requests for exceptions when it is believed that the exception should have been granted and/or the standard changed.

That said, even though architectural standards would be developed with the objective of controlling costs across the enterprise, there must still be a process in place to request exceptions to evaluate opportunities for improvement. If an exception does not violate the interests of another stakeholder and is clearly advantageous cost-wise over the potential life of the design, then the exception should be approved. Likewise, if the standard can be improved to better control costs or protect the interests of stakeholders across the enterprise, then the process to update the standard should be engaged.

We will now discuss a set of candidate architectural disciplines to be evaluated for inclusion into a modern information systems architecture practice.

3.1.1   TECHNOLOGY PORTFOLIO MANAGEMENT

Technology portfolio management (TPM) is the discipline of managing the technology assets of an enterprise in a manner that is somewhat analogous to managing a portfolio of securities, whose focus is to optimize present and future value while managing risk.

At the onset, this is somewhat more challenging than one might expect as financial securities have consistent measurement criteria and technology products do not, at least not without a good amount of work as no industry standard has yet been established.

The challenge is that consistent measurement is only possible when comparing technologies that belong to the same area of technology and provide the same or overlapping capabilities. The development of standard categories is only beginning to emerge with tools for administrating TPM, such as the typical TPM tools. That said, the small number of categories that have been identified out of the box by the typical TPM tools is simply not granular enough to support the needs of large organizations, as the high-level categories should correspond directly with the architectural discipline that is most closely aligned to its core capability.

Once allocated to their associated architectural discipline, the subcategories, and in some cases, the sub-subcategories of technologies are best determined by the SME responsible for the particular architectural discipline.

For example, the subcategories for many operations and infrastructure components can be any combination of the hardware environment categories, such as mainframe; mid-range application server, database server, network server, or security server.

An example within the architectural discipline of workflow automation, technologies can be categorized as business process modeling notation (BPMN) tools, business process modeling (BPM) technologies, or workflow automation (WFA) tools, which we will discuss in the section that addresses the architectural discipline of workflow automation.

One approach to begin managing a portfolio of technology is to first develop an inventory of technologies in use across your company. This is not always easy as there may be technologies purchased and administered by business that may not be apparent to IT personnel. A thorough review of procurement contracts globally and incoming annual maintenance fees to accounts payable are typically required.

As the list of technologies is being assembled from across the globe, a variety of information associated with each technology can be gathered, noting that much of this information can further evolve repeatedly over time. The basic information that one would start with should include information from the last point in time payment was effected.

This should include exact name of the product, the name of the vendor, a vendor supplied product identifier, the product versions purchased, when each version was acquired, the platforms it was acquired for, and date of last update to the records of this product, and a high-level statement of the product's capabilities.

One should also analyze each application system and the particular technologies that support them in production, as well as the technologies that support them in the development and deployment life cycle. To do so however, there needs to be a clear understanding of the distinction in definition between an application and a technology.

To do this we must first be careful with the use of terms. The term "business capability" refers to the business functions that are performed within a given department using any combination of manual procedures and automation. A department receives a "request" corresponding to a "business capability" that it is responsible to perform, such as the business capability for accepting and processing a payment, or the business capability of effecting a payment.

Just as business departments perform business capabilities, IT departments perform business capabilities as well, such as the business capability of a Help Desk providing advice and support to users for personal computer equipment and software.

A given business capability may be performed manually, with automation, or using a combination of manual operations with automation. The automation itself, however, may be an application, such as a funds transfer application which executes business rules specific to the business capability of funds transfer, or a technology, such as the Internet which executes generic capabilities of the particular technology.

As such, the business rules of an application must be maintained by an application development team. The application development team can be within the enterprise either onshore or offshore; it may be outsourced to a vendor.

So here's the critical distinction that we are making. A technology does not contain business-specific business rules that support a business capability, whereas an application does contain business-specific business rules. Therefore, there are numerous software products that are technologies, such as rules engines, spreadsheets, and development tools (e.g., MS Access). These are simply technologies. However, once business rules are placed within a given instance of such a technology, then that instance becomes an application, which should be managed and maintained by an application development team as a production asset.

So to clarify, once a spreadsheet contains complex formulas that is used to support a business capability, that instance of that spreadsheet is an application that should be tested, its source should be controlled, it should be backed up for recovery purposes, and it should be considered as an inventory item in a disaster recovery (DR) plan.

However, if the spreadsheet is simply a document or a report, such as any word processing document like an MS Word file or Google Doc that do not contain business rules, then those instances are simply electronic documents and cannot be classified and managed as an application.

This means that the each application must also be analyzed to determine the specific technologies that ultimately support the automation needs of a given business capability. This includes network software, database software, operating systems, and security software, as well as the various types of drivers that integrate different components together.

Also included should be document management systems, and the development and testing tools, as well as monitoring tools that support the development as well as maintenance process for supporting automation upon which business capabilities rely.

3.1.1.1 Organizing Technologies into Portfolios

Portfolios of technologies represent a way to group technologies so that they are easier to manage. In general, the better the framework of portfolios, the more evenly distributed the technologies should be into those portfolios.

Organizing technologies into portfolios may be approached either bottom up, by first identifying the inventory of technologies and then attempting to compartmentalize them into portfolios, or top down. Once an inventory of technologies has been established, no matter how large it may be, the process of identifying the portfolio that they belong to may be conducted.

The number of technologies can be large; we have seen it even in the thousands. Although a number of classification schemes can be used to identify portfolios, the approach that we have seen that has been best for us is to classify them into portfolios that most closely match the a particular architectural discipline.

It is important to classify technologies into portfolios that correspond directly with architectural disciplines for a number of reasons. First and foremost is that there is a major difference in the result of managing technologies using a team of generalists, such as by individual solution architects, versus having an SME managing the portfolio in which they are expert.

This approach has been the best we've seen for managing a large portfolio of existing technologies, and when it comes to the selection of new technologies, or the selection of a future state set of technologies, it is also best.

As discussed earlier, a team of generalists, who know a great deal about many architectural disciplines, but no one discipline to the extent that they could be considered an expert, will repeatedly demonstrate a propensity to select the most expensive technology for any given capability. The approach that they take can be quite methodical, although flawed.

The approach of most generalists is to begin by getting a list of the leading technologies for a given capability from a major research company. Depending upon how this list is used, this can be the first misstep for a couple of reasons.

First, the criteria that research companies use are necessarily a best guess as to what the important characteristics are to an average enterprise, although it is difficult to define what an average enterprise may be. Unless your enterprise meets the criteria of being close to the average, it will not likely be as pertinent to your organization as you might like. Your enterprise may have particular strategies and technology direction that can easily outweigh the criteria used by an average organization.

Second, one must frequently take into account the relationship that research companies have with vendors, as some vendors represent large cash streams to the research company who sometimes hire research companies for consulting services. The advice of these firms may not be intentionally slanted at all, but we have seen at least one situation where the recommendation of a major research company was the result of deception, negligence, or incompetence.

Unfortunately, generalists are at an unfair disadvantage to detect questionable research, whereas an SME will tend to spot it immediately.

The next potential misstep performed by generalists is that they tend to use the product feature list from marketing literature as a substitute for requirements and evaluation criteria. This has a number of problems associated with it. While the evaluation criteria itself may not conform to the evaluation criteria most appropriate for your enterprise, the potentially bigger issues are that the feature list identified within the marketing literature is likely to be slanted toward the evaluation criteria used by the research company, and the evaluation criteria of the research company may actually be influenced by the vendor to favor themselves during the product evaluation process while working with the research analyst.

The final potential misstep performed by generalists is that they may not understand the all-in costs of a technology over the life of the technology. Introductory discounts and prices can distort the true cost structure, and the business benefits ofthe technology are often not realized due to tool complexity and hidden costs.

Vendor marketing personnel are the best at what they do. They are familiar with many of the financial ROI analysis approaches used by large organizations. Although most technical people do not enjoy performing a detailed financial analysis of a technology that is under evaluation, it is extremely important that this step is performed carefully in an impartial manner.

3.1.1.2   Architecture ROI Framework

When it comes to analyzing the all-in cost of each vendor technology, the SME will already have valuable insight into what other customers have experienced with a given technology, why and what the costs and benefits are. Even armed with that knowledge, it is still advisable for the SME to make use of a framework to evaluate the various aspects from an architectural perspective using an architecture ROI framework.

An architecture ROI framework can contain a number of categories with which to evaluate costs and benefits. Foremost, the appropriate SMEs should determine each technology's compatibility with the application strategy, technology strategy, and data strategy. If the technology is not compatible with strategy of the enterprise, the technology can be rejected and the architecture ROI need not be performed.

If, however, the technology is compatible with the strategy of the enterprise, then we recommend that the architecture ROI framework minimally addresses the following with the minimum of a 3-year projection:

- application impact
  - costs include new application licensing, maintenance, implementation, and decommissioning
  - savings include decommissioned application license reduction, reallocation, and maintenance
- infrastructure impact
  - costs include new infrastructure purchases, maintenance, installation and setup, decommissioning
  - savings include decommissioned infrastructure reduction, reallocation, annual charges, and infrastructure avoidance
- personnel impact
  - costs include additional employees, time and materials consultant labor, SOW costs, travel expenses, training costs, conference fees, membership fees, and overtime nonexempt charges
  - savings include employee hiring avoidance, employee attrition, employee position elimination, consultant hiring avoidance, consultant personnel reduction, training avoidance, travel expense avoidance, conference fee avoidance, and membership fee avoidance
- vendor impact
  - costs include hosting fees, service subscription fees, usage fee estimates, setup fees, support fees, appliance fees, and travel
  - savings include hosting fee reduction, service subscription fee reduction, usage fee reduction, appliance fee reduction, and travel expense reduction
- operational workflow impact
  - costs include increased rate of inbound incidents/requests, estimated increase in processing time, and average incident/request cost increase
  - savings include decreased rate of incoming incidents/requests, estimated decrease in processing time, and average incident/request cost decrease
- business impact
  - costs include estimated business startup costs, estimated losses from periodic loss of business capabilities, estimated loss from customer dissatisfaction, and estimated exposure from regulatory noncompliance
  - savings include value of additional business capabilities, value of improved customer satisfaction, and value of enhanced regulatory reporting

Additionally, each cost and benefit should have a visual illustration of a 3- to 5-year projection associated with it, such as in the cost illustration in red, and savings illustration in green, shown in Figure A.

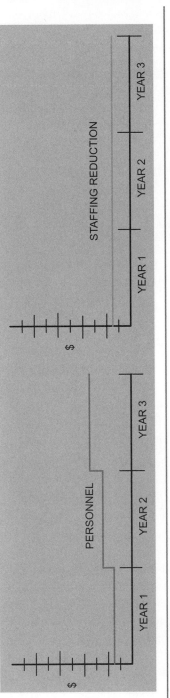
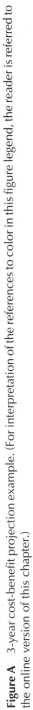

Figure A 3-year cost-benefit projection example. (For interpretation of the references to color in this figure legend, the reader is referred to the online version of this chapter.)

Once the figures have been reasonably verified, then it is time to prepare subtotals for each category followed at the end by a grand total chart to depict the net costs and savings of all categories, showing an architecture ROI cost, as illustrated in Figure B.

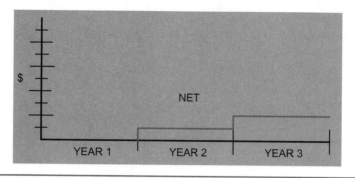

Figure B Net cost and savings. (For color version of this figure, the reader is referred to the online version of this chapter.)

The assumption associated with the architecture ROI framework is that it does not consider:

- after tax implications,
- net present value (NPV) to account for the future value of money,
- internal rate of return (IRR) to compare two or more investments,
- personnel severance costs as negotiated by HR,
- the distinction between airfare and lodging rates, and
- subjective measures of earnings and capital assumptions.

At this point, the architecture ROI is ready to go to finance to be included into their financial framework.

In conclusion, one or few experts will select technologies that will provide the greatest business value, as it is more likely to satisfy the capabilities actually required, to be less complex, be a vendor whose core capability more closely corresponds to what is needed to satisfy the pertinent business capability, and to have a better understanding of the all-in cost over the life of the technology.

Another important reason to classify technologies into portfolios that correspond directly with architectural disciplines is that it is much easier to identify a point of responsibility for a given technology that can perform the role and add real value to the users of the particular technology.

Once the appropriate portfolios for classifying technologies have been determined, it is a straightforward process to allocate those technologies that have a clear focus. It should be noted that some technologies have such a number of capabilities such that they begin to spread into multiple architectural disciplines.

When this occurs, it is important to take note which capabilities a technology was acquired and approved for. Identifying which capabilities that a technology is to be used for is another role that experts within architectural disciplines are well suited for.

3.1.1.3 Enhanced TPM

After each technology has been allocated to the most appropriate architectural discipline, there are a few of basic steps to follow that will help with managing the content of that portfolio. Depending upon the particular architectural discipline, technologies can be further organized in useful ways.

If we consider the architectural discipline "Content Management Architecture" as an example, the technologies that could be allocated to that discipline can be organized into enterprise content management systems (aka document management systems) may include:

- Web content management systems,
- mobile content management,
- collaboration management,
- component content management,
- media content management (e.g., audio, video), and
- image management systems.

By organizing technologies of a portfolio by further allocating them in a diagram into such technology categories, it now becomes easy to visually illustrate technologies by these technology categories to readily depict gaps, overlaps, and oversaturation of technologies within each technology category of the particular portfolio.

The characteristics used to create technology subcategories within each portfolio are best determined by the SME that manages the particular architectural discipline. To speak to it generally however, the characteristics of the subcategories used should provide a good distribution of the technologies that have been allocated to the specific architectural discipline.

When the technologies belonging to a particular portfolio have been organized in such a manner, the SME is better positioned to identify technology strategy that is optimal for the particular portfolio.

Now that the various technologies have been organized into subcategories within their associated architectural discipline, it is time to consider technology metadata and metrics. Since all architectural disciplines need to acquire many of the same metadata about their respective technologies, it is best to develop a shared process and repository developed by the architectural discipline TPM.

As one would expect, products that have a high concentration of adoption within a line of business are not readily subject to a change in technology direction, whereas technologies that have few users and instances within a line of business can be subject to a rapid change of technology direction.

Basic metadata can include vendor name, technology name, supported hardware and operating system environments, approved usage, whether there are any special considerations for failover or DR, and the degree to which it is compatible with each line of business application strategy, technology strategy, and data strategy.

Basic metrics can include licenses purchased, licenses consumed, annual maintenance fees, cost of additional licenses, lines of business that use the technology, the level of experience across the users, degree of user training required, number of outstanding product issues, the frequency of product patches and new releases, and the number of hours consumed to provide administration for the product.

With this information, the SME can take into consideration, the costs associated with the potential disruption of each potential change to determine the most beneficial future state for the organization within each line of business. It then becomes possible to develop a roadmap to achieve the intended future state which optimizes business value, ultimately affecting the competitiveness of the company within the marketplace, as these practices accumulatively influence the infrastructural costs of the enterprise.

Additionally, publishing these artifacts as part of a policy of full transparency is the best way to illustrate the direction and strategy of technology within each technology portfolio. Imparting knowledge of the future state roadmap and the supporting metrics of a technology portfolio communicates all of the necessary information in the appropriate context as opposed to generalists assigning a status of buy, hold, or divest to each technology to drive toward the future direction with minimal knowledge and a lack of gathered information.

One last interesting topic to consider in TPM is to understand the circumstances when technologies drive the application strategy and when applications drive the technology strategy.

Although there are always exceptions, it is much more common to see a particular line of business drive the entire IT infrastructure relative to their line of business because applications for a given line of business have mostly evolved on some platforms more than in others. For example, an Investments line of business within an insurance company is far more likely to be Windows and Microsoft centric than IBM mainframe or Oracle centric, whereas HR within a large company is more likely to be Oracle UNIX centric than Microsoft centric. Once the suite of applications within a given line of business determines the dominant applications and their associated environments, the technology stack simply follows their lead.

In contrast, there are still occasions when technology leads the selection of applications and environment. This may help to explain IBM's motivation to get into the Big Data space so that IBM hardware can play more of a central role in the high-end Hadoop world within large enterprises.

3.1.2 REPORTING ARCHITECTURE

Developing reports in the early years of IT was rather easy, especially since the volume of data available in a digital form at that time was relatively low. As the volume of information increased soon, it became valuable to report on historical data and the depiction of trends, statistics, and statistical correlations.

It was not long before reports went from batch to online transaction processing (OLTP) reporting, with applications generating reporting journals, which were simply flat file records generated during normal processing to support easy reporting afterward. The earliest advancements in the analysis of larger amounts of data were propelled by the business advantages that could be had within the most competitive industries, such as among the advertising and financial investment firms.

Soon new terms emerged; some of these terms emerged out of necessity, as the term "reporting" would prove too general and extremely ineffective within Internet search engines. Hence, a variety of more specific terms entered the language.

These included:

- statistical analysis,
- online analytical processing (OLAP),
- BI,
- nonstatistical analysis (e.g., neural networks),
- data mining,
- predictive analytics (aka forecasting models),
- operational data stores (ODS),
- data warehouse (DW),
- data marts (DM),
- geographic information systems (GIS), and more recently,
- Big Data, and
- mashup technology.

New techniques using hardware were developed in an attempt to deal with the ability of the already existing hardware to process large amounts of data.

These included the emergence of:

- approximately a dozen levels of a redundant array of independent disks (RAID),
- solid state drives,
- vector processing,
- parallel processing,
- supercomputers,
- multiprocessing,
- massively parallel computing (MPP),
- massively parallel processing arrays (MPPA),

- symmetric multiprocessing (SMP),
- cluster computing,
- distributed computing,
- grid computing,
- cloud computing, and
- in memory computing.

To further advance the handling of larger quantities of data, file access methods and file organizations gave way to database technologies, with a variety of database types, such as:

- transactional,
- multidimensional,
- spatial, and
- object oriented.

Alongside these technologies came a variety of database architectures, such as:

- hierarchical,
- network,
- inverted list,
- relational,
- columnar-relational hybrids, and
- true columnar (where relational database management system overhead is eliminated).

Although this can seem overly complex initially, it is not difficult to understand any reporting software architecture as long as you begin at the foundation of the technology, which is to first establish a good understanding of the I/O substructure and its performance specifications. Performance specifications vary with the type of operation, but they basically consist of two types of access, which are sequential access and random access.

From the foundation you build up to understanding programs that access the data, called access methods, as well as the way that they organize data on storage media, called file organizations.

Once access methods and file organizations are understood, then you are ready to understand the types of indexes, database architectures, and the architectures of database management systems including how they manage buffers to minimize the frequency with which the CPU must wait for data to move to and from the storage devices through the I/O substructure.

An expert in this discipline should be able to accurately calculate how long it will take to do each type of report by estimating the amount of time it takes for each block of data to traverse through the various parts of the I/O substructure to the CPU core. In this manner an expert can tell if a given technology will be sufficient for the particular type of report and quantity of data.

3.1.2.1   Data Warehouse Architecture

Before the volume of data grew beyond the capacity of standard reporting technologies data was read directly from their associated production transaction system files and databases. As data volume grew a problem emerged in that reporting and transactional activity shared the same production files and databases. As this resource contention grew, the need to replicate data for reporting purposes away from transactional systems grew.

When transactional systems were relatively few, replication of data for reporting was first implemented with the generation of files that could each would be used to create a particular report. With the growth in number of these files a more consolidated approach was sought, and from that the concept of the data warehouse emerged as a means to support many different reports.

As the variety of transaction system grew, along with the volume of data and number of reports, so did the complexity of the data warehouse. Soon more than one data warehouses were needed to support reporting requirements.

The complexity of creating and maintaining additional data warehouses creates opportunities for data inconsistencies across data warehouses. This led the industry to conclude that manageable collections of transaction systems should have their data integrated into ODS where it should be easier to resolve data inconsistencies because they were from similar transaction systems. Once the first wave of consolidation issues had been resolved then multiple ODSs could be further consolidated into a data warehouse.

With numerous transaction systems acting as the source of data bound for data warehouses, ODSs served as an intermediate step that could act as a mini-data warehouse for a collection of related transaction systems. These mini-data warehouses were easier to implement because the database designs of related transaction systems tended to be less disparate from one another than more distantly related transactions systems. Additionally, a number of reports could be supported from the layer of ODS databases, thereby reducing the load and complexity placed upon a single consolidated data warehouse.

With the emergence of an ODS layer, the data warehouse could return to its role of supporting the consolidated reporting needs of the organization that any could only be otherwise supported using a combination of one or more ODSs. In this approach, ODSs would house the details associated with their collection of transaction system databases, and the data warehouse would house the details associated with the collection of the ODS layer.

Needless to say, housing such a large accumulation of detail data from across several transaction systems poses a major challenge to database technologies that were designed to best address the needs of transaction processing.

Using database technology designed for transactional processing, the ability to read the detail data necessary to calculate basic totals and statistics in real time was soon lost. Data warehouses needed either a new technique to support the types of reports that focused on data aggregation, or it needed a new breed of hardware, software and databases that could support analytical processing, and a new breed of hardware, software and database technologies were born.

Data warehouse architecture deals with an array of complexities that occur in metadata, data and databases designs.

In metadata, issues include anomalies such as:

- ambiguously named fields,
- multiple terms that mean the same thing,
- one term that has multiple meanings,
- terms that do not represent an atomic data point such as compound fields,
- terms that have incorrect, missing, or useless definitions.

In data, issues include anomalies such as:

- sparseness of data where few values were populated for specific fields,
- invalid data like birth dates in the future,
- invalid or inconceivable values like a month of zero,
- partial loss of data due to truncation,
- invalid formats like alphabetic characters in a numeric field,
- invalid codes like a state code of ZZ,
- one field populated with data belonging to a different field like surname in first name,
- application code is required to interpret the data.

In individual databases, issues include anomalies such as:

- children records with no association to parent records
- children associated with the wrong parent
- duplicate records having the same business data
- schema designs that do not correctly correlate to the business
- indexes that point to incorrect rows of data
- loss of historical data

In multiple databases, issues include anomalies such as:

- inconsistent code values for the same idea like New Jersey = "99" or "NJ"
- incompatible code values for the same idea like New Jersey = Northeast US

■ non matching values for the same fields like the same person having different birth dates

■ incompatible structures that intended to represent the same things

The process of untangling metadata, data, and database issues may require tracing the data back to the online forms and batch programs that populated the values to be able to decipher the source and meaning of the data, often requiring knowledge of data discovery techniques, data quality expertise, data cleansing, data standardization and data integration experience.

3.1.2.2   BI Architecture

BI architecture is generally a discipline that organizes raw data into useful information for reporting to support business decision making, frequently using forms of data aggregation, commonly referred to as online analytical processing (OLAP).

OLAP comprises a set of reporting data visualization techniques that provide the capability to view aggregated data, called aggregates (aka rollups), from different perspectives, which are called dimensions. As an example aggregates, such as "sales unit volumes" and "revenue totals" may be viewed by a variety of dimensions, such as:

■ "calendar period,"
■ "geographic region,"
■ "sales representative,"
■ "product,"
■ "product type,"
■ "customer,"
■ "customer type,"
■ "delivery method," or
■ "payment method."

The choice of aggregates and dimensions is specified by the user, and the results are displayed in real time.

To deliver results in real time however, the initial approach to support data aggregation techniques was somewhat primitive in that all of the desired aggregates and dimensions that would be needed had to be predicted in advance and then precalculated typically during batch process usually performed overnight. This also means that although the responses were in real time, the data was from the day before and would not include anything from today until the next day.

Since unanticipated business questions cannot be addressed in real time, there is sometimes the tendency to overpredict the possible aggregates and dimensions and to precalculate them as well. This technique has grown to such an extent that the batch cycle to precalculate the various aggregates by the desired dimensions has become so time consuming that it frequently creates pressure to extend the batch window of the system.

Data mart load programs literally have to calculate each aggregate for each dimension, such as totaling up all of the "sales unit volumes" and "revenue totals" by each "calendar period," "geographic region," "sales representative," "product," "product type," "customer," "customer type," "delivery method," "payment method," and every combination of these dimensions in a long running overnight batch job.

Precalculated aggregates were stored in a variety of representations, sometimes called data marts, star schemas, fact tables, snowflakes, or binary representations known as cubes.

The feature that these approaches had in common was that dimensions acted as indexes to the aggregates to organize the precalculated results. A number of books have been written on this approach where they will also refer to a number of OLAP variants, such as MOLAP, ROLAP, HOLAP, WOLAP, DOLAP, and RTOLAP.

In contrast, the new breed of hardware, software, and databases approaches this problem now in new ways. The two major approaches include a distributed approach to have many servers working on the many parts of the same problem at the same time, and an approach that simply compresses the data to such an extent that the details of billion rows of data can be processed in real time on inexpensive commodity hardware, or trillions of rows of data in real time at a somewhat higher cost on mainframes.

As a result, physical data marts and the need to precalculate them are no longer necessary, with the added advantage that these new technologies can automatically support drill-down capabilities to illustrate the underlying detail data that was used to determine the aggregated totals.

The new breed of specialized hardware is typically referred to as an appliance, referring to the fact that the solution is an all included combination of software and hardware. Appliance solutions are higher priced, often significantly so in the millions of dollars, and have higher degrees of complexity associated with them particularly in areas such as failover and DR. That said, BI architecture encompasses more than just the capabilities of data aggregation.

BI can be expansive encompassing a number of architectural disciplines that are so encompassing themselves that they need to stand alone from BI architecture. These include topics such as data mining, data visualization, complex event processing (CEP), natural language processing (NLP), and predictive analytics.

Data mining is an architectural discipline that focuses on knowledge discovery in data. Early forms of data mining evaluated the statistical significance between the values of pairs of data elements. It soon grew to include analysis into the statistical significance among three or more combinations of data elements.

The premise of data mining is that one ever knows in advance what relationships may be discovered within the data. As such, data mining is a data analysis technique that simply looks for correlations among variables in a database by testing for possible relationships among their values and patterns of values. The types of relationships among variables may be considered directly related, inversely related, logarithmically related, or related via statistical clusters.

One challenge of data mining is that most statistical relationships found among variables do not represent business significance, such as a correlation between a zip code and a telephone area code. Therefore, a business SME is required to evaluate each correlation.

The body of correlations that have no business significance must be designated as not useful so that those correlations may be ignored going forward. The correlations that cannot be summarily dismissed are then considered by the business SME to evaluate the potential business value of the unexpected correlation.

Hence, examples of some potentially useful correlations may include the situations, such as a correlation between the numbers of times that a customer contacts the customer service hotline with a certain type of issue before transferring their business to a competitor, or a correlation among the value of various currencies, energy product prices, and precious metal commodity prices.

An active data mining program can cause business executives to reevaluate the level of importance that they place upon information when it is illustrated that valuable information for decision making lays hidden among vast quantities of business data. For example, data mining could discover the factors that correspond to the buying patterns of customers in different geographic regions.

Data visualization is an architectural discipline closely related to BI architecture that studies the visual representation of data, often over other dimensions such as time. Given the way that human brain works, taking data that exists as rows of numbers into different visual patterns across space, using different colors, intensities, shapes, sizes, and movements, can communicate clearly and bring to attention the more important aspects. Some of the common functions include drill downs, drill ups, filtering, group, pivot, rank, rotate, and sort. There are hundreds of ways to visualize data and hundreds of products in this space, many of which are highly specialized to particular use cases in targeted applications within specific industries.

A partial list of visual representations includes:

- cluster diagrams,
- terrain maps,
- architectural drawings,
- floor plans,
- shelf layouts,
- routes,
- connectivity diagrams,
- bubbles,
- histograms,

- heat maps,
- scatter plots,
- rose charts,
- cockpit gauges,
- radar diagrams, and
- stem and leaf plots.

3.1.2.3 Predictive Analytics Architecture

Predictive analytics is another architectural discipline that encompasses such a large space that it is worthy of its own discipline. Predictive analytics encompasses a variety of techniques, statistical as well as nonstatistical, modeling, and machine learning. Its focus, however, is identifying useful data, understanding that data, developing a predictive or forecasting capability using that data, and then deploying those predictive capabilities in useful ways across various automation capabilities of the enterprise.

Usually, the breakthroughs that propel a business forward originate on the business side or in executive management. There are a handful of factors that can lead to breakthroughs in business, where competitive advantages in technology can suddenly shift to one company within an industry for a period of time until the others catch up.

The basic types of competitive breakthroughs involve innovations in products, processes, paradigms, or any combination of these. Breakthroughs in paradigms are the most interesting as for the most part they facilitate a different way of looking at something. Some of the companies that have done particularly well involving breakthroughs in paradigms are companies such as Google, Apple, Facebook, and Amazon.

In a number of cases, however, a breakthrough in paradigm can be caused by mathematics, such as the mathematical developments that eventually led to and included the Black-Scholes options pricing model, which is where most agree that the discipline of quantitative analysis emerged.

The ability of a statistical model to predict behavior or forecast a trend is dependent upon the availability of data and its correct participation in the statistical model. One advantage that statistical models have to offer is their rigor and ability to trace the individual factors that contribute to their predictive result. Statistical methods however require individuals to be highly skilled in this specialized area.

The architectural discipline of predictive analytics is deeply engrained in statistics and mathematics, with numerous specialty areas.

Some examples of a specialty area include:

- longitudinal analysis, which involves the development of models that observe a particular statistical unit over a period of time,

- survey sampling models, which project the opinions and voting patterns of sample populations to a larger population, and
- stimulus-response predictive models, which forecast future behavior or traits of individuals.

While knowledge of statistical methods is essential for this discipline, it should not be without knowledge of nonstatistical methods, such as neural network technology (aka neural nets).

Neural networks are nonstatistical models that produce an algorithm based upon visual patterns. To be useful, numerical and textual information are converted into a visual image. The role of the algorithm is ultimately to classify each new visual image as having a substantial resemblance to an already known image.

Similar to statistical models, the ability of a neural network to predict behavior or forecast a trend is dependent upon the availability of data and its participation in the nonstatistical model to properly form the "visual image."

Neural nets are essentially complex nonlinear modeling equations. The parameters of the equations are optimized using a particular optimization method. There are various types of neural nets that use different modeling equations and optimization methods. Optimization methods range from simple methods like gradient descent to more powerful ones like genetic algorithms.

The concepts of neural networks and regression analysis are surprisingly similar. The taxonomy of each is different, as is usually the case among the disciplines of artificial intelligence.

As examples, in regression analysis, we have *independent variables*; in neural networks, they are referred to as "*inputs.*" In regression analysis, you have *dependent variables*; in neural nets, they are referred to as "*outputs.*" In regression analysis, there are *observations*; in neural nets, they are referred to as "*patterns.*"

The patterns are the samples from which the neural net builds the model. In regression analysis, the optimization method finds *coefficients*. In neural nets, the coefficients are referred to as *weights*.

Neural network "training" results in mathematical equations (models) just like regression analysis, but the neural network equations are more complex and robust than the simple "polynomial" equations produced by regression analysis. This is why neural networks are generally better at recognizing complex patterns.

That said, it should also be noted that it is often a trial-and-error process to identify the optimum type of neural network and corresponding features and settings to use given the data and the particular problem set. This tends to drive the rigorous statistician insane. Although early neural networks lacked the ability to trace the individual factors that contributed to the result, which also drove many a statistician insane, modern neural networks can now provide traceability for each and every outcome.

Early neural nets required highly specialized personnel; however, the products and training in this space have become user friendly for business users and even IT users to understand and use.

An early adopter of neural nets was American Express. Early on credit card applications were evaluated manually by clerical staff. They would review the information on the credit card application and then based upon their experience judge whether or not the applicant was a good credit risk.

The paradigm breakthrough that AMEX created was that they envisioned that the data on credit card applications could be converted to digital images that in turn could be recognized by a neural network. If the neural net could learn the patterns of images made by the data from the credit card applications of those that proved good credit risks, as well as patterns corresponding from bad credit risks, then it could potentially classify the patterns of images made by the data from new credit card applications as resembling good or bad credit risks correctly, and in a split second.

AMEX was so right. In fact, the error rate in correctly evaluating a credit card application dropped significantly with neural nets, giving them the ability to evaluate credit card applications better than any company in the industry, faster, more accurately, and at a fraction of the cost. At that time, AMEX was not a dominant global credit card company, but they rapidly became the global leader and continue to endeavor to maintain that status.

Regardless of the particular technique that is adopted, the use of predictive analytics has become essential to many businesses. Some insurance companies use it to identify prospective customers that will be profitable versus those that will actually cause the company to lose money.

For example, predictive analytics have been successfully deployed to determine which customers actively rate shop for insurance policies. If customers attain an insurance policy and then defect to another carrier within a relatively short period of time, then it ends up costing the insurance company more than they have made in profits for the given time period.

Today, retailers use predictive analytics to identify what products to feature to whom and at what time so as to maximize their advertising expenditures. Internet providers use predictive analytics to determine what advertisements to display, where it should be displayed, to whom. There are numerous applications across many industries, such as pharmaceuticals, health care, and financial services.

3.1.2.4   Big Data Architecture

The term "big data" means different things to different people. In its most simple form, big data refers to sufficient amounts of data that it becomes difficult to analyze it or report on it using the standard transactional, BI, and data warehouse technologies. Many of the "big data"-specific technologies, however, require significant budgets and usually require an extensive infrastructure to support. As such, it is critical for enterprise architecture to oversee it with the appropriate business principles to protect the interests of the enterprise.

In the context of control systems, big data is generally understood as representing large amounts of unstructured data. In this context, the true definition of unstructured data refers to the types of data that do not have discrete data points within the data that can be designed to map the stream of data such that anyone would know where one data point begins and ends after which the next data point would begin.

In a control system, the concept of a "record" housing unstructured data is different, as it represents a specific continuum of time when the data was recorded. In contrast, a record within an information system context will typically represent an instance of something.

In the context of information systems, big data is generally understood to be structured data and semistructured data, which is often referred to as unstructured data, as there are few examples of true unstructured data in an information system paradigm.

That said, it is important to clearly define what is meant by structured, unstructured, and semistructured data.

Structured data is the term used when it is clear what data elements exist, where, and in what form. In its most simple form, structured data is a fixed record layout; however, there are variable record layouts, including XML that make it clear what data points exist, where, and in what form.

The most common form of structured data is file and database data. This includes the content of the many databases and files within an enterprise company where there is a formal file layout or database schema. This data is typically the result of business applications collecting books and records data for the enterprise.

The next most common form of structured data refers to the content of machine generated outputs (e.g., logs), that are produced by various types of software products, such as application systems, database management systems, networks, and security software. The ability to search, monitor, and analyze machine generated output from across the operational environment can provide significant benefit to any large company.

Unstructured data is the term used when it is not clear what data elements exist, where they exist, and the form they may be in. Common examples include written or spoken language, although heuristics can often be applied to discern some sampling of structured data from them.

The most unstructured data does not even have data elements. These forms of unstructured data include signal feeds from sensors involving streaming video, sound, radar, radio waves, sonar, light sensors, and charged particle detectors.

Often some degree of structured data may be known or inferred with even these forms of unstructured data, such as its time, location, source, and direction.

Semistructured data is the term used when it is clear that there is some combination of structured and unstructured data, which often represents the largest amount of data in size across most every enterprise. As an example, I have frequently seen as much 80% of the data across all online storage devices within a financial services company be classified as semistructured data.

The most common forms of semistructured data include electronic documents, such as PDFs, diagrams, presentations, word processing documents, and spreadsheet documents, as distinct from spreadsheets that strictly represent flat files of structured data. Another common form of semistructured data includes messages that originate from individuals, such as e-mail, text messages, and tweets.

The structured component of the data in semistructured data for files is the file metadata, such as the file name, size, date created, date last modified, date last accessed, author, total editing time, and file permissions. The structured component of the data in e-mails includes the e-mail metadata, such as the date and time sent, date and time received, sender, receiver, recipients copied, e-mail size, subject line, and attachment file names, and their metadata.

The unstructured component of the data in semistructured data refers to the content of the file and/or body of the message. This form of unstructured data, however, can be transformed into structured data, at least in part, which is discussed in more detail within the discipline of NLP architecture, where automation interprets the language and grammar of messages, such as social media blogs and tweets, allowing it to accurately and efficiently extract data points into structured data. Opportunities to strategically convert the unstructured component of semistructured data to structured data provide significant competitive advantages.

Big data deals with any combination of structured, unstructured, and semistructured data, and the only thing in common between the ways that big data deals with extremely large volumes of data is that it does not rely upon file systems and database management systems that are used for transaction processing.

Regarding the more precise definition of big data, it is the quantity of data that meets any or all of the following criteria:

- difficult to record the data due to the high velocity of the information being received,
- difficult to record the data due to the volume of information being received,
- difficult to maintain the data due to the frequency of updates being received—although this tends to eliminate MapReduce as a viable solution,
- difficult to deal with the variety of structured, unstructured, and semistructured data,
- difficult to read the necessary volume of data within it to perform a needed business capability within the necessary time frame using traditional technologies,

- difficult to support large numbers of concurrent users running analytics and dashboards,
- difficult to deal with the volume of data in a cost-effective manner due to the infrastructure costs associated with transaction processing technologies.

3.1.2.4.1 OldSQL vs. NoSQL vs. New SQL

3.1.2.4.1.1 OldSQL The term *OldSQL* refers to the traditional transactional database management systems, regardless of their particular architecture (e.g., hierarchical, such as IMS, network, such as IDMS, inverted list, such as Adabas, or relational, such as SQL Server, DB2, Oracle, and Sybase). In relation to one another, all of these databases are forms of polymorphic data storage. This simply means that although the data is stored using different patterns, the information content is the same.

These products have developed from traditional file access methods and file organizations, such as IBM's DB2 database management system, which is built upon VSAM.

These OldSQL databases were designed to handle individual transactions, such as airline reservations, bank account transactions, and purchasing systems which touch a variety of database records, such as the customer, customer account, availability of whatever they are purchasing, and then effect the purchase, debiting the customer, crediting the company, and adjusting the available inventory to avoid overselling. Yes, if you were thinking that airline reservation systems seem to need help, you are correct although the airlines intentionally sell a certain number of additional seats than they have to compensate for some portion of cancellations and passengers that do not show up on time.

OldSQL databases have dominated the database industry since the 1980s and generally run on elderly code lines. The early database management systems did not have SQL until the emergence of SQL with relational databases. The query language of these early transaction systems was referred to as data manipulation language (DML) and was specific to the brand of database. These codes lines have grown quite large and complex containing many features in a race to have more features than each of their competitors, which all now feature SQL as a common query language.

A longer list of transaction database features includes such things as:

- SQL preprocessors,
- SQL compilers,
- authorization controls,
- SQL query optimizers,
- transaction managers,
- task management,
- program management,
- distributed database management,

- communications management,
- trace management,
- administrative utilities,
- shutdown,
- startup,
- system quiescing,
- journaling,
- error control,
- file management,
- row-level locking,
- deadlock detection and management,
- memory management,
- buffer management, and
- recovery management.

As one can imagine, having large numbers of sophisticated features means large amounts of code that takes time to execute and manage lists of things like locks that all contribute to overhead that can slow a database down, such as having to maintain free space on a page to allow for a record to expand without having to move the record to another page, or to add another record to the page that is next in sort sequence or naturally on the same page due to a hashing algorithm.

Diagram OldSQL database page with free space. (For color version of this figure, the reader is referred to the online version of this chapter.)

3.1.2.4.1.2 NoSQL A number of nontraditional database and BI technologies have emerged to address big data more efficiently. At a high level, these new breed of database management system architectures often take advantage of distributed processing and/or massive memory infrastructures that can use parallel processing as an accelerator.

Interestingly, they are called NoSQL because they claim that the SQL query language is one of the reasons why traditional transactions systems are so slow. If this were only true, then another query language could be simply developed to address that problem. After all, SQL is merely a syntax for a DML to create, read, update, and delete data.

Vendors of NoSQL database products are slowly moving their proprietary query languages closer and closer to SQL as the industry has caught on to the fact that speed and query language are unrelated. To adjust to this, the term *NoSQL* now represents the phrase "not only SQL."

The aspects that do slow down OldSQL include:

■ many extra lines of code that get executed to support many features that are specific to transaction systems,
■ row-level locking and the management of lock tables,
■ shared resource management, and
■ journaling.

Aside from stripping away these features, NoSQL databases usually take advantage of parallel processing across a number of nodes, which also enhances recoverability through various forms of data redundancy.

Aside from SQL, there is another unfounded excuse given for the poor performance of OldSQL transaction databases, namely, "ACID." I am often amazed at how frequently ACID compliance is often falsely cited as something that hinders performance.

To explain what ACID is in simple terms, if I purchase a nice executive looking leather backpack from Amazon to carry my 17 inch HP laptop through the streets of Manhattan, and Amazon only has one left in stock, ACID makes sure that if someone else is purchasing the same backpack from Amazon that only one of us gets to buy that backpack.

To briefly discus what each letter in ACID stands for:

■ Atomicity refers to all or nothing for a logical unit of work,
■ Consistency refers to adherence of data integrity rules that are enforced by the database management system,
■ Isolation refers to the need to enforce a sequence of transactions when updating a database, such as two purchasers both trying to purchase the last instance of an item, and
■ Durability refers to safeguarding that information will persist once a commit has been performed to declare successful completion of a transaction.

The topic of big data is rather vast much like big data would imply. Some of the topics it includes are the following:

■ infrastructure design of multinode systems
    ■ where each node is a server, or
    ■ SMP,
    ■ MPP, or

- asymmetric massively parallel processing (AMPP) systems, which is a combination of SMP and MPP.
- large-scale file system organization,
- large-scale database management systems that reside on the large-scale file system,
- data architectures of Hadoop or Hadoop like environments,
- metadata management of the file system and database management system,
- distributed file system (DFS) failures and recovery techniques,
- MapReduce, its many algorithms and various types of capabilities that can be built upon it.

MapReduce is an architectural discipline in itself. Some of the topics that a MapReduce Architect would have to know include:

- maps tasks,
- reduce tasks,
- Hadoop Master controller creating map workers and reduce workers,
- relational set operations,
- communication cost modeling to measure the efficacy of algorithms,
- similarity measures,
- distance measures,
- clustering and networks,
- filtering, and
- link analysis using page rank.

And then of course, it has close ties to various other architectural disciplines, such as reporting architecture, data visualization, information architecture, and data security.

3.1.2.4.1.3 NewSQL NewSQL is the latest entrant of database management system for OLTP processing. These modern relational database management systems seek to provide the same scalable performance of NoSQL systems for OLTP workloads while still maintaining the ACID guarantees of a traditional database system.

As for features that give NewSQL high performance and usefulness, NewSQL:

- scales out to distributed nodes (aka sharding),
- renders full ACID compliance,
- has a smaller code set,
- includes fewer features, and
- supports transactional processing.

3.1.2.4.2 Big Data—Apache Software Foundation

The focus of big data has recently moved to the software frameworks based on Hadoop, which are centrally managed by a U.S.-based nonprofit corporation incorporated in Delaware in June 1999 named Apache Software Foundation (ASF). The software available from ASF is subject to the Apache License and is therefore free and open source software (FOSS).

The software within the ASF is developed by a decentralized community of developers. ASF is funded almost entirely from grants and contributions, and over 2000 volunteers with only a handful of employees. Before software can be added to the ASF inventory, its intellectual property (IP) must be contributed or granted to the ASF.

The ASF offers a rapidly growing list of open source software. Rather than listing them, to give an idea as to what types of open source offering they have, consider the following types of software and frameworks:

- access methods,
- archival tools,
- Big Data BigTable software,
- BPM and workflow software,
- cloud infrastructure administration software,
- content management/document management software,
- database software,
- documentation frameworks,
- enterprise service bus (ESB) software,
- file system software,
- integration services,
- job scheduling software,
- machine learning/artificial intelligence software,
- search engines,
- security software,
- software development software,
- version control software,
- Web software, and
- Web standards.

A handful of companies represent the major contributors in the ASF space. They all base their architectures on Hadoop which in turn are based upon the Google's MapReduce and Google File System (GFS) papers.

Hadoop, or more formally Apache Hadoop, as a term refers to the entire open source software framework that is based in the Google papers. The foundation of this framework is a file system, Hadoop Distributed File System (HDFS). HDFS as a file system is fairly rudimentary with basic file permissions at the file level like in UNIX, but able to store large files extremely well, although it cannot look up any one of those individual files quickly. It is important to be aware of the fact that IBM has a high-performance variant of HDFS called GPFS.

On top of HDFS, using its file system is a type of columnar database, HBase, which is a type of NoSQL database analogous to Google's BigTable, which is their database that sits on top of the GFS. HBase as a database is fairly rudimentary with an indexing capability that supports high-speed lookups. It is HBase that supports massively parallelized processing via MapReduce. Therefore, if you have hundreds of millions of rows or more of something, then HBase is one of the most well-known tools which may be well suited to meet your needs. Yes, there are others, but that's the topic for yet another book.

To focus on the Apache Foundation, the number of software components and frameworks that are part of the Apache Software Framework (ASF) that integrates with HDFS and HBase is roughly 100. We will not go through these, except for the few that are most important in our view. However, first let's ask the question, "Do we need a hundred software components and frameworks, and are the ones that exist the right ones?" The way to understand this is to first follow the money. To do this, we should look at how companies make money from software that is free.

The pattern for this model is Red Hat in November 1999 when it became the largest open source company in the world with the acquisition of Cygnus, which was the first business to provide custom engineering and support services for free software.

A relatively small number of companies are developing software for the ASF in a significant way so that they can position themselves to provide paid custom engineering and support services for free software. Many of the software components in the ASF open source space are not what large enterprises tend to find practical, at least not without customization.

When one of these companies illustrates their view of the Hadoop framework, we should not be surprised if the components that are more prominently displayed are components that they are most qualified to customize and support or include software components that they license. Hence, the big data software framework diagram from each vendor will, for practical purposes, look different.

There are also a relatively large number of companies, which are developing **licensed soft-ware in this space**, sometimes only after the software enters a production environment. Instead of vying for paid custom engineering and support services, the goal of these companies is to sell software in volume.

If we now return to the question, "Do we need a hundred software components and frameworks, and are the ones that exist the right ones for a large enterprise?" the answer may resonate more clearly.

First, of the roughly 100 components of the ASF, there are ones that are extremely likely to be more frequently deployed in the next several years, and those that are likely to decline in use.

We will begin by defining a handful of candidate ASF components:

- R Language—a powerful statistical programming language that can tap into the advanced capabilities of MapReduce,
- Sqoop—provides ETL capabilities in the Hadoop framework (though not the only one),
- Hive—a query language for data summarization, query, and analysis,
- Pig—a scripting language for invoking MapReduce programs, and
- Impala—provides a SQL query capability for HDFS and HBase.

Let's speculate regarding the viability of a sampling of the ASF:

Let's being with "R." The "R Programming Language" was created at the University of Auckland, New Zealand. It was inspired by two other languages "S" and "Scheme" and was developed using C and FORTRAN. "R" has been available as open source under the GNU General Public License (aka GNU GPL or GPL) and Free Software Foundation (FSF), which are organizations distinct from the ASF. The GPU offers the largest amount of free software of any free or open source provider.

To provide an example of what R Language looks like, let's create the following real life scenario with a little background first.

Prime numbers are taught to us in school as being whole numbers that cannot be factored with other whole numbers (aka integer) other than the number 1 or itself. In other words, if we take a whole number such as the number 18, it is not a prime number simply because it can be factored as 9 times 2, or 3 times 6, which are all whole numbers. In contrast, the number 5 is a prime number because it cannot be factored by any whole number other than 1 or 5. Using this definition, the list of prime numbers begins as 1, 2, 3, 5, 7, 11, 13, 17, and 19. That said, some include the number 1, some exclude it. This is where prime number theory basically begins and ends, although I disagree that it should end here.

In my view, there is a second rule involving prime numbers that is not yet recognized, except for by myself. To me, prime numbers are not only whole numbers that cannot be factored with other whole numbers other than by the number 1 or itself, but prime numbers also represent volume in three-dimensional space whose mean (aka average) is always an integer (Luisi Prime Numbers).

Hence, primes in my view are a relationship among spatial volumes of a series of cubes beginning with a cube of 1 by 1 by 1. It also excludes all even numbers as being nonprimes, thereby eliminating the number "2." Visually in one's mind the sum of the volume of each prime divided by the number of cubes is always a simple integer.

To provide an example of what R language looks like, let's code for the mean of primes, which can be stated in pseudo code as the AVERAGE (first prime**3, second prime**3, and so on to infinity) is always a simple integer.

To go one step further, let's say that this new mathematical theory intends to say that any other number added on the end of the sequence that is the next "potential" prime number will only have a remainder of zero when the number added to the prime number series is the next prime number in the sequence. Since this is my theory, I choose to call these numbers "Luisi Prime Numbers," which can be useful when we discuss NP-complete and NP-hard problems.

Although "Mersenne Prime Numbers" are among the largest presently known prime numbers, the Luisi Prime Numbers are a major improvement over Mersenne Prime Numbers as Mersenne Prime Numbers are simply based on testing for a prime that is the number two raised to some exponential power and subtracting one from it. The first four Mersenne Prime Numbers are "3" (based on $2^2 - 1$), "7" (based on $2^3 - 1$), "31" (based on $2^5 - 1$), and "127" (based on $2^7 - 1$), which miss all the prime numbers in between one less than a power of two such as 11, 13, 17, 19, 23, and so on.

I could begin to test out the basic theory easily enough with R Language as follows:

■ > x <− c (1)	place in variable 'x' the first prime number
■ > y <− x×3	cube the prime number list
■ > print (x)	print the vector in variable 'x'
■ > print (y)	print the vector in variable 'y'
■ > mean (y)	average the cube of the 1 prime number
■ > [1] 1.0000000000	mean (y) with no receiving variable
■ > x <− c (1, 3)	place in variable 'x' a vector of prime numbers
■ > y <− x×3	cube the prime number list
■ > print (x)	print the vector in variable 'x'
■ > print (y)	print the vector in variable 'y'
■ > mean (y)	average the cube of the 2 prime numbers
■ > [1] 14.0000000000	mean (y) with no receiving variable
■ > x <− c (1, 3, 5)	place in variable 'x' a vector of prime numbers
■ > y <− x×3	cube the prime number list
■ > print (x)	print the vector in variable 'x'
■ > print (y)	print the vector in variable 'y'
■ > mean (y)	average the cube of the 3 prime numbers
■ > [1] 51.0000000000	mean (y) with no receiving variable

And so on, at least until I learn how to create a do loop in R

■ > x <− c (1, 3, 5, 7, 11, 13, 17, 19, 23)	place in variable 'x' a vector of prime numbers
■ > y <− x×3	cube the prime number list
■ > print (x)	print the vector in variable 'x'
■ > print (y)	print the vector in variable 'y'
■ > mean (y)	average the cube of the 9 prime numbers
■ > [1] 3,107.0000000000	mean (y) with no receiving variable

As is the practice for certain types of open source software, a company named Revolution Analytics began offering support for the R programming language and additionally developed three paid versions, including:

- Enhanced Open Source,
- Enterprise Workstation, and
- Enterprise Server.

The popularity of R grew rapidly in the analytics community, and it now uses a large library of R extensions that have been assembled under "The Comprehensive R Archive Network (CRAN)," with an inventory presently in excess of 5500 R extensions.

In my opinion, "R" will enjoy increased use within the industry. Although it is not obvious or intuitive how to use R as a programming language in the short term, once the developer understands it, it is an extremely efficient way to develop software that takes advantage of the powerful capabilities of MapReduce.

Next are the ETL capabilities of "Sqoop." A strong competitor to Sqoop is the ETL product space, which has an attractive distributed architecture for their conventional ETL and has an open source version in both the Hadoop and conventional space.

Last are "Hive," "Pig," and "Impala." These components have a variety of limitations pertaining to their access and security capabilities as well as runtime restrictions involving available memory, but new versions are on the way. There are also emerging products that use a free license preproduction and licensed in production, that support full SQL, including insert, update, and delete capabilities as well as support for data security using "grant" and "revoke."

Since support is necessary for any set of automation that supports important business capabilities, particularly in a large enterprise, it should be clear that the option for technology to be free is realistically not an option, except for the small company or home user.

3.1.2.4.3   Competing Hadoop Frameworks

I should note that this is among the few chapters where vendor names are used. To remain vendor agnostic, the names are being used simply for a historical perspective, without any preference shown for any vendor over another and purely with a journalistic perspective.

For the most part, there are six major competing frameworks in the Hadoop space and then a myriad of additional companies that offer products within these or similar frameworks. Of the six major frameworks, they include the following.

3.1.2.4.3.1   Cloudera Although Yahoo developed Hadoop in 2006, the first company to form after Yahoo developed, it was Cloudera in 2009. It was formed by three engineers, one each from Google, Yahoo, and Facebook.

Cloudera has a framework that features their licensed components and the open source components that they are competent to support and customize for other organizations.

The way Cloudera depicts their framework, they organize their components into five major groups:

- Cloudera Support,
- Cloudera Navigator,
- Cloudera Manager,
- Cloudera Distribution including Apache Hadoop (CDH), and
- Connectors (e.g., Microstrategy, Netezza, Oracle, Qlikview, Tableau, Teradata)

(See the most current version of the diagram on www.cloudera.com).

3.1.2.4.3.2   Hortonworks Two years later, 2011, the next one that formed was Hortonworks. Hortonworks received over 20 engineers from the Hadoop team of Yahoo and partnered with Microsoft, Informatica, and Teradata. One of their differentiators from the other frameworks is that Hortonworks is the only one that is staunchly open source.

Due to the fact that Hortonworks has a framework that features only open source components, all of their revenue comes from support, customization, and consulting services of the Apache Foundation stack. The Hortonworks approach is to provide all of their contributions involving the Hadoop framework to the Apache Foundation to support and customize these products and frameworks for other organizations. As a result, Hortonworks version of Hadoop is the trunk version of Hadoop.

The way Hortonworks depicts their framework, they organize their components into five major groups:

- Hortonworks Operational Services,
- Hortonworks Data Services,
- Hortonworks Core,
- Hortonworks Platform Services, and
- Hortonworks Data Platforms (HDP)

(See the most current version of the diagram on www.hortonworks.com).

3.1.2.4.3.3   MapR Around the same time in the same year, 2011, the company MapR formed as a team with EMC and Amazon to distribute an EMC-specific distribution of Apache Hadoop. A specific distribution refers to the fact that a branch has been taken off the trunk, which is a version of Hadoop has been selected which becomes a stable version of Hadoop off of which MapR may develop additional components.

In theory, even though a branch has been selected off the trunk, the ability to take a new more current branch of Hadoop always exists and it should always be compatible.

The differences seen in the MapR framework are due to the MapR specifically licensed software components that they have developed.

The way MapR depicts their framework, they organize their components into three major groups:

- Apache Projects with fifteen Apache Foundation open source components,
- MapR Control System, and
- MapR Data Platform

(See the most current version of the diagram on www.mapr.com).

MapR offers three different versions of Hadoop known as M3, M5, and M7, with each successive version being more advanced with more features. While M3 is free, M5 and M7 are available as licensed versions, M7 having the higher price point.

3.1.2.4.3.4   IBM By November 2011, IBM announced its own branch of Hadoop called IBM BigInsights within the InfoSphere family of products.

The way IBM depicts their framework, they organize their components into six major groups:

- Optional IBM and partner offerings,
- Analytics and discovery,
- Applications,
- Infrastructure,
- Connectivity and Integration, and
- Administrative and development tools

(See the most current version of the diagram on www-01.ibm.com/software/data/ infosphere/biginsights/).

The IBM BigInsights framework includes:

- Text analytics—providing advanced text analytics capabilities,
- BigSheets—providing a spreadsheet like interface to visualize data,
- Big SQL—providing a SQL interface to operate MapReduce,
- Workload Optimization—providing job scheduling capabilities,
- Development tools—based on Eclipse, and
- Administrative Tools—to manage security access rights.

The framework offered by IBM has fewer open source components depicted as compared to licensed components as IBM is in the process of integrating a number of their products into the Big Data ecosystem to provide enterprise grade capabilities, such as data security using their Infosphere Guardium product to potentially support data monitoring, auditing, vulnerability assessments, and data privacy.

3.1.2.4.3.5 Microsoft The fifth framework is that of Microsoft's HDInsight. This framework is unique in that it is the only one that operates in Windows directly instead of Linux. *(See the most current version of the diagram on www. windowsazure.com/en-us/documentation/services/hdinsight/?fb=en-us.)*

HDInsight supports Apache compatible technologies, including Pig, Hive, and Sqoop, and also supports the familiar desktop tools that run in Windows, such as MS Excel, PowerPivot, SQL Server Analysis Services (SSAS), and SQL Server Reporting Services (SSRS), which of course are not supported in Linux.

In the interest of full disclosure, we should note that Microsoft SQL Server also has various connectors that allow it to access Hadoop HBase on Linux through Hive.

3.1.2.4.3.6 Intel The sixth framework is that of Intel's distribution of Apache Hadoop, which is unique for it being built from the perspective of its chip set. Intel states in its advertising that it achieves:

- up to a 30-fold boost in Hadoop performance with optimizations for its CPUs, storage devices, and networking suite,
- up to three and a half fold boost in Hive query performance,
- data obfuscation without a performance penalty, and
- multisite scalability.

3.1.2.4.3.7 Summary All six are outstanding companies. As for architectural depictions, if you view their respective framework diagrams, they all share a common challenge. They all demonstrate an inconsistent use of symbols and diagramming conventions.

If these diagrams were drawn using a consistent set of symbols, then they would communicate the role of each component relative to each other component and more rapidly understood.

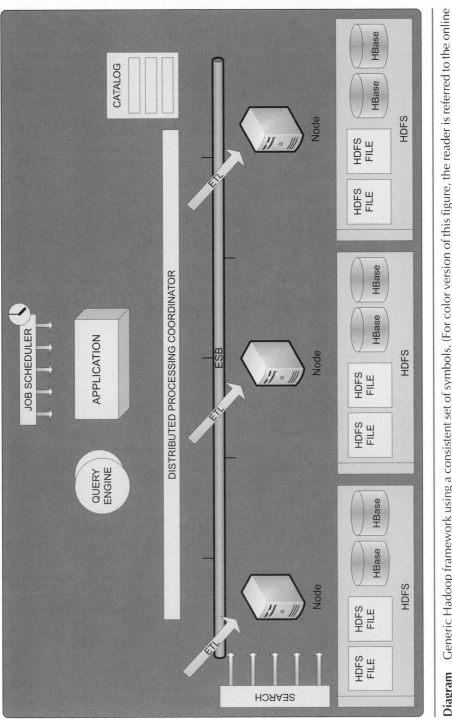

Diagram   Generic Hadoop framework using a consistent set of symbols. (For color version of this figure, the reader is referred to the online version of this chapter.)

In any event, these are the basic types of components that each framework contains. From here, one can color code the Apache Foundation components that are available through free open source licenses versus the components that are available through other open source providers and/or paid licenses.

It is important to note that companies should choose carefully which framework they will adopt. The reason for this is that if you choose a framework with proprietary components, any investment that you make in those proprietary components is likely to be lost.

When in doubt, the best choice is to not choose a framework or employ proprietary components until the implications have been determined and a strategic direction has been set. Each vendor offering proprietary components within their big data framework has an attractive offering. The ideal solution would be to have the ability to integrate combinations of proprietary components from each of the vendors, but presently that option is not in alignment with the marketing strategy of the major vendors.

There are also products and vendors that operate under the covers to improve the performance of various components of the Hadoop framework. Two examples of this class of component are Syncsort for accelerating sort performance for MapReduce in Hadoop and SAS for accelerating statistical analysis algorithms, both of which are installed on each node of a Hadoop cluster.

3.1.2.4.4 Big Data Is Use Case Driven

As one can already sense, there are perhaps an unusually large number of products within the big data space. To explain why this is the case, we only need to look at the large variety of use case types that exist. As one would expect, certain use case types are best handled with technologies that have been designed to support their specific needs.

The common use case types for big data include, but are not limited to:

- Data discovery,
- Document management/content management,
- Knowledge management (KM) (aka Graph DB),
- Online transaction processing systems (NewSQL/OLTP),
- Data warehousing,
- Real-time analytics,
- Predictive analytics,
- Algorithmic approaches,
- Batch analysis,
- Advanced search, and
- Relational database technology in Hadoop.

3.1.2.4.4.1   Data Discovery Use Case Type Data discovery falls into one of three basic types of discovery, which include:

■ novelty discoveries,
■ class discoveries, and
■ association discoveries.

Novelty discoveries are the new, rare, one-in-a-million (billion or trillion) objects or events that can be discovered among Big Data, such as a star going supernova in some distant galaxy.

Class discoveries are the new collections of individual objects or people that have some common characteristic or behavior, such as a new class of customer like a group of men that are blue-collar workers but also particularly conscious of their personal appearance or hygiene, or a new class or drugs that are able to operate through the blood-brain barrier membrane utilizing a new transport mechanism.

Association discoveries are the unusual and/or improbable co-occurring associations, which may be as simple as discovering connections among individuals, such as can be illustrated on Linked-in or Facebook.

Big Data offers a wealth of opportunity to discover useful information among vastly large amounts of objects and data.

Among the entrants for this use case type are included any of the technologies that have either some variant of MapReduce across a potentially large number of nodes or certain architectures of quantum computing.

3.1.2.4.4.2 Document   Management/Content   Management   Use   Case Type Document management is a type of use case that usually requires a response to a query in the span of 3-5 seconds to an end user, or a response in hundreds of milliseconds to an automated component which may deliver its response directly to an end user or a fully automated process. The use case type of document management/content management refers to an extensive collection of use cases that involve documents or content that may involve structured, unstructured, and/or semistructured data.

These can include:

■ government archival records
  ■ official documents of government agencies
  ■ legislative documents of congress
  ■ content generated by politicians and staff
  ■ government contracts

- business document management
  - loan applications and documents
  - mortgage applications and documents
  - insurance applications and documents
  - insurance claims documents
  - new account forms
  - employment applications
  - contracts
- IT document management
  - word processing documents
  - presentation files
  - spreadsheet files
  - spreadsheet applications
  - desktop applications
  - standards documents
  - company policies
  - architectural frameworks
- customer document management
  - diplomas
  - copies of birth certificates
  - marriage, divorce, and civil union certificates
  - insurance policies
  - records for tax preparation

Once the specific use case(s) of document management/content management have been identified, then one has the ability to start listing requirements. Basic document requirements start with simple things, such as the maximum size of a document and the number of documents that must be managed but it continues into an extensive list that will determine the candidate Big Data products that one may choose from.

Potential document management/content management requirements include:

- maximum document size
- maximum document ingestion rate
- maximum number of documents
- file types of documents
- expected space requirements
- maximum concurrent users retrieving documents
- document update/modification requirements
- peak access rate of stored documents
- number of possible keys and search criteria of documents

- local or distributed location of users
- multi-data center
- fault tolerance
- developer friendly
- document access speed required

In fact, the potential list of requirements can extend into every nonfunctional type of requirement listed in the nonfunctional requirements section discussed later in this book.

Needless to say, there are many Big Data products in the space of document management/content management, each with their own limits on document size, number of keys, index ability, retrieval speed, ingestion rates, and ability to support concurrent users.

Among the entrants for this use case type are included:

- Basho Riak,
- MarkLogic,
- MongoDB,
- Cassandra,
- Couchbase,
- Hadoop HDFS, and
- Hadoop HBase.

The use case of document management however can become much more interesting.

As an example, let's say that your organization has millions of documents around the globe in various document repositories. It is also rather likely that the organization does not know what documents it has across these repositories and cannot locate the documents that they think they have.

In this type of use case, there are big data tools that can crawl through documents that can propose an ontology for use to tag and cluster documents together into collections. If done properly, these ontology clusters can then be used to give insight into what documents actually represent so that it can be determined which documents are valuable and which are not.

3.1.2.4.4.3   KM Use Case Type (aka Graph DB) Imagine the vast storage available within Hadoop as a clean white board that not only spans an entire wall of a large conference room, but as one that continues onto the next wall. To a great extent, Hadoop is such a white board, just waiting for Big Data architects to create an architecture within that massive area that will support new and/or existing types of use cases with new approaches and greater ease.

KM is a use case type that itself has many use case subtypes. To illustrate the extremes, let's say the continuum of KM ranges from artificial intelligence use cases that require massive amounts of joins across massive amounts of data to collect information in milliseconds as input into various types of real-time processes, to use cases that require even more massive amounts of knowledge to be amassed over time and queried on demand within minutes. It is this latter end of the KM continuum that we will explore now.

This use case subtype begins with the ingestion of documents and records from around the globe into the bottom tier (aka Tier-1), including files, documents, e-mails, telephone records, text messages, desktop spreadsheet files, desktop word processing files, and so on.

Each one of the files ingested will create a standard wrapper around each part of discrete content consisting of a header and footer that houses metadata about the content, such as its:

■ source,
■ frequency of extraction,
■ object type,
■ file type,
■ file format,
■ schema for structured data,
■ extraction date, and
■ ingestion date.

This bottom level of the Hadoop architecture framework can accommodate any number of documents, and with the metadata wrappers around them, they can be easily searched and indexed for inspection by applications that are driven by artificial intelligence techniques or by human SMEs. The essential point of the wrappers is that the metadata within those wrappers has oversight by a data dictionary that ensures metadata values are defined and well understood, such as file types and so on.

Another important way to think about the bottom layer of the architecture is that this layer houses "data," as opposed to "information," "knowledge," or "wisdom."

In contrast, the middle layer of this Hadoop framework (aka Tier-2) houses "information." It houses information one fact at a time in a construct that is borrowed from the resource description framework (RDF), called "triples." Triples are a subset of the RDF, which is a type of rudimentary data model for metadata that houses knowledge, in this particular case gleaned from the "data" collected in the bottom layer (see the below diagram).

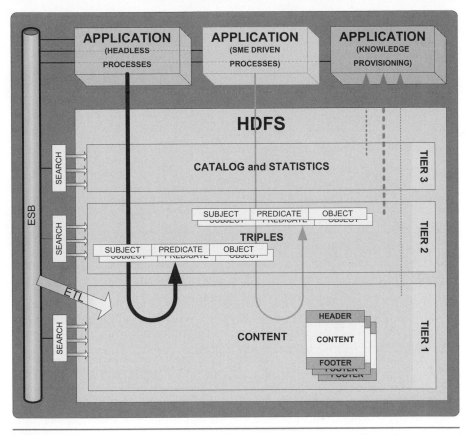

Diagram Hadoop 3-tier architecture for knowledge management. (For color version of this figure, the reader is referred to the online version of this chapter.)

Triples belong to a branch of semantics and represent an easy way to understand facts that are composed of three parts.

Each triple includes one:

- subject,
- predicate, and
- object.

The "subject" of the triple is always a noun. Rules must be established to determine the setoff things that are permissible to use as a "subject." The subject can be something as simple as a person or organization, or it may include places or things, as in a noun is a person place or a thing.

The "predicate" of a triple is always a trait or aspect of the "subject" expressed in relationship to the "object," which is another noun. The set of permissible predicates must be appropriately managed to ensure that they are consistent, defined, and well understood. Rules must also be established to determine the setoff things that are permissible to use as an "object."

This represents a collection of use cases that are closely aligned to intelligence gathering activities on individuals and organizations. The resulting KM capabilities offer a variety of commercial and government capabilities.

Imagine the applications for triples, such as:

- "Jim" *"knows"* "Peter"
- "Peter" *attends* "downtown NYC WOW"
- "Fred" *"attends"* "downtown NYC WOW"
- "Peter" *"makes-shipments-to"* "Jim"
- "Peter" *"owns"* "Firearms Inc."

Although triples can be stored in HDFS, they can also be stored in HBase, or any other Big Data database using any effective technique or combination of techniques for accelerating storage and retrieval. There are competitions (e.g., IEEE) for being able to manage and effectively use billions of triples.

The top level of our Hadoop architecture contains our catalog and statistics about the other two layers of the architecture. It can reveal how many triples exist, how many times each predicate has been used including which ones have not been used, and so on. As such, the top level (aka Tier-3) contains knowledge about our information (Tier-2) and our data (Tier-1).

At a high level, this architectural framework supports the ingestion of data, while simultaneously building information about the data using "headless" processes and SMEs, for use by business users to ask questions about the information being gleaned by the "headless" processes and SMEs.

3.1.2.4.4.4 Data Warehousing (DW) Use Case Type Data warehousing is a type of use case that usually requires a response to a query in the span of 3-5 seconds to an end user. The use case type of data warehousing refers to an extensive collection of use cases that involve content that usually involves structured data but may also involve unstructured, and/or semistructured data.

These can include use cases found within the industry sectors of:

- financial services industry
  - insurance underwriting
  - loan underwriting
  - insurance fraud detection
  - insurance anti-money laundering (aka AML) detection
  - know your customer (aka KYC)
  - global exposure

- science-based industries
  - pharmaceutical development
  - pharmaceutical testing
  - pharmaceutical market research
  - genetics research
- marketing
  - customer analytics
  - merger and acquisition (M&A) decision making
  - divestiture decision making
  - direct and mass marketing campaign management
  - customer analytics
- government
  - material management
  - intelligence community
  - human disease management
  - livestock disease management
  - agricultural disease management

Once the specific use case(s) of data warehousing (DW) have been identified, then one has the ability to start listing specific requirements. Similar to document management, the requirements for basic data warehousing also begins with simple things, such as the number of source systems, the topics of data, the size of the data, and the maximum number of rows, but it also continues into an extensive list that will determine the candidate Big Data products that one may choose from.

Potential data warehouse requirements include:

- maximum space required
- maximum data ingestion sources
- maximum data ingestion rate
- identifying the optimal source for each data point
- data quality issues of each source
- data standardization issues of each source
- data format issues of each source
- database structure issues of each source
- data integration issues of each source
- internationalization (e.g., Unicode, language translation)
- index support
- drill downs
- sharding support
- backup and restorability
- disaster recoverability
- concurrent users

- query access path analysis
- number of columns being returned
- data types
- number of joins
- multi-data center support

In fact, the potential list of requirements for data warehousing can also extend into every nonfunctional type of requirement listed in the nonfunctional requirements section discussed later in this book.

Needless to say, there are many Big Data products in the space of data warehousing on both the Hadoop and non-Hadoop side of the fence, each with their own limitations on data size, number of keys, index ability, retrieval speed, ingestion rates, and ability to support concurrent users.

3.1.2.4.4.5 Real-Time Analytics Use Case Type Real-time analytics is a type of use case that usually requires a response to a query in the span of 1-5 seconds to an end user, or a response in milliseconds to an automated component which may deliver its response directly to an end user or a fully automated process. The use case type of real-time analytics refers to an extensive collection of use cases that involve content that usually involves structured data but may also involve unstructured and/or semistructured data.

These can include use cases found within the industry sectors of:

- financial services industry
    - investment risk
    - operational risk
    - operational performance
    - money desk cash management positions
    - securities desk securities inventory (aka securities depository record)
    - financial risk
    - market risk
    - credit risk
    - regulatory exception reporting
    - trading analytics
    - algorithmic trading (i.e., older versions of algorithmic trading)
    - real-time valuation
- government
    - intelligence
    - homeland security
    - human disease management
- marketing
    - opportunity-based marketing

- dynamic Web-based advertising
- dynamic smartphone-based advertising
- dynamic smartphone-based alerts and notifications
- social media monitoring

Once the specific use case(s) of real-time analytics have been identified, then one has the ability to start listing specific requirements for the applicable use cases. Similar to document management and data warehousing, the requirements for basic real-time analytics begin with simple things, such as the number of source systems, the volume of data, the size of the data, and the maximum number of rows, but it also continues into an extensive list that will determine the candidate Big Data products that one may choose from.

Potential real-time analytics requirements include:

- types of real-time data analytics
- number of concurrent dashboards
- number of concurrent pivots
- number of concurrent data mining requests
- number of concurrent advanced analytics
- maximum space required
- maximum data ingestion sources
- maximum data ingestion rate
- identifying the optimal source for each data point
- number of additional metrics to be generated
- temporal requirements for additional metrics to be generated
- data quality issues of each source
- data standardization issues of each source
- data format issues of each source
- database structure issues of each source
- data integration issues of each source
- internationalization (e.g., Unicode, language translation)
- index support
- drill downs
- sharding support
- backup and restorability
- disaster recoverability
- concurrent users
- query access path analysis
- number of columns being returned
- data types
- maximum number of joins
- multi-data center support

Again, the potential list of requirements for real-time analytics can also extend into every nonfunctional type of requirement listed in the nonfunctional requirements section discussed later in this book.

There are many Big Data products in the space of real-time analytics, although at present they are mostly on the non-Hadoop side of the fence, each with their own limitations on data size, ingestion rates, retrieval speed, costs, and ability to support concurrent users.

In fact, the usual suspects in this use case type include:

- SAP Hana,
- HP Vertica,
- Greenplum, and
- Teradata.

3.1.2.4.4.6 Predictive Analytics Use Case Type Predictive analytics is a type of use case that usually requires a response to a query in the span of milliseconds or nanoseconds to an automated component which may deliver its response directly to an end user or a fully automated process when the predictive analytic is fully operationalized.

The use case type of predictive analytics refers to an extensive collection of use cases that involve some set of predictive data points that are being rendered to a statistical or nonstatistical mathematical model, or high-speed CEP engine.

These can include use cases found within the industry sectors of:

- financial services industry
  - capital markets fraud detection
  - wholesale banking fraud detection
  - retail banking fraud detection
  - market risk forecasting
  - market opportunity forecasting
  - operational defect forecasting
- marketing
  - customer lifetime value (LTV) scoring
  - customer defection scoring
  - customer lifetime event scoring
- government
  - terrorist group activity forecasting
  - terrorist specific event forecasting
- engineering and manufacturing
  - equipment failure forecasting
- commerce
  - open source component forecasting

- 3D printer component design forecasting
- employee collusion forecasting
- supplier collusion forecasting
- customer collusion forecasting

Once the specific use case(s) of predictive analytics have been identified, one has the ability to start listing specific requirements for the applicable use cases. Similar to prior use case types, the requirements for predictive analytics begins with simple things, such as the number of sources, the volume of data, the size of the data, and the maximum number of rows, but again it continues into an extensive list that will determine the candidate Big Data products that one may choose from.

Potential predictive analytics requirements include:

- transaction rates within the operational system
- learning set size
- learning set updates
- traceability
- integrate ability
- deploy ability

Again, the potential list of requirements for predictive analytics can also extend into every nonfunctional type of requirement listed in the nonfunctional requirements section discussed later in this book.

There are many Big Data products in the space of predictive analytics; they are mostly on the non-Hadoop side of the fence, each with their own limitations on operational execution speeds, learning rates, result accuracy, and result traceability.

As a sampling among the entrants for this use case type include:

- Fair Isaac's HNC predictive models offering,
- Ward Systems,
- Sybase CEP engine, and
- SAS CEP and statistical package offering.

3.1.2.4.4.7 Algorithm-Based Use Case Type Algorithm based is a type of use case that does not require real-time or near real-time response rates.

The use case type of algorithm-based Big Data refers to an extensive collection of use cases that involve some set of advanced algorithms that would be deployed by quants and data scientists.

These can include use cases found across industries (e.g., science-based industries, financial services, commerce, marketing, and government) involving the following types of algorithms:

- matrix vector multiplication,
- relational algebraic operations,

- selections and projections,
- union, intersection, and difference,
- grouping and aggregation,
- reducer size and replication rates,
- similarity joins, and
- graph modeling.

If these sound strange to you, and there are many more that are even more unusual, I would not worry, as these terms are generally used by experienced quants and/or data scientists.

The types of candidate requirements that one encounters in this specialized area are generally the set of formulas and algorithms that will support the required function.

Some options for this use case type include:

- IBM Netezza for hardware-based algorithms,
- Hadoop HDFS for advanced MapReduce capabilities, and
- Hadoop HBase also for advanced MapReduce capabilities.

3.1.2.4.4.8 Online Transaction Processing (NewSQL/OLTP) Use Case Type Online transaction processing (NewSQL/OLTP) is a type of use case that usually requires a response to a query in the span of 1-3 seconds or milliseconds to an automated component which may deliver its response directly to an end user or a fully automated process.

The use case type of NewSQL OLTP refers to a collection of use cases that involve some set of transaction processing involving Big Data volumes of data and/or transaction rates.

These can include use cases found within the industry sectors of:

- e-Commerce
  - global Web-based transaction systems
  - global inventory systems
  - global shipping systems
- consumer Products and Services
  - in-home medical care systems
- marketing
  - RFID supply chain management
  - Opportunity-based marketing
  - smartphone and tablet transaction systems
  - Google glasses applications
- government
  - military logistics
  - homeland security

Additional nonfunctional requirements can include:

- peak transactions per second
- maximum transaction lengths
- system availability
- system security
- failover
- DR
- complex transaction access paths
- internationalization (e.g., Unicode and language translation)
- full text search
- index support
- sharding support

The potential list of requirements for NewSQL OLTP can also extend into any number of nonfunctional type of requirement listed in the nonfunctional requirements section discussed later in this book.

There are several Big Data products in the space of NewSQL OLTP.

Among the candidates for this use case type are:

- Akiban,
- Clustrix,
- Google Spanner,
- NuoDB,
- SQLFire, and
- VoltDB.

3.1.2.4.4.9 Batch Analytics Use Case Type Batch analysis is a type of use case that usually requires a response to a query in minutes or hours.

The use case type of batch analysis refers to a collection of use cases that involve volumes of data reaching into the petabytes and beyond.

These can include use cases found within the industry sectors of:

- financial industry
  - financial crime
  - anti-money laundering
  - insurance fraud detection
  - credit risk for banking
  - portfolio valuation
- marketing
  - customer analytics
  - market analytics

- government
  - terrorist activity forecasting
  - terrorism event forecasting
- science-based
  - genetic research
- commerce
  - employee collusion detection
  - vendor collusion detection
  - customer collusion detection

The batch analysis type of use case is often the least costly type of use case as it often has fixed sets of large amounts of data with ample time for Big Data technologies to work the problem.

That said, the potential list of requirements for batch analytics can also extend into any number of nonfunctional type of requirement listed in the nonfunctional requirements section discussed later in this book.

There are several Big Data products in the space of batch analytics.

Among the candidates for this use case type are:

- Hadoop HDFS, and
- Hadoop HBase.

3.1.2.4.4.10 GIS Use Case Type GIS is a type of use case that ranges from batch to real time.

The use case type of GIS refers to a collection of use cases that involve Big Data volumes of data reaching into the terabytes of geographical information and beyond.

This can include use cases involving:

- address geocoding
  - warrant servicing
  - emergency service
  - crime analysis
  - public health analysis
- liner measures event modeling
  - road maintenance activities
  - roadway projects
  - traffic analysis
  - safety analysis
- routing
  - evacuation planning
  - towing services
  - snow removal services
  - refuse removal services
  - police, fire, and ambulance services

- topological
  - cell phone tower coverage
  - elevation data
  - orthophotography
  - hydrography
- cartography
  - hazardous materials tracking
  - taxable asset tracking (e.g., mobile homes)

The GIS type of use case includes nonfunctional requirement types, such as:

- user friendliness
- ACID compliance
- full spatial support (i.e., operators involving physical proximity)
  - near
  - inside
  - between
  - behind
  - above
  - below
- flexibility

That said, the potential list of requirements for batch analytics can also extend into any number of nonfunctional type of requirement listed in the nonfunctional requirements section discussed later in this book.

There are several products in the space of GIS analytics.

Among the candidates for this use case type are:

- Neo4j,
- PostGIS
  - open source
  - geographic support
  - built on PostgreSQL
- Oracle Spatial
  - spatial support in an Oracle database
- GeoTime
  - temporal 3D visual analytics (i.e., illustrating how something looked over time)

3.1.2.4.4.11 Search and Discovery Use Case Type Search and Discovery is a type of use case that usually requires a response to a query or many subordinate queries in the span of 1-3 seconds or milliseconds.

The use case type of Search and Discovery refers to a collection of use cases that involve some set of searching involving Big Data volumes of data.

These can include use cases found across industries involving:

- Web site search
- internal data source identification and mapping
- external data source identification and mapping
- discovery (i.e., searching for data categories across the data landscape of a large enterprise)
- e-discovery

There are few competitors in this space, including:

- Lucidworks (i.e., built on Solr with an enhanced GUI for common use cases)
- Solr
- Splunk (i.e., for machine generated output)

3.1.2.4.4.12 Relational Database Technology in Hadoop Use Case Type In contrast to the technique of a relational database management system operating outside Hadoop, such as SQL Server Polybase with access to data within HDFS using something like Hive, Pig, or Impala, a relatively recent type of use case is that of supporting a full relational database capability within and across a Hadoop cluster.

This use case type is particularly interesting as it facilitates real-time queries over extremely large relational databases to be deployed across a Hadoop cluster in HDFS, using MapReduce behind the scenes of a standard SQL interface.

There are few competitors in this space as well including:

- Splice Machine (full SQL), and
- Citus Data (append data only).

The architecture of this class of product is that it essentially requires software on each node of the Hadoop cluster to manage the SQL interface to the file system.

There are several advantages of this use case type especially where full SQL is supported, including:

- use of existing SQL trained personnel,
- ability to support extremely large relational database tables,
- distributed processing that leverages the power of MapReduce,
- a full complement of SQL capabilities, including
  - grant and revoke,
  - select, insert, update, and delete

3.1.2.4.4.13 Big Data Is Use Case Driven—Summary The most important point I hope you take away here is that approaching Big Data tool selection from the tool side, or trying to make one product support the needs of all use cases, is clearly the wrong way to address any problem.

It would be like a pharmaceutical company suggesting on television that you try a particular drug that they manufacture for any and every aliment you have, when you need to begin by consulting a physician with the symptoms and then work toward a potential solution that meet your particular set of circumstances, such as not creating a conflict with other medications you may already be taking.

Unfortunately, the tool approach is too frequently adopted as people have a tendency to use the one or few tools that they are already familiar or enamored with. As architects, we should never bypass the step of collecting requirements from the various users, funding sources, and numerous organizational stakeholders.

Those who adopt a tool as their first step and then try to shoehorn it into various types of use cases usually do so to the peril of their organization. The typical result is that they end up attempting to demonstrate something to the business that has not been properly thought through. At best, the outcome is something that is neither as useful and as cost-effective as it could have been, nor as useful an educational experience for the organization that it could have been. At worst, the outcome represents a costly exercise that squanders organizational resources and provides management with a less than pleasant Big Data technology experience.

That said, there is much value in exercising a variety of Big Data tools as a means to better understand what they can do and how well they do it. New products in the Big Data space are being announced nearly every month and staying on top of just the marketing information perspective of each product requires a great deal of knowledge and energy. More important than the marketing materials however is the ability to understand how these products actually work and the ability to get the opportunity to experiment with the particular products in which the greatest potential utility exists to meet your needs.

If you have a Big Data ecosystem sandbox at your disposal, then you are in luck within the safety of your own firewalls, but if you are not fortunate enough to have a Big Data ecosystem sandbox at your disposal, then the next best thing or possibly better is to be able to rent resources from a Big Data ecosystem sandbox externally to your enterprise, such as from Google, Amazon, or Microsoft, where you may be able to rent access to whatever Big Data product(s) you would like to experiment with using your data in a secure environment.

3.1.2.4.5 Organizing Big Data into a Life Cycle

The landscape of Big Data tools is reminiscent of when DOS commands were the only command interface into the world of the personal computer. At that time, humans had to mold their thinking to participate in the world of the computer, whereas Finder and Windows eventually molded the computer to what humans could instinctively understand so that it could interact more effectively in our world.

Although the landscape for Big Data will continue to rapidly evolve into the near future, its proper deployment will continue to be anything but trivial for some time into the future. Before we get into what a proper deployment model looks like, let's first look at an "ad hoc" deployment model.

3.1.2.4.5.1 Ad hoc Deployment Each ad hoc deployment is actually quite simple, at least initially. It generally begins with the identification of a possible use case.

The use case that is chosen is usually an interesting one that advertises to solve some problem that could not previously be solved, such as the challenge of consolidating customers across an area of an insurance company, where the number of insurance policy applications makes it particularly labor intensive to consolidate each additional few million customers on a roadmap to a hundred million customers.

A popular big data database tool is chosen, such as MongoDB or Cassandra, and a partial solution is achieved within a 6-month time frame with relatively low cost and effort. We all know the way this story continues. It is increasingly difficult and expensive to compete the customer consolidation effort, so folks lose interest in that project and then start looking for the next ad hoc big data project.

This ad hoc process is repeated for either the same use case in other countries and for new use cases, all of which also achieve partial solutions within short time frames with relatively low cost and effort. As we advance forward in time, we find ourselves with numerous partially completed efforts cluttering the IT landscape, with each delivering great business benefit to small pockets of customers and business users across that as an aggregate are ultimately inconsequential to the overall capabilities and efficiency of the organization.

3.1.2.4.5.2 Big Data Deployment Big Data deployment should be driven by a set of principles that serve to help frame the discussion.

Big Data deployment principles include:

- deployment of big data technologies follow a defined life cycle
- metadata management is a consideration at each step of the life cycle
- iterations of a big data life cycle generate lessons learned and process improvement
- projects involving Big Data must adhere to the same ROI standards as any other
- deployments of Big Data require the same if not additional governance and oversight
- Big Data should leverage shared services, technologies, and infrastructures
- operational frameworks should quarantine business users to only "approved" use cases

Now that we have a basic set of principles to help provide considerations for the deployment of Big Data, we will organize our discussion into sections for:

- Plan,
- Build, and
- Operate.

3.1.2.4.5.3   Big Data Deployment—Plan   The "Plan" phase of Big Data begins with business selecting the business use case type(s) that they need to advance the business in the direction they wish to go or to address specific a business pain point. Either way, they will need to quantify the business value of what they wish to accomplish.

Associated with business use case type(s), there are a list of technologies that specialize within that area of Big Data. Although the list of technologies is constantly evolving with new licensed and open source possibilities, that list should be reassembled every couple of months.

If products that have been incorporated into the Big Data ecosystem are no longer the better choice, a retirement plan will have to be developed to decommission it from the ecosystem. Given the fact that Big Data technologies are so volatile, the process of decommissioning products should become a core competence of every organization that does not wish to accumulate an inventory of young yet obsolete products, and its associated infrastructure.

At this juncture, the business in partnership with enterprise architecture must identify the nonfunctional requirement types that must be provided for use case types under consideration distinct from the nonfunctional requirement types that are merely nice to have (see the section 8.1.1).

Given the nonfunctional requirement types that are unambiguously required, candidate technologies will be disqualified as unable to support mandatory nonfunctional requirement types. The product or products that remain should be fully eligible to address the particular Big Data use case types. If more than one product is eligible, then they should all continue through the process to the ROI assessment.

In the event that new Big Data technologies must be introduced into the ecosystem, the architecture team should develop frameworks to incorporate the new Big Data technology into the ecosystem, and the operations area should be consulted to begin determining the new support costs for the eligible technologies.

The activities up to this point are supported by the business area, enterprise architecture, and operations staff as part of the services that they provide, and may not be a formal project.

By this time however, a project with a project manager should be formed encompassing the following activities under a modest planning budget:

- specific business use cases are determined by business analysts
- business value is determined for each business use case by business
- business requirements are recorded by business analysts
- candidate systems of record are identified as potential data sources
- specific business users and/or business user roles are identified for each use case
- interests of various stakeholders are incorporated into standards
  - enterprise architecture
  - compliance

- legal
- chief data officer
- assess the capacity of the environment
- operations provides costs and schedules for
  - adding capacity to an existing Big Data technology or
  - standing up a new technology
- business analysts identify specific sources of data to support each use case
  - assess whether
    - data will be fully refreshed each time
    - data will be appended to existing data
    - data will be updated
    - data will be deleted
- eligible technologies undergo an architecture ROI assessment
- stakeholders assess the implications of the particular combination of data sources
  - legal
  - auditing
  - compliance
  - chief data officer
  - data owner
- approval to leverage data from each data source for each use case is acquired
  - legal
  - auditing
  - compliance
  - chief data officer
  - data owner
- detailed nonfunctional requirements are recorded by business analysts
- enterprise architecture presents product recommendation
- vendor management determines cost associated with
  - product licensing and/or open source support
  - training
- architecture ROI is leveraged to complete the ROI analysis
  - business ROI
  - finance ROI
- product selection is finalized
  - business management
  - IT management
- identify funding requirements for
  - build phase
    - software costs (e.g., licenses and/or open source support agreements)
    - hardware costs
    - data owner application development (AD) support

- data extraction
- data transport to landing zone
- Big Data application development (AD) team support
  - determine whether files will be encrypted
  - determine whether files will be compressed
  - metadata data quality checks
    - column counts
    - field data types and lengths are present
  - file data quality checks
    - record counts and check sums
    - special character elimination
  - row-level data quality checks
    - metadata row-level validations
    - prime key validations
    - prime foreign key validations
    - foreign key validations
  - column data quality checks
    - data profiling
    - data cleansing
      - domain values
      - range and min-max edits
    - data standardization
      - reference data lookups
    - data reformatting/format standardization
    - data restructuring
    - data integration/data ingestion
  - testing and migration team support
  - Big Data architecture support
  - Big Data operations setup
  - helpdesk setup
  - business support costs
- operate phase
  - ongoing operations support
  - ongoing helpdesk support
  - business operational costs
- future decommission phase
- present the project to the planning board
- funding assessment
  - funding approval
  - funding rejection
  - returned for re-planning

3.1.2.4.5.4   Big Data Deployment—Build The "Build" phase of Big Data begins with an overall project manager coordination multiple threads involving oversight and coordination of the following groups, each led by a domain project manager:

- operations—operations project manager,
- vendor(s)—vendor project manager(s),
- business—business project manager,
- data source application development teams—data source AD team project manager(s),
- Big Data application development team—Big Data AD team project manager, and
- test/migration team—test/migration team project manager.

The operations team supports the creation of a development, user acceptance test (UAT), and production environment with the capacity required to support the intended development and testing activities. Prior to production turnover operations will test system failover, and the various other operational administrative tasks that fall to them.

Vendors support the architecture, design, and implementation of the products they support, including installation and setup of the software in the development, UAT, production environment, and the training and mentoring of business users and IT staff in the use and administration of the product, and participate in the testing of operational procedures for the administration of the system.

Business supports the business analysts and the Big Data AD team in their efforts to profile the data so that data cleansing, data standardization, data reformatting, and data integration decisions can be made to best support the needs of the business for their use cases. During this process, business will also identify the metadata and metrics about process that will help accomplish their objectives. The business will also test the set of administrative functions that they are responsible for to support their use cases.

Ultimately, business must evaluate the extent to which data quality checks of each type should be performed based upon the use case, its business value, and business data associated with each use case.

The data source AD team(s) support the identification of required data within their source systems and then develop the software to extract the data either as a one-time effort or in accordance with the schedule of extracts to meet the needs of one or more specific use cases that have been approved. The data is then transported to the required location for additional processing by the Big Data AD team.

The Big Data AD team coordinates the receipt of data from the various data owners and works with the business and business analysts to profile and process the data for ingestion into the Big Data product set in the development environment. Once the appropriate metadata and metrics are also identified and collected, this AD team will conduct unit testing to ensure that the various components of data and technology can perform their function. When unit testing is complete, the data and software are passed to the test and migration team as a configuration of software and data. The Big Data AD team will also test the set of administrative functions that they are responsible for to support the Big Data capabilities.

The test and migration team accepts the data and software from the Big Data AD team and identifies the components as a configuration that will undergo user acceptance testing and then migration to production. Prior to this however, the test migration team works with the business and business analysts to develop a test plan that will ensure that all of the components operate together as they should to support each and every use case.

The configuration management components of the Big Data project include:

- software products that are used including their versions
- applications including
  - Java code
  - Flume interceptors
  - HBase coprocessors
  - user-defined functions
- software syntax
  - parameters and associated software product or application
  - programming code and associated software product or application
  - data transformation code
    - file-level cleansing
    - field-level cleansing and edits
    - data standardization
    - reformatting and restructuring
- inbound data sources and outbound data targets
  - file names
  - schemas including their versions
- approved business use cases
  - complete description of each use case
  - description of permissible production data
  - individual approver names and dates

Once the system has been tested by business users and possibly business analysts in the user acceptance environment, the test results are reviewed by the various stakeholders. Included within these tests are test cases to confirm the appropriate nonfunctional requirements of the Big Data application have been met, such as security, usability, and data obfuscation requirements.

These overall lists of stakeholders that must render their approval include:

- business management,
  - business users who participated in testing each use case

- IT development management,
- legal,
- auditing,
- compliance,
- chief data officer,
- data owner(s) of the sourced data,
- test and migration management, and
- IT operations management

3.1.2.4.5.5 *Big Data Deployment—Operate* The "Operate" phase of Big Data begins with the "go live" decision of the stakeholders, where the various components of the configuration are migrated from the configuration management folders representing UAT environment to the production environment including the data used in UAT. Once migrated, an initial test is performed in production to test the production infrastructure including startup and shutdown, job scheduling capabilities, and the administrative functions that each respective area is responsible for.

If critical issues arise, the system may remain unavailable for production use until at least the critical issues are resolved.

When successful, the data used for testing will be removed and a full complement of production data will be introduced using the normal operational processes associated with production. At this point, the production system is made available for production operation for use by the business.

3.1.2.4.5.6 *Big Data Deployment—Summary* The important thing to note after following a proper Big Data deployment plan is that the appropriate stakeholders have confirmed that the compliance and regulatory needs have been met, and that the proper audit controls have been put in place.

At this point, if there is an audit from a regulator, everyone has performed the due diligence required of them, including the approval of specific use cases, use of specific data sources, and most importantly the combination of specific data sources and data for use in specific use cases.

There are quite a number of considerations and complexities when establishing Big Data development, integration test, UAT, and production environment, and few vendors with a handle on this space that would be suitable for a financial services company or large enterprise with rigorous regulatory oversight and mandates across the globe.

3.1.2.4.6 Metadata of a Big Data Ecosystem

There are 20 basic topic areas of metadata that pertain to Big Data, and within those, there are hundreds of metadata data points.

The basic topic areas of Big Data include:

- use case planning/business metadata,

- use case requirements metadata (e.g., data and applications),
- internal data discovery metadata/locating the required data across the enterprise,
- external data discovery metadata/locating the required data from external data providers,
- inbound metadata,
- ingestion metadata,
- data persistence layer metadata,
- outbound metadata,
- technology metadata,
- life cycle metadata,
- operations metadata,
- data governance metadata,
- compliance metadata,
- configuration management metadata,
- team metadata (e.g., use case application team, technology provisioning application team, data provisioning application team)
- directory services metadata,
- ecosystem administrator metadata,
- stakeholder metadata,
- workflow metadata, and
- decommissioning metadata.

As a sampling of the metadata contained within, let's explore the first several topics of metadata.

3.1.2.4.6.1 Use Case Planning/Business Metadata The use case planning/business metadata category of metadata encompasses the information about the use case beginning with the business concept and the anticipated business benefit. As such, it would discuss its informational requirements with suggestions as to which lines of business may be able to supply data from within the organization, and suggestions as to which data providers may be able to meet its data requirements from outside the organization.

External sources may include any combination of sources, such as:

- academic organization,
- administrative jurisdiction (e.g., states, provinces),
- specific company with whom an agreement to provide data has been negotiated,
- data reseller whose primary business is reselling data,
- industry group,
- international organization (e.g., United Nations)
- treaty zone,
- national government,

- news organization, and
- social media source (e.g., Facebook, Twitter).

3.1.2.4.6.2 Use Case Requirements Metadata The use case requirements category of metadata encompasses the information about the data sources identified and the candidate technologies that support the type of use cases desired.

Regarding data sources, the metadata identifies the specific sources from which the necessary data is available to be sourced. For many use cases, the degree to which data source availability exists or has been identified will determine the viability of the use case at this point in time.

Regarding the candidate technologies, the metadata identifies the minimum and desired set of capabilities that technologies will have to provide to facilitate the processing of the data and its associated data volumes and data velocity. For many use cases, the degree to which technology availability exists or has been specifically identified will also determine the viability of the use case at this point in time.

3.1.2.4.6.3 Internal Data Discovery Metadata The internal data discovery metadata category of metadata encompasses the information about data discovery across the data landscape. Although effective technologies exist in this space, the most frequent method for identifying locations from across the enterprise is manually supported by collaboration and word of mouth.

3.1.2.4.6.4 External Data Discovery Metadata The external data discovery metadata category of metadata encompasses the information about data discovery outside the organization across the data landscape. For this category of data discovery, a complete product has not yet emerged, although the parts of such a product in fact are available for integration.

At present, the most only method for identifying locations external to the enterprise is manually supported by research into companies and online data providers from across the Internet.

3.1.2.4.6.5 Inbound Metadata The inbound metadata category of metadata encompasses the information about the data being transported to the Big Data ecosystem.

This begins with the transport mechanism, such as whether it is over an ESB, ETL product, file transport protocol (FTP), utility, developed program, or physically carried medium (e.g., tape, cartridge, drive). It also includes every useful piece of information that will be needed to process the file once received, such as the file name(s), encryption or decompression algorithm, and a long list of details that will be required about the file (e.g., file type, file format, delimiting character) including the taxonomy of the file name that may incorporate many of the metadata characteristics within its taxonomy.

3.1.2.4.6.6 Ingestion Metadata The ingestion metadata category of metadata encompasses the information about the "process" used to accept the data being delivered to the Big Data ecosystem.

This metadata involves a wealth of metadata surrounding "initial profiling," data cleansing, data standardization, data formatting, data restructuring, data integration, and file readiness. It is useful to collect a variety of metrics on the raw data for analysis and subsequent reporting to help facilitate business awareness and their data governance activities.

3.1.2.4.6.7 Data Persistence Layer Metadata The data persistence metadata category of metadata encompasses the information about the data landed into the Big Data ecosystem.

This metadata contains a collection of data points such as the:

- file name(s) of the landed data and its taxonomy,
- HDFS Hive directory,
- HDFS pathname,
- HDFS table name,
- HDFS staging directory,
- HDFS raw directory,
- received date,
- temporal requirements (aka history),
- applicable compression algorithm,
- file splittability,
- archive begin date,
- file permissions, and
- data sensitivity profile.

3.1.2.4.6.8 Outbound Metadata The outbound category of metadata is a topic area of metadata that assumes a particular architectural framework where the Big Data space accumulates source data from within the enterprise as well as from external sources with the intent to extract it into a quarantined use case production container. The container can be of any style of Big Data, including any of the traditional Big Data, Hadoop based, or any of the other open source or proprietary technologies, such as those that perform high-speed joins across large numbers of tables or ones that perform complex algorithms in a sophisticated appliance solution.

3.1.2.4.6.9 Technology Metadata The technology category of metadata encompasses a wealth of Big Data technology-related metadata for each of the products that are part of the development, integration test, quality assurance, and production ecosystem.

Sample technology metadata can overlap and extend the information that is typically captured as part of a technology portfolio practice:

- product name,
- product version/release,
- origin of source code,
- support agreement,
- document name for standards governing development use,
- document name for standards governing its operation,
- component list of reusable functions under management,
- product limitations,
- product run book, and
- product run time parameters.

3.1.2.4.6.10   Life Cycle Metadata The life cycle category of metadata encompasses information about the various life cycle environments and the metadata associated with the approvals to promote data, programmed components, and product versions.

The level of maturity of operational metadata that will be needed depends largely on the regulatory requirements of your particular organization's industry.

Sample life cycle metadata may include:

- test plans and their versioning,
- test results and their versioning,
- test team approvals by component,
- architectural approvals,
- business approvals,
- operations approvals,
- helpdesk approvals,
- PMO approvals,
- compliance approvals, and
- audit approvals.

3.1.2.4.6.11   Operations Metadata The operations category of metadata encompasses information about operations readiness. The level of maturity of operational metadata that will be needed depends largely on the regulatory requirements of your particular organization's industry.

Sample operations metadata may include:

- equipment delivery dates,
- equipment installation dates,
- equipment setup dates,
- environment readiness dates,
- product installation dates,
- product setup dates,
- job scheduling planning dates,
- job scheduling setup dates,

- failover testing dates,
- DR testing dates,
- use case application installation guides, and
- use case application operation guides.

3.1.2.4.6.12   Data Governance Metadata The data governance category of metadata encompasses information about the data governance program. Even though this area of metadata is often omitted, from the perspective of usefulness, this is the single most important area of metadata to get right. Correspondingly, when one looks at any of the numerous initiatives that fail, it is almost guaranteed that this area of metadata, along with the use case planning metadata, is generally nowhere to be found. The most obvious reason for this is that there is little that can be achieved from analysis of data that the data scientist or data analyst does not understand.

Sample data governance metadata may include:

- business data glossary entry names for each inbound schema data point,
- business data glossary entry names for each subsequently derived data point,
- business metadata percent completeness for each business data glossary entry,
- data source evaluation(s),
- data lineage, and
- data steward associated with each data source.

3.1.2.4.6.13   Compliance Metadata The compliance category of metadata encompasses information pertinent to the various areas of scope overseen by compliance, such as human resource compliance, legal compliance, and financial compliance.

Sample compliance metadata may include:

- data sensitivity associated with individual data points used in combination for a use case,
- regulatory jurisdiction(s),
- information input to compliance,
- compliance assessment of input,
- compliance decision, and
- compliance decision date.

3.1.2.4.6.14   Configuration Management Metadata The configuration management category of metadata encompasses the basic information that identifies the components of each Big Data environment and each use case and application.

Sample configuration management metadata may include:

- required Big Data technology ecosystem,
- source files,
- data transport components,
- initial data profiling components,

- data cleansing components,
- data standardization components,
- data standardization code table components,
- data reformatting components,
- data restructuring components,
- data integration components,
- product versions,
- customized product components,
- source code of developed programs and product syntax, and
- product run time parameters.

3.1.2.4.6.15 Team Metadata The team metadata category of metadata encompasses the application development team that is associated with the use case, technology provisioning, and data provisioning.

The use case application development team is the team focused on the business problem and is responsible for understanding it and addressing it more than any other development team.

The technology provisioning team is the Big Data team that is focused on managing and supporting the technology portfolio across the Big Data ecosystem, which may entail a large number of technologies and products involving traditional Big Data, Hadoop-based Big Data, and specialized proprietary technologies.

The data provisioning application development team is each application development team associated with the applications that originate or process the data downstream from where it originates.

3.1.2.4.6.16 Directory Services Metadata The directory services metadata category of metadata encompasses the permissions aspects of the data, applications, and products within each environment of the life cycle.

At its basic level, it consists of the IT user groups, users, and assignments of users to user groups, as well as use case owner groups, use case owner users, and assignments of use case owner users to the use case owner user groups.

At a more advanced level, it consists of the history and attrition of users and approvers, user recertification, and approver recertification metadata.

3.1.2.4.6.17 Ecosystem Administrator Metadata The administrator metadata category of metadata encompasses the various aspects related to sustaining the life cycle environments at an agreed-to service level that facilitates development and production activities.

Sample configuration management metadata may include:

- ensuring product and technology licensing coverage, including freeware licenses,
- product and technology maintenance agreement coverage,
- evaluating and applying software upgrades,

- applying hardware upgrades and configuration modifications,
- ensuring backups of data and software,
- restoring backed up data and software when required,
- incident tracking and problem management, and
- providing support to users within the various environments for system-level services.

3.1.2.4.6.18   Stakeholder Metadata The stakeholder metadata category of metadata encompasses the tracking of designated owners and approvers that have interests that must be represented and protected. This includes identification of individuals that must provide budgets and approvals.

Sample stakeholder metadata may include:

- use case owners,
- compliance,
- legal,
- auditing,
- architecture,
- operations,
- use case application development teams,
- business data owners,
- data owner application development teams, and
- Big Data ecosystem application development team.

3.1.2.4.6.19   Workflow Metadata The workflow metadata category of metadata encompasses the various types of information related to the processes that must be performed and adhered to.

Sample workflow metadata may include:

- services catalog that services may be requested from,
- requests for services,
- process steps,
- inputs to process steps,
- outputs from process steps,
- department originating each request,
- contact person submitting the request,
- request date time,
- request approvals from either business or IT,
- group assigned to service support the request,
- individual assigned to support the request,
- estimated hours of labor to complete the request,
- estimated completion date,
- actual hours of labor to complete the request,

- actual completion date,
- requestor approval and request closure,
- reopening of closed requests,
- requests that failed to complete and the reason associated with the failure,
- request reassignment date,
- request cancellation date, and
- request modification date.

3.1.2.4.6.20 Decommissioning Metadata The decommissioning metadata category of metadata encompasses the information associated with retire any combination of the following:

- Big Data ecosystem,
- use case,
- a particular use case application,
- a particular quarantined production area,
- Big Data technology or product,
- data file source, and
- data file instance.

The information collected will include backups of the items being decommissioned to the extent required by records information management (RIM) guidelines and regulatory requirements associated with the particular organization.

3.1.2.4.6.21 Metadata Summary The topic of Big Data metadata is somewhat large, and it is best to grow into the various metadata maturity levels over time, starting with the metadata required on day one, which can vary significantly depending upon the regulatory oversight required of your organization. Additionally, there are various methods for collecting metadata using automation that can accelerate any Big Data initiative.

The best approach to navigate these topics appropriately for the industry in which your organization belongs is to engage SMEs in this space, of which there are a few excellent choices of vendors who have SMEs that address these topics.

3.1.2.4.7   Big Data—A Little Deeper

Whether the Big Data approach is based upon Hadoop or a proprietary data persistence layer, the speed with which they offer their various capabilities is dependent upon solid architectural techniques and some permutation of the same five fundamental accelerators.

For example, use case types that employ reference data in their processing must replicate reference data on each node to keep them from going out to a shared resource.

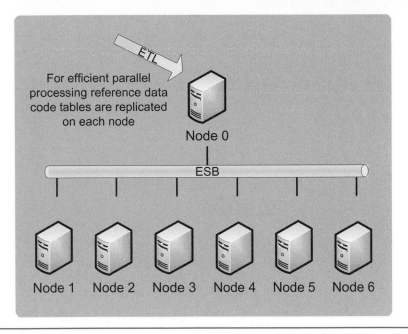

Diagram Parallel processing requires reference data replication. (For color version of this figure, the reader is referred to the online version of this chapter.)

In total, the five fundamental Big Data accelerators include:

- **parallel and distributed processing,**
- **reduced code set that eliminates large amounts of DBMS code,**
- **fewer features than OldSQL transaction databases that reduce the work being performed,**
- **compression, and**
- **proprietary hardware that perform algorithms on processors that are co-located on the data persistence layer.**

To illustrate what we mean, we will take one of these and drill it down in simple steps to a level that most enterprise information architects never thought possible.

3.1.2.4.7.1 Compression—Background Compression is not only a large topic, but it is also more fundamental to the Big Data accelerators than the others for a simple reason.

Computers are comprised of three fundamental components, which are one or more CPUs, memory, and a bus, which is a circuit that connects two different parts together where in this case it is the bus that connects the CPU to the memory. More than most components, the essential factors in determining computer speed are the CPU speed and the speed of the bus.

One obvious way to make computation faster is to make faster CPUs and bus circuits. As the components of computers shrink in size to the molecular and atomic level, the physical limitations of designing faster CPUs and bus circuits are approaching nature's limit for the speed of light.

However, another obvious way to make computing faster is the ability to pass far fewer bits of data and machine instructions through the bus to the CPU. Due to the way computer technology has boot strapped each new technology on top of older technologies, for the most part today's computers pass thousands of times more bits through the bus to the CPU than is absolutely necessary to perform each calculation. Hence, the concept of "least number of bits" (LNBs) as a totally new and comprehensive architecture.

Its scope spans compression optimal concepts across all hardware and software. For software, this includes the operating system, the executables (aka binaries) that are run on the operating system, data, metadata, network and bus traffic, and any content that must travel over a bus to interact with each CPU. The concept of compression within each of these areas is essentially the same, which is to reduce the size of these artifacts, whether executables, data, or metadata so that they take up less space.

The techniques to achieve compression vary by type of artifact, and the ability to compress an artifact is largely determined by whether the artifact is being compressed individually in isolation to everything around it, or jointly with respect to its ecosystem where compression across the components of the ecosystem is being coordinated to be optimized.

For example, an advanced form of application architecture called process normalization can significantly reduce the number of lines of code in large information systems. However, process normalization itself leverages other disciplines such as a well-formed logical data architecture (LDA) and an appropriate combination of service-oriented architecture (SOA) and object-oriented architecture (OOA). When combined, an SOA focus is applied to user functions and an OOA focus is applied to system services, such as data services involving data persistence layers.

Another important point about compression is that its optimization is not always about achieving an artifact of the smallest size.

Optimization with respect to compression is the overall result that achieves the LNBs summed up (in total instructions plus data) having to be presented to the CPU to achieve a defined unit of work.

This definition takes into consideration the additional overhead of compression and decompression algorithms, as well as any mathematics that are performed as an alternative to executing I/O operations.

Since this is a topic of an entire book on its own, we will take the reader on a brief journey into the topic of "data compression" as an introduction to these concepts.

3.1.2.4.7.2   Data Compression—Background The topic of data compression is generally poorly understood even among data experts with a lifetime of experience.

The notion of compression that is assumed by many is the type of data compression that one gets from eliminating repeating bytes of characters, which in its most simple form are data strings or fields containing repeating blanks (e.g., hexadecimal "40"), zeros (e.g., hexadecimal "F0"), or low values (e.g., hexadecimal "00"). The early commercial compression tools available for personal computer used a form of data compression that is far more effective by using an algorithm called LZ77 (and later LZ78) and Huffman coding.

The basic concept behind Huffman coding is simple. It creates a b-tree of the alphabet that is to be compressed using a form of encoding and represents its characters in a binary tree based upon the frequency with which these characters occur within streams of data (see the below diagram).

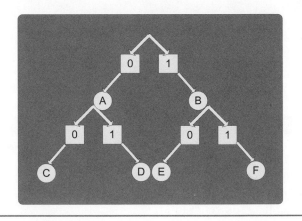

Diagram   Huffman table concept.

Using the Huffman Table Concept diagram, letters would be encoded in binary as follows:

- Alphabet character "A"＝Binary "0,"
- Alphabet character "B"＝Binary "1,"
- Alphabet character "C"＝Binary "00,"
- Alphabet character "D"＝Binary "01,"
- Alphabet character "E"＝Binary "10," and
- Alphabet character "F"＝Binary "11."

The algorithms would encode streams of characters into an encoded (and usually compressed) output stream and decode the encoded stream into an uncompressed stream.

3.1.2.4.7.3 Data Compression—Columnar Databases in a Relational DBMS If we recall the format of the OldSQL database page, depending upon the size of the page, the length of each record, and the amount of free space that was designated during the initial database load, only a certain number of records would be able to fit on the same page.

Let's assume one of the most common database page sizes of 4K (i.e., 4096 bytes) and a hypothetical record size of 750 bytes. This would give us five records per page totaling 3750 bytes with 346 bytes left over for the database page header, page footer, and free space.

Diagram OldSQL database page with five records. (For color version of this figure, the reader is referred to the online version of this chapter.)

In this scenario, let's also assume that there are some number of fields on each record, where one field is State Code.

Diagram State code and household income amount field per record. (For color version of this figure, the reader is referred to the online version of this chapter.)

If this was a Big Data database with 120 million households in the USA, then we would have to read a 4K page for every five State Codes and Household Income Amount fields. To do the arithmetic that would be 120,000,000 divided by 5 pages, or 24 million 4K pages that would have to be read. This amounts to 98,304,000,000 bytes, which we will round up to 100 gigabytes for ease of calculation purposes.

There are various architectures of columnar databases. The most basic form of columnar database, which is also the one that takes the least amount of software development to achieve a columnar database, is one that leverages the infrastructure of an existing relational database management system.

In this basic form of columnar database, the rows of a table are redesigned tohouse an array of only one field. In the example below, the row has been redesigned to house an array of 10 fields representing the same column of data.

For drawing purposes, we have illustrated an array of 10 columns per row. With five rows per page, this allows us to store 50 fields on each database page.

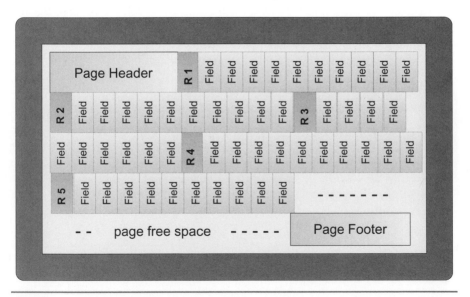

Diagram Columnar database implemented in a relational DBMS. (For color version of this figure, the reader is referred to the online version of this chapter.)

More realistically though, if the field was a two-character State Code, then we should be able to store 375 State Codes per row, or 1875 State Codes per 4K page instead of our original 5.

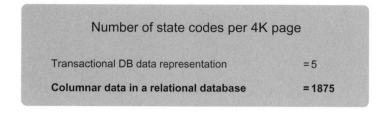

Diagram   Two-character state codes in a columnar-relational DB. (For color version of this figure, the reader is referred to the online version of this chapter.)

From a high-level perspective, the columnar approach in a relational database is 375 times more efficient (i.e., 1875/5) because the I/O substructure only had to render one 4K page to get 1875 State Code values, whereas it only acquired 5 State Codes after reading a 4K page when it was a standard OldSQL transaction database.

3.1.2.4.7.4   Data Compression—Columnar Databases in a Columnar DBMS   As we already know, when one designs a database management system from the ground up, it can take advantage of clearing away any excess infrastructural components and vestiges of transactional database management technology, or even the file access method and file organization technology and conventions that it is built upon. If we draw our diagram again with only columns one after another, we can now accommodate additional columns per page.

Diagram   Columnar database implemented in a columnar DBMS. (For color version of this figure, the reader is referred to the online version of this chapter.)

Again, more realistically though, if the field was a two-character State Code, then we should be able to store 2048 State Codes per 4K page instead of our original 5 per page.

Number of state codes per 4K page	
Transactional DB data representation	= 5
Columnar data in a relational database	= 1875
Columnar data in a columnar database	**= 2048**

Diagram   Two-character state codes per 4K page. (For color version of this figure, the reader is referred to the online version of this chapter.)

From a basic architectural perspective, the columnar approach in a columnar database is 409 times more efficient (i.e., 2048/5) because the I/O substructure only had to render one 4K page to get 2048 State Code values, whereas it only acquired 5 State Codes after reading a 4K page when it was a standard OldSQL transaction database.

This initial perspective on a columnar database will serve as our starting point as we drill deeper into data compression in the context of columnar databases.

3.1.2.4.7.5   Data Compression—Summary   There are a myriad of additional techniques to consider when optimizing the compression of data into what can mathematically be referred to as the LNB format (aka hyper-numbers, hyper-compression). While many of basic techniques do not require profiling the data, a number of extremely effective techniques require advanced data profiling to determine the true LNB storage strategy to employ.

The concepts of LNB and its ensuing branch of mathematics first began as a means to address what are called NP-complete problems, where the NP stands for nondeterministic polynomial time. The concept of NP-complete however is quite simple.

NP-complete represents all mathematical formulas, including any computational algorithms, where (a) it can be mathematically proved that the formula or algorithm will determine the correct results, (b) when the results are determined, the accuracy of those results can be proved in a reasonably short span of time, but (c) to execute the formula or algorithm on even the fastest computers to get the accurate result set will take a greater span of time than one has, which in many cases would be billions of years after the sun is expected to go supernova.

The most famous NP-complete problem is the traveling salesman problem (TSP). Given *n* number of cities and the length of roadway between each city, determine the shortest path that can be traversed to visit all *n* cities. Although challenging to a computer, there are algorithms using a number of concepts from LNB that can solve these problems where *n* can be as large as many thousands. The greater the number of LNB concepts deployed on NP-complete problems, the greater the ability to calculate accurate results in a reasonable span of time.

For example, 1 join of 15 tables containing a million rows per table can fully occupy a dedicated mainframe computer for days when using conventional database technologies, whereas the same or smaller computing platform reasonably architected using LNB concepts will perform a join across 30 tables containing a hundred million rows per table in seconds, such as on a Windows Intel box. This difference in performance is made possible by the extremely few number of bits traveling through the bus and CPU from data, metadata, and machine instructions. The total bits required to get the correct result set are several magnitudes less when employing an LNB architecture.

When advanced compression is combined with the other four fundamental Big Data accelerators, then the resulting computational performance pushes even deeper into realm of transforming NP-complete problems into those that can be completed in a short span of time.

This is an area of great specialization, and given the huge value to industries such as capital markets, and the defense industry there are surprisingly few companies that specialize in data compression and encoding, where among the few there are a couple of boutique companies in the USA and one in Europe.

3.1.2.4.7.6 Big Data—Summary Big Data is still in its infancy.

New products and new versions of existing products are being introduced every month and will continue until the combination of the database acceleration techniques is exploited to their logical conclusion and combined together, including:

- parallel and distributed processing,
- reduced code sets using "process normalization,"
- the right DBMS features,
- advanced data compression and encoding,
- new hardware architectures including servers, CPUs, networks, I/O substructures, and
- highly compact and innovative software infrastructures (e.g., operating systems, security software packages, job schedulers, configuration management software, etc.).

3.1.2.4.7.7 Big Data—The Future The future for Big Data will likely be one that merges with advanced compression technologies, such as LNB (aka hyper-numbers, hyper-compression) to optimize computing platforms.

Possibly, the future Big Data product will be a type of parallel LNB database built on a normalized LNB set of instructions with LNB hardware customization built into LNB parallel processing smart phones and tablets simultaneously switching between multiple LNB carriers, cellular towers, and storage in the cloud.

The final Big Data product will be rearchitected from the ground up capable of supporting all use case types, driven by the principles and concepts of LNB information theory, which is yet another book for a niche audience. Hopefully, this information architecture-based science will be taught among universities as a routine part of building the foundation of our future workforce.

However, the future of Big Data is also likely to be paired with a big calculation capability that leverages quantum computing.

3.1.2.4.8   Quantum Computing—A Lot Deeper

3.1.2.4.8.1   Quantum Computing—The Present As we mentioned earlier, there are certain types of problems that get classified as being NP-complete for their lengthy span of computation time, often because the number of possible results is extremely large, such as 2 to the power of n, where only one or few results are the optimal result.

Sample use cases for types of problems requiring a lengthy span of computation time using conventional computers that can be approached more effectively on a quantum computing platform include:

- cryptography (aka code breaking)
- prime number generation
- TSP patterns
- labeling images and objects within images
- NLP capabilities including extracting meaning from written or verbal language
- identifying correlations in genetic code
- testing a scientific hypothesis
- machine learning for problem solving (aka self-programming)

A quantum computing platform is fundamentally a different type of information system in that it is probabilistic. This means that answer it returns has a probability of being correct or incorrect. The accuracy of the answer can sometimes be confirmed using a conventional computer and the accuracy may also be confirmed by issuing the same question multiple times to determine if the same result set occurs. In quantum computing, the more frequently the same result set is returned, the higher the confidence level of the result.

3.1.2.4.8.2   Quantum Computing—System Architecture At present, there are two competing system architectures for quantum computing; there is the gate model (aka quantum circuit) and adiabatic quantum computing (AQC). Although they are different architectures, they have been shown mathematically shown to be equivalent in that both architectures will operate correctly. From a practical perspective, the only difference that results is efficiency. As such, an AQC can be used to perform the same function that a gate model can perform efficiently, although it may take the AQC a longer span of time to generate the results than one would achieve using the best conventional computer.

The gate model is a design that is optimal for code breaking, particularly an algorithm known as Shor's algorithm. The existing gate model implementations have few qubits and gates demonstrated, and the growth rate of qubit and gate implementations from year to year is linear. It has a complete error correction theory, which it apparently needs as it is more susceptible to decoherence. In quantum mechanics, decoherence means a loss of ordering of phase angles of electrons which determine its state and ultimately the internal value of its associated qubits giving the appearance of a wave function collapse, which for all practical purposes is simply information loss.

In contrast, AQC is optimal for discrete combinatorial optimization problems also known as NP-complete, as well as the problems that are more difficult to check which are referred to as NP-hard problems. Let's take a moment to discuss a basic area of nomenclature from mathematics.

First we should define a few terms. These terms may seem complicated but don't pass out as they are truly simple.

Any algorithm or formula has two basic properties: One is the effort or length of time it takes to *solve* a given problem to determine an answer using a formula, and the other is the effort or length of time it takes to *check* or verify the accuracy of an answer.

In this context, a problem that one can *solve* within a reasonable duration of time is labeled with the letter "**P**" to represent the term "polynomial time." Problems labeled as "**P**" are considered as being easy problems.

In contrast, a problem that one cannot solve within a reasonable duration of time is labeled with the letters "**NP**" to represent the term "nondeterministic polynomial time." These problems are so complicated to solve that it can take billions or trillions of years for a computer to solve them.

However, once an answer has been determined, if one is able to *check* the answer within a reasonable duration of time, then it is labeled "**NP-complete**." However, if an "**NP**" problem is difficult to *check* in a reasonable duration of time, then it is labeled "**NP-hard**."

For example, imagine we have quickly identified "Luisi Prime Numbers" up to primes that are 900 digits in length. To test each prime number with a *check* that attempts to divide the prime number by a series of integers can take quite some time.

AQC opens problem solving to a wide variety of use cases involving real world problems. The existing AQC implementations involve up to a 128 qubit (D-Wave One) called a "Rainier 4" and 512 qubit version (D-Wave Two) called a "Vesuvius 3,"

the first commercially available quantum computer systems. AQC has low suscep-
tibility to decoherence, and although it does not yet have a complete theory of quantum error correction, it has not needed one to this point.

With respect to quantum computing, Rose's law is the quantum computing equivalent regarding the number of qubits per processor doubling every year to Moore's
law for conventional computers regarding the number of transistors on integrated
circuits doubling every 2 years.

3.1.2.4.8.3   Quantum Computing—Hardware Architecture Approaching the hardware architecture in a top-down manner, we begin with a shielded room that is
designed to screen out RF electromagnetic noise. Other than shielded power lines,
the only path for a signal to enter and exit the room are digital optical channels to
transport programming and information in and computational results out.

The present commercially available quantum computer system is a black cube
measuring approximately $10' \times 10' \times 10'$ sitting in the shielded room.

The majority of the 1000 cubic feet are part of the high-tech cooling apparatus
(e.g., dry dilution refrigerator) that uses a closed liquid Helium system to achieve
temperatures that are approximately 100 times colder than interstellar space.
Although it can take hours to initially achieve the necessary operating temperature,
once cooled the temperature is maintained within its operating range for months or
years. The same helium is condensed again using a pulse-tube technology, thereby
making helium replenishment unnecessary.

The deployment model is considered to be a cloud computing model because the
system can be programmed remotely from any location via an internet type connection. Each quantum computer system has its own conventional computer outside the
shielded room to provide job scheduling capabilities for multiple other systems
and users.

When programming and data enter the room on the fiber optic channel, it is transitioned into low-frequency analog currents under 30 MHz and then transitioned
again to superconducting lines at supercooled temperatures with low-frequency filters for removing noise. The I/O subsystem inside the quantum processor is constructed of superconducting materials, such as the metals tin (Sn), titanium (Ti),
and niobium (Nb) (aka columbium (Cb)) when operating between 80 and 20mK,
where 20 mK is the ideal for performance that can be achieved in a cost-effective
manner. 20 mK is 20,000 of one Kelvin degree. This is colder than the temperature
of interstellar space (aka temperature of the cosmic background radiation in interstellar space) which is approximately 2.75 K (i.e., 2750 or 2730 mK warmer than a quantum processor).

The quantum processor is additionally shielded with multiple concentric cylin-
drical shields that manage the magnetic field to less than 1 nanoTesla (nT) for the
entire three-dimensional volume of the quantum processor array of qubits.

The qubit (aka *S*uperconducting *QU*antum *I*nterference *D*evice (SQUID)) is the smallest unit of information (a bit) in a quantum transistor that contains two magnetic spin states having a total of four possible wave function values (i.e., "$-1-1$," "$-1+1$," "$+1-1$," "$+1+1$"), double that of a conventional computer bit (i.e., "0," "1").

Qubits are physically connected together using two couplers that envelop the qubit on four sides and are also manufactured of superconducting materials. According to the quantum computing manufacturer, qubits are analogous to neurons and couplers are analogous to synapses, where programming tutorials show how to use the brain-like architecture that help solve problems in machine learning. The other significant part of the circuitry that surrounds each qubit is numerous switches (aka Josephson junctions) with over 180 Josephson junctions per qubit in each three-dimensional quantum chip.

3.1.2.4.8.4   Quantum Computing—Software Architecture The emergence of quantum computing hardware introduces the need for quantum computing software that effectively leverages this new advancement in quantum computing hardware technology. As one would expect, programming any computer at the machine language level, never mind a quantum computer, is difficult and quite limiting. Although the quantum computing software framework is still evolving, at present it is represented in the following diagram.

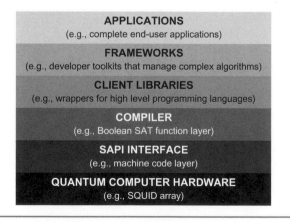

Diagram   Quantum computing software framework.

3.1.2.4.8.5   Quantum Computing Hardware Layer Discussing this framework bottom-up, we begin with the quantum computer hardware layer. This layer contains an array of qubits ready to receive initialization from a machine language program. This process represents the setting of each qubit to one of its four possible values. The next step is introduction of the function. The function is essentially a mathematical formula that represents the energy state of the system for which you have programmed a Boolean SAT (aka Boolean satisfiability).

SAT was the first documented example of an NP-complete problem where there are no known algorithms that can solve the particular problem in a reasonable span of time using conventional computers.

In this step, a Boolean expression is constructed using variables and basic operators, such as AND, OR, and NOT, to represent the desired optimization function.

The next step is the annealing process. This is a slow step, where the slower the better as slower tends to yield the optimum result as opposed to near optimal result. Once you have let the appropriate amount of time elapse, which can vary depending upon the number of variables and the Boolean SAT formula, you will want to acquire the result. In this step, you inspect the values of the qubits as that represents the result set.

You may wonder whether you have given it enough time, whether the answer is correct, and how you might be able to test the result.

Results are typically tested using the conventional computer, and confidence in the result being optimal is achieved by running the same question again to see how often you get the same result set. While quantum computing is not necessarily fast in the same terms that we think about conventional computing in, depending on the characteristics of the problem, they can save you more than billions or trillions of years.

3.1.2.4.8.6 SAPI Interface The system application program interface (API) is the machine code layer of the quantum computer that communicates directly to the quantum computer hardware. Learning QC machine language is extremely difficult even for the scientists who have an intimate understanding of the underlying quantum physics.

Programming at this level is required when new functions, fundamental physics, or QC computer science experiments are being explored or implemented.

3.1.2.4.8.7 Compiler The compiler layer facilitates the implementation of Boolean SAT formulas without requiring any knowledge of machine code, QC physics, or QC hardware. As such, this layer allows the user to focus solely on the problem they are solving in terms of bit strings and mathematics. It is not a compiler in the way the term is used in conventional computing.

3.1.2.4.8.8 Client Libraries For most developers, this is the most natural layer to start with. This layer allows the use of the same standard high-level programming languages that are found in conventional computers. This layer can be used to more easily implement the Boolean SAT formulas and work with the bit strings.

3.1.2.4.8.9 Frameworks Complex functions that have been previously developed can be reused by wrapping the client library code into functions that comprise a toolkit for developers that have been bundled into easy to use libraries, such as supervised binary classification, supervised multiple label assignment, and unsupervised feature learning.

3.1.2.4.8.10 Applications This is the layer where an end user would interact using a graphical user interface (GUI) with the applications that have already been developed for their use.

3.1.2.4.8.11 Quantum Computing Summary Useful tutorials and books are already emerging for quantum computing programming. From an enterprise architecture perspective, quantum computing has many applications for various types of enterprises and in certain industries should be considered as an additional participant within the computing ecosystem if it is not already a part of your enterprise.

3.1.2.5 Mashup Architecture

Big data comes from a large variety sources across the Internet (e.g., Twitter feeds, RSS feeds), Intranet, a variety of external data providers, and a variety of internal data providers persisted in various types of transactional database, data warehouses, and traditional and Hadoop big data repositories. The counterpart to big data sources and repositories is the capability to visualize this data across any of these sources and persistence platforms, and hence the term "mashup" is born.

The term "mashup" refers to an interactive Web environment where data from various sources may be selected and combined by a business end user using drag-and-drop capabilities into the presentation style of their choice. It is the newest breakthrough in enterprise reporting offering several compelling advantages.

3.1.2.5.1 Data Virtualization Layer
The first capability that makes "mashup" technology distinct from "portal" technology is that it has a data virtualization layer on its front end that allows it to source data simultaneously from data sources from around the enterprise from within the firewall, from files and feeds that are externally located outside the firewall, such as from the servers of business partners, and from anywhere on the Internet, and then combine any combination of those feeds into a visualization.

3.1.2.5.2 Cross Data Landscape Metrics
The second capability that makes "mashup" technology a long-term direction is its ability to report on reports from across the IT landscape.

Few realize the fact that there are often tens of thousands or even hundreds of thousands of reports across a large enterprise. If we look at the number of reports that exist within a large enterprise and compare that number to the number of reports that are currently in use, or even just compare it to the number of users across the entire enterprise, we see an interesting relationship we call the "iceberg phenomenon."

The iceberg phenomenon occurs as the number of reports that are in use stay relatively proportional to the overall number of users across the enterprise, while the number of reports that fall out of use continues to grow, thereby forming the underwater portion of the iceberg.

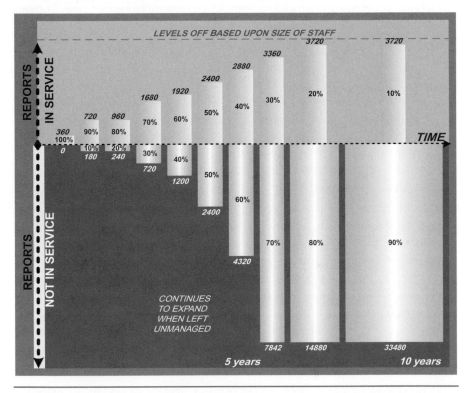

Diagram   Iceberg phenomenon results from report duplication, falling out of use due to user attrition, changes in needs, lack of report traceability, and lack of report true ups.

A good "mashup" technology will eliminate the pressure on business users to develop countless desktop database application reports and spreadsheet reports that can violate business compliance guidelines involving the presence of production data outside the production environment. When this occurs, the number of reports can rapidly grow beyond tens of thousands, each using disparate data sources, some originating their own production data not in production, with all lacking testing procedures, source code control and data security, as desktop reporting tool files can be attached to an e-mail.

The alternative for business users prior to the emergence of mashup technology was a time-consuming process of working with business analysts to design a report, determine the data points needed, locate these data points from across the data landscape, scrub the data to make it usable for reporting, integrate the same data originating from more than one source, and format the final output with the appropriate totals and statistics.

The capabilities of mashup start with self-service reporting for nontechnical users, end user-defined dynamic data mashups, dashboards, scorecards, what-if and ad hoc reporting, drill-down reporting with personalized views based on role, group, and other selections, with the option for scheduled execution, and the generation of report files exported into controlled document repositories.

3.1.2.5.3 Data Security
The third capability that makes "mashup" technology distinct from "portal" technology is that it has a variety of data security capabilities built into it. This begins with having an LDAP lookup capability built into it, with the ability either to pass the permissions to the data sources or, our favorite, to apply the data permissions dynamically for any ad hoc query where the permissions are controlled by business owners with oversight from legal and regulatory compliance.

3.1.2.5.4 Wealth of Visualization Styles
The fourth capability that makes "mashup" technology distinct from "portal" technology is that "mashup" provides a full complement of presentation styles, such as charts, graphs, maps, and reports immediately available out of the box without requiring time consuming and costly IT development support.

Most reporting products focus on the interests of the individuals creating and consuming the reports. While this is an important part of the task, the key differentiator to "mashup" technology is that it addresses the interests of many additional stakeholders besides those creating and consuming reports, such as:

- information and data security architecture—to manage ad hoc access to data
- information architecture—to understand which data is being used and not used
- business compliance—to understand who uses what production data and to ensure that it is sourced from a production environment
- legal—to understand which individuals may be involved in legal holds (LHs)
- executive management—to readily understand what data is available to them for decision making

3.1.2.5.5 End User Self-service at a Low Cost
The fifth aspect of mashup technology distinct from other reporting and BI tools is its low cost structure and high self-service as its core characteristic. Mashups generally support a large number of users after a rapid implementation using just a Web browser for end users and developers. It should have a low learning curve with simplicity for end users and advanced capabilities for data scientists.

So now that we know what is meant by the term "mashup," mashup architecture offers us a glimpse into how architectural disciplines themselves can meet the needs of other architectural disciplines and fit into their architectural frameworks.

As an example, mashup architecture is also one of the key components of a forward-thinking data governance framework that empowers business users to become self-reliant to support a majority of their informational needs.

The components of the data governance framework are further explained in the sections that address the 10 capabilities of data governance. Likewise, the components of data virtualization are further explained in the section 4.1.9.1, which also resides within the disciplines of information architecture.

3.1.2.6 *Compliance Architecture*

Internal and external big data sources of data, persistence layers, and mashup technologies to visualize and report on that data can lead the legal and compliance departments to wish for a simpler way of life.

Depending upon whether an organization is public or private, the jurisdictions in which an enterprise operates and where it is domiciled it may be subject to economic treaty zone, national (aka federal), state (aka province), and local legislation, regulatory oversight, financial oversight, and financial reporting requirements.

In response, these requirement organizations have had to establish a variety of corporate officers and departments to focus on some area of responsibility. Within the business departments, this is largely performed by departments responsible for legal, business compliance, financial reporting, and the various communications departments, such as regulatory communications with the Office of the Comptroller of the Currency (OCC) if the enterprise has been incorporated under the banking charter in the USA. These areas then engage with the sources of regulation, understand the requirements, and then take action within and across the enterprise to ensure that compliance is attained so that:

- the brand and reputation of the organization are protected,
- financial penalties are not incurred by the enterprise,
- business operations are not restricted or ceased, and
- officers of the company do not become subject to criminal penalties.

Regardless of which area of compliance is involved, the challenge comes down to being able to influence the activities of many individuals across the many departments among the various lines of business of the enterprise. Moreover, these individuals must understand how to incorporate this influence into their daily and cyclical activities.

While the level of maturity for monitoring activities across business departments is often high, the ability of these stakeholders to monitor and influence the many activities of IT is less mature, even when an IT compliance function has been put in place.

While most architects have awareness of many of these requirements, most IT developers across various application development teams are focused on technology and not the regulations, never mind the flow of modifications that stream from each source within each jurisdiction of the enterprise.

Some of the standards and frameworks include:

- ISO 17799
- ISO 27000
- Committee of Sponsoring Organizations of the Treadway Commission (COSO)

Compliance architecture is a discipline that collaborates with the other various architectural disciplines, such as information architecture and application architecture, to address the various requirements from the various stakeholders across the various jurisdictions. This is usually implemented by including guidance within the standards and frameworks of the pertinent architectural disciplines.

To help give some context as to the scope, let's begin with sources of compliance restrictions to address topics ranging from anti-terrorism to nondiscrimination.

These include, but are certainly not limited to:

- Office of Foreign Assets Control (OFAC) within the Treasury department,
- United and Strengthening America by Providing Appropriate Tools Required to Intercept and Obstruct Terrorism—specifically Section 314(a) USA PATRIOT Act,
- Office of Federal Contract Compliance Programs (OFCCP),
- Equal Employment Opportunity Act (EEOA),
- Financial Stability Board (FSB),
- Global Financial Markets Association (GFMA),
- Bank Secrecy Act (BSA),
- Regulation E of the Electronic Fund Transfer Act (EFTA),
- Dodd-Frank,
- Securities and Exchange Commission (SEC),
- Federal Trade Commission (FTC),
- OCC,
- Commodity Futures Trading Commission (CFTC),
- International Swaps and Derivatives Association (ISDA),
- Sarbanes Oxley (SOX),
- Basel II, and
- Solvency II.

To help give some context as to what specifically can be involved, let's begin with lists of customer and vendor restrictions to address economic sanctions, embargos, terrorists, and drug traffickers.

These include, but are certainly not limited to:

- Blocked Persons List,
- Targeted Countries List,
- Denied Persons List,
- Denied Entities List,
- FBI's Most Wanted,
- Debarred Parties List,
- Global Watch List, and
- Politically Exposed Persons (PEP).

Anti-money laundering/know your client (AML/KYC), which is a part of client activity monitoring, pertains to regulations that require organizations make a reasonable attempt to be aware of who their customers are and any customer transactions that may be attempting to hide the sources of illegally acquired funds, requiring a suspicious activity report (SAR) to be filed for transactions of $10,000 and over.

The Customer Identification Program (CIP), introduced by Dodd-Frank, is a requirement to know who the counterparties are on a swap contract. The DTCC, which is a holding company established in 1999 to combine the Depository Trust Corporation (DTC) and the National Securities Clearing Corporation (NSCC), along with SWIFT, which is the Society for the Worldwide Interbank Financial Telecommunication, is implementing Legal Entity Identifier (LEI) and its immediate predecessor the CFTC Interim Compliant Identifier (CICI), which are intended to uniquely identify counterparty entities.

The requirement for LEI began in Dodd-Frank and assumed that the SEC would regulate the security-based swaps, and the CFTC would regulate all other types of swaps, such as:

- interest rate swaps,
- commodities swaps,
- currency swaps, and
- credit default swaps.

Compliance architecture also includes RIM. These are categories of data, almost data subject area like, some pertaining to particular lines of business and some pertaining to common topics such as HR. In RIM, each category is associated with a description and a corresponding retention period that it must be held for prior to its proper disposal. It is the responsibility of the enterprise to safeguard and retain a reporting capability on RIM data for the corresponding retention period to be able to support inquiries from either the government or regulators. Depending upon the category of data, the number of years can vary usually somewhere between 2 and 12 years.

Another topic within the scope of compliance architecture is LHs. LHs involve the protection of all paper and electronic records pertaining to litigation that has been filed, as well as any litigation involving matters that have a reasonable expectation of being filed. The financial penalties for improper management of such data can range into the hundreds of millions of dollars.

There are numerous other topics that must be addressed by compliance architecture, enough for several books. Additional topics include the large area, such as LHs, Governance Risk and Compliance (GRC) architecture, and XBRL financial reporting to the SEC, which includes Forms 10-Q, 10-K, 20-F, 8-K, and 6-K to be transmitted to the SEC.

This is why compliance architecture is a distinct architectural discipline, potentially requiring further specialization into legal compliance architecture, HR compliance architecture, and financial compliance architecture.

As an example for the qualifications of a compliance architect, on our team in a top-10 bank, the individual held a Juris Doctorate (JD) from Georgetown University.

3.1.2.7 Application Portfolio Architecture

Application portfolio architecture (aka applications architecture with a plural) is a discipline that was commonly created early on as a part of an enterprise architecture practice. Sometimes, application portfolio architecture is combined with the discipline of TPM. Perhaps this occurred as a result of confusion over the distinction between an application and technology, or maybe it occurred due to the potentially strong bonds that technologies and applications can have with one another.

To briefly recap the distinction between a technology and an application, a technology does not contain business rules that support a business capability, whereas an application does. There are numerous software products that are technologies, such as rules engines, spreadsheets, and development tools (e.g., MS Access) that we classify simply as technologies. However, once business rules are placed within any given instance of such a technology, then that specific instance of a rules engine, spreadsheet, or MS Access file is an application, which should be maintained by an application development team.

So to clarify, once a spreadsheet contains complex formulas that are used to support a business capability, that instance of that spreadsheet should formally transition into becoming an application.

As an application it should be tested, its source code should be controlled in a production repository, it should be backed up for recovery purposes, and so on. However, if the spreadsheet is simply a document or report, in a manner similar to any word processing document like an MS Word file or Google Doc, which does not contain business rules, then those instances are simply "electronic documents" that should not be classified as an application. At most, depending upon what role they play, they should be classified as production reports.

Application portfolio architecture has a "macro" and a "micro" application portfolio management (APM) perspective, and both are important. The more common of the two is the "micro" perspective, which involves the maintenance of an application inventory with all of its relevant information. In the micro view, each application stands alone. In a more mature state, it links to the technology portfolio to illustrate which technologies a given application is dependent upon.

The less common perspective is the "macro" view of applications. In this view, applications are associated with the business capabilities they support in their current state, as well as a number of alternatives from which a future state can be chosen. In its more mature state, the current state of the application portfolio and alternatives by business capability has been assessed for their relative cost-benefit risk analysis over time.

As many in enterprises have observed, costs of applications tend to grow over time as the maintenance of software grows more complex, and licenses for older packages and their supporting technologies correspondingly increase in cost as the vendor's customer base declines.

Unless an application can eventually be retired as part of its normal end of life, the choices are to maintain the increasing cost of maintenance, or replace the application or potentially consolidate the application with others that will provide a lower lifetime cost.

When managed properly, this architectural discipline provides any enterprise a way to accurately project automation costs for a given line of business to facilitate advanced planning of business direction and budgeting.

3.1.2.7.1   Workflow Architecture

Usually, a department with a large enterprise is a collection of related business capabilities that as an aggregate have an overall annual budget allocated to it and every large enterprise will have quite a number of departments. Operational workflows within each department represent the activities that conduct and support business for the organization.

Depending upon the department and the particular business capability, a workflow may be completely manual, completely automated, or comprised of a combination of manual activities and automation. Whether processes are manual or automated, competitive advantages stem from the design of better operational processes.

Workflow processes can be improved incrementally, even with the most subtle change. Although the business advantages to identifying, collecting, and illustrating information regarding operational processes are high, few companies pay any attention to it unless it represents a high-volume process that is core to their business.

It is no surprise then that the companies that collect and analyze data about their operational processes as a matter of normal operating procedure tend to grow most rapidly through acquisition by demonstrating a high degree of competence at integrating acquired businesses into their existing operational workflows. The reason they are so effective is that they already know a great deal about their existing workflows because of the metrics that they've collected. Without those metrics, and without an in-depth understanding of their workflows, management can only guess at what to do and how well it worked.

The discipline of workflow architecture is comprised of three major areas. The first is BPMN, which forms a foundation for the remaining areas.

3.1.2.7.1.1 Business Process Modeling Notation BPMN is a standardized notation that graphically represents processes modeling the operational workflow and potentially encompassing the business rules that get performed within the operational workflow, regardless of whether those business rules are manual or automated, potentially generating workflow automation or BPM technology syntax for either simulation purposes or implementation. The role of BPMN therefore is to document workflows.

Using this notation, one may document workflows that represent the current operational processes, proposed operational processes, or transitional processes. They may pertain to manual processes, automated processes, or the integration of manual and automated processes.

Depending upon the workflow documented and the particular product used to document the workflow, if the resulting BPMN syntax meets the criteria of workflow automation, then it may be forward engineered into workflow automation or BPM technology. However, if the BPMN syntax meets the criteria of BPM technology, then it can only be forward engineered into BPM technology, whereas the differences pertain to scope, which we shall soon see.

3.1.2.7.1.2 Workflow Automation The second major area of workflow architecture is workflow automation, which standardizes the operational steps of a business or IT department within software to mirror the steps of an operational workflow excluding business rules. Operational workflows include requests entering a department, the transfer of request activities, including signature cycles, through to the eventual completion of the request.

The first characteristic that defines workflow automation is that it is restricted only to aspects of the workflow. The best way to understand this is with an example.

Let's select a particular department that is found in all major companies, regardless of industry, products and services, such as a data services department (e.g., enterprise data management). A data services department typically receives requests for a variety of services from application development teams. To name just a few, some of these services include requests for a new database to support a new application, a change to an existing database design, or an increase in size to accommodate a substantially larger number of data records than previously anticipated.

In its manual form, the person making the request of data services walks over to the person that handles this type of request for them. Occasionally, instead of walking over the requester sometimes phones, sends e-mail, or sends a paper document through interoffice mail.

Once received within data services, the person handling the request sends a message to the requestor regarding the amount of time it will take the various participants to do and when it can be fit into their respective work schedules.

The individual making the request then takes note of the time it will take and when it will be scheduled, and then either approves or enters into a discussion to have the request supported sooner.

When the work is actually performed, the tools that are used by data services include a CASE tool, where the department's naming and database design standards will be applied, and a DBMS product, within which the physical database will be created or altered where the department's physical design standards will be applied.

The data services contact then notifies the person the request originated with that their activities have been completed and that they can check it to determine if everything appears to be working properly.

In the example above, the business rules performed by data services were conducted in the CASE tool and DBMS product, where all of the other activity is operational workflow. What is interesting is that there are almost an infinite number of possible operational workflows, depending upon how the manager of the data services department wants to organize the staff members of the department and the sequence in which they perform their work. What don't change, no matter which operational workflow is used, are the business rules that are performed by the department using the CASE tool and DBMS product.

As such, if the manager of the data services department were to document the operational workflow using BPMN, then the documented workflow could be automated using a WFA tool (e.g., Service-now.com) to result in something like the following.

In its automated form, the person making the request of data services enters their request into the data services workflow application. The request then shows up on the summary screen of data services outstanding requests.

Someone in data services assigns the request to them and returns an estimated number of hours and an estimated completion date that goes back to the requestors screen for their approval.

Once the approval is returned to data services, the work activities are performed in the appropriate software applications, tools, and products, and then the requestor is notified upon completion. The requester validates the work and closes the request as complete.

In this scenario, the WFA tool kept metrics of all requests coming into the department, from whom, with a record of who in data services satisfied the request, tracking the duration and completion dates and tracking whether the estimates were accurate.

The department manager can see what his department was doing, what work was in the pipeline, what his department had accomplished, how many times his department got it right, and how many requests required rework. Perhaps most importantly, the manager sees what percentage of his resources are being consumed by other departments and could compare the funding he received from those departments.

3.1.2.7.1.3   BPM Technology The third major area of workflow architecture is BPM technology, which is a technology involving multiple architectural disciplines that constitute a robust application development environment. BPM technology automates both workflow automation and its associated business rules often as a way to integrate applications that reside across disparate technological environments, thereby coupling workflow automation to the applications involved.

There are a number of issues that arise with BPM technologies that do not occur with workflow automation, starting with recoverability of BPM technology applications as it often requires synchronization across multiple application databases and BPM technology databases, files, and queues.

The first reason why workflow architecture must govern BPMN, workflow automation, and BPM technology is that use of the wrong technology can significantly raise the complexity and infrastructural costs of automation. The second reason is that the guiding principles of these three areas are completely different from one another.

Examples of guiding principles for BPMN include: processes are assets of the business requiring management as such, process models provide business value even when they remain manual, and distinctions exist between operational workflow and their associated business rules.

Examples of guiding principles for workflow automation include: workflows are defined and repeatable, operational metrics are collected in an unintrusive manner, operational workflows and their efficiency are rendered transparent with automation, and BI on operational metrics provide operational radar.

Examples of guiding principles for BPM technology include: BPM technologies provide competitive advantages when the circumstances are appropriate, and they must balance the needs of business architecture, APM, TPM, application architecture, database architecture, and DR* architecture.

Workflow architecture is frequently faced with the use of several BPM technologies and sometimes multiple WFA tools, although frequently without its associated foundation of BPMN documentation.

3.1.2.7.2 Application Architecture

In any discussion of application architecture (i.e., application architecture in its singular form), it is important to remind ourselves to maintain the important distinction between applications and technologies mentioned in the TPM and application portfolio architecture sections; technologies do not contain business rules, whereas applications do.

As such, application architecture (i.e. application architecture with a singular application) refers to the manner in which an application is put together.

This includes:

- the degree to which an application employs modules to package it capabilities
- how business requirements are packaged into the modules of the application
- how technical requirements are packaged into modules of the application
- how error handling is integrated into the application's framework
- whether and how performance monitoring may be integrated into the application

The way requirements are packaged and packages organized depends largely on the type of application, influencing the potential number of software layers and objects, functional grouping, and tiers, such as a graphics tier, application tier, data virtualization, and database tier.

For information systems, there are a number of common application types, such as portals, Web applications, online transaction processing applications, batch applications, workflow automation applications, BPM technology applications, simulations, games, and autonomic computing applications, some overlapping and most making use of databases. Among these types of applications, a variety of application architectures and types of programming languages exist.

One way to classify types of programming languages is to group them into one of the five "generations of programming languages," such as:

- machine language (i.e., first-generation language),
- assembly languages (i.e., second-generation language),
- Cobol, Fortran, PL/I (i.e., third-generation language),
- MS Access, PowerBuilder (i.e., fourth-generation language), and
- mashup technologies (e.g., drag-and-drop self-service).

A richer although rather overlapping taxonomy for the types of programming languages consists of approximately 50 programming language types, such as array (aka vector), assembly languages, command line interfaces, compiled languages, interpreted languages, DMLs, object-oriented languages, scripting languages, procedural languages, and rules engines. These types of programming languages then have numerous subtypes and architectures of their own.

For example, rules engine types include data governance rules engines, data manipulation rules engines, business applications, reactive rules engines, BPM rules engines, CEP rules engines, game rules engines, and business rule management system and reasoning rules engines.

Rather than getting overly directed toward the large number of details of these different information systems application types and their application architectures, we will discuss why they need architecture and the resulting frameworks that each should have.

3.1.2.7.2.1 Requirements Traceability Depending upon the needs of the company, the first priority for application architecture is software maintainability, particularly since the investment that a company makes in software development is so high. That said, requirements traceability is perhaps one of the largest contributors to improved software maintainability, but oddly it is among the least likely to occur in software architectures among large companies that do not see themselves as having a core competency of software development and technology.

In fact, business requirements are rarely treated as the valuable asset they truly are. Too frequently, business requirements are poorly documented, and consequently, poorly labeled and organized within the applications that implement them. Without traceability back to requirements, it becomes obvious why the many resulting automation lines of code are overly labor intensive to adjust as requirements change and new requirements are added.

To understand this in terms of real cost through staffing levels, approximately 10,000 lines of code represent the upper limit that a typical developer can maintain, which are based upon estimates from the U.S. Government. To maintain an application developed by someone else, the developer must first understand how the original developer approached the packaging of requirements and their organization. This translates into the fact that every one million lines of code must be maintained by a staff of a hundred developers.

Depending upon the technologies involved and the annual cost of a developer, the cost per developer can be anywhere between 80,000 and 180,000 per year. Given the fact that a typically large enterprise can have many millions of lines of code, this translates to hundreds of developers whose cost must be added to the price of the products and services offered by the enterprise.

Error handling—Regarding one aspect of application architecture, it is often said that error handling represents nearly half of all application code. A standard approach to error handling can be established for each type of application architecture commonly used within the enterprise. Some application types include batch, OLTP, and Web based. When application architecture establishes standards and reusable frameworks for basic capabilities, such as error handling and application security, it acts as an accelerator to both development and maintenance.

Software reuse—This brings us to the most challenging aspect of application architecture, software reuse. Government agencies and universities have attempted several times to create repositories of software specifically for reuse.

In fact, many companies, universities, and government agencies have studied at great depth the topic of software reuse in information systems. When viewed from the perspective of control systems or electronics, the notion of software reuse seems relatively simple. However, unlike control systems that associate software capabilities to the tangible world, information systems are often far too nonstandard in its architecture. The most significant difference, however, is that control systems associated with particular types of mechanical devices, such as anemometers and other sensors, encounter nearly identical structured and unstructured data.

To begin, software components must be architected first to be reusable. In fact, any naming convention for software modules that do not share the same rigorous LDA cannot overcome the reality that the software parts are by definition incompatible. One of the things we will learn from the discipline of data architecture is that the only glue that can hold software modules together is the data. That said, then how can application architecture address the challenge of software reuse?

Of the infinite number of ways that applications may be architected, there are three methods that can achieve true software reuse. To discuss these, let's assume for a moment that we have dozens of application systems that support the same business capabilities.

Let's also assume that we accumulated, through several acquisitions of smaller companies, an inventory of purchased and homegrown applications dependent upon a variety of older technologies.

Each of these information system applications is likely to have database designs that do not resemble one another. In addition, aside from some differences within the business requirements themselves, probably every characteristic that makes up an application's architecture is probably vastly different, such as:

- the degree to which an application employs modules to package it capabilities
- how business requirements are packaged into the modules of the application
- how technical requirements are packaged into modules of the application
- how error handling is integrated into the application's framework
- whether and how performance monitoring may be integrated into the application

To attain reuse in information system applications, architects and developers must employ a level of standardization that they are not used to. Part of the challenge is mindset, as even today, most people consider software development an art form as opposed to an engineering discipline. However, to achieve reuse in an information system, a variety of frameworks are required.

The first and most important framework is the LDA, which we will discuss in detail separately. The critical thing to know about an LDA is that it encompasses every category of data that any application must deal with. As a framework, it fully addresses the data perspective of operational workflows, transactions, business data, and data analytics.

The second most important aspect are the frameworks of the application architecture itself. This means that the application design patterns chosen must be standardized into frameworks as well. Although a somewhat technical subject to discuss in a book intended to include a business user audience, we will touch upon application design patterns in the next section.

The third most important consideration is the interfaces that support various services across a variety of other architectural disciplines.

The fourth most important aspect is the frameworks of the system infrastructure, including the operating system environments and possible programming languages.

Hence, software reuse within the information systems paradigm only becomes attainable once each of these four areas has been addressed as rigorous engineering disciplines.

3.1.2.7.3   Application Architecture Design Patterns

Each major application type (e.g., batch, OLTP, and Web based) may employ almost any combination of architectural design patterns, most of which have names. Among the most common and/or useful design patterns to be aware of are:

- *integration pattern*—identifies whether the application is a silo application, is fully integrated into a unified framework of applications and shared databases, or stand alone but sharing common subsystems (aka subsystem interface pattern)
- *distribution pattern*—identifies whether the application is nondistributed, distributed, peer-to-peer (P2P) distributed (e.g., pure, hybrid, or centralized peer to peer), grid, and/or running in the cloud inside or outside the firewall
- *tier pattern*—identifies whether the application is single tier, two tier, three tier, or four tier, where these may be any combination of presentation layer, application layer, data virtualization layer, and data layer
- *procedural pattern*—identifies whether the application is unstructured, structured, object-oriented (OO), service-oriented architecture (SOA), 4-GL, rule-based (expert system), statistical model, or nonstatistical model (neural network)

  Object-oriented procedural patterns employ what is called the "Law of Demeter" or "Principle of Least Knowledge," which is a layered architecture that does not permit a program to reach further than an adjacent layer of the architecture, and hence it is said that each program can only talk to its friends.
- *processing pattern*—identifies whether the application is single-threaded or belonging to one or more of several parallel processing styles (e.g., tightly coupled parallel processing (e.g., SMP), loosely coupled parallel processing (e.g., MPP, grid computing)

- *usage pattern*—identifies whether the application is consumer to consumer (C2C), consumer to business (C2B), business to business (B2B), business to employee (B2E), business to government (B2G), government to citizen (G2C), government to business (G2B), government to government (G2G), or local usage
- *analytical pattern*—identifies whether the application is statistical, neural network, or simply multidimensional; however, neural networks as an example have at least two dozen design patterns associated with them, each tending to be useful for different types of problems, types, and distributions of data
- *interactive pattern*—(aka synchronous versus asynchronous) identifies whether the application is conversational, which waits for a response, or pseudo-conversational, which does not wait, but instead starts a new instance of a task to handle the response if and when it arrives
- *data communication pattern*—identifies whether the application transmits data using a push approach, such as an ESB that transmits data as it occurs; a pull approach, such as with extract, transform, and load (ETL) that transmits data in a batch on demand or scheduled; or a hybrid approach, such as using ETL within an ESB
- *message dissemination pattern*—identifies whether the application sends information directly to a predetermined recipient or subscribing recipients, or indirectly through publishing or broadcasting
- *resource sequence pattern*—identifies whether the application's processing sequence intentionally orders the locking of shared resources in a particular sequence as a means to proactively prevent the possibility of a deadly embrace across logical units of work
- *pipeline pattern* (aka pipe and filter)[1]—identifies whether the applications, whether multiprocessor pipeline or single processor "pseudo" pipeline, are patterns architected as a series of queues that enter their respective routines

    The queues that messages travel on are referred to as pipes, and the processes that reside at the end of each pipe are referred to as filters. Each filter process messages sequentially in a first-in-first-out fashion, although parallelism can be achieved by instantiating more than one filter for a given inbound pipe.

---

[1]This is an architectural style that divides a larger processing task into a sequence of smaller, independent processing steps, referred to as "filters," which are connected by channels, referred to as "pipes." Each filter exposes a very simple interface receiving inbound messages from an inbound pipe, then processes the data, and then generates a message on an outbound pipe. The pipe connects one filter to the next, until the processing is complete. There are a number of architectural subpatterns based on pipeline patterns, such as the aggregator subpattern, which is a special filter that receives a stream of messages and correlates the ones that are related, aggregates information from them, and generates an outbound message with the aggregated information. In contrast, a splitter subpattern is a special filter that separates messages into subsets that can be routed to distinct outbound pipes.

These patterns are typical in operating systems, such as MVS, UNIX, VM/CMS, and Windows, as well as "mini-operating systems" such as OLTP environments, such as CICS and IDMS/Central Version, but are a pattern that is used among other types of applications.

For additional messaging patterns and subpatterns, refer to *Enterprise Integration Patterns: Designing, Building, and Deploying Messaging Solutions* by Gregor Hohpe and Bobby Woolf.[2] Although nearly 700 pages, it is well written, organized, and comprehensive for this architectural niche.

- *event-driven pattern*—identifies whether the application triggers processes implicitly or explicitly when events come into existence

  Explicit invocations occur when a process invokes a subsequent process directly, whereas implicit invocations occur when a process stores data in a shared location or transmits a message for other processes to detect on their own

- *MV patterns*—are a family of applications consisting of MVC (model-view-controller), MVP (model-view-presenter), MVVM (model-view-view-model), HMVC (hierarchical-model-view-controller), and PAC (presentation-abstraction-control) that organize responsibility for different user interface elements within an application, such as in a shopping cart application, to facilitate independent development, testing, and maintenance of each component

- *blackboard patterns*—are applications where a deterministic strategy is not known for approaching a problem; thus, the framework is to invoke a diverse set of processes to render partial solutions to a problem into a shared buffer, which is then monitored by one or more other processes that attempt to recognize a solution to the overall problem from the information continually evolving within the buffer

One of the most advantageous approaches to application architecture is to blend different architectural patterns, such as SOA for the front end and OO on the back end to achieve an application with an optimum set of characteristics.

3.1.2.7.4 Integration Architecture

As the number of application systems, environments, and technologies grew that had to communicate with one another, so emerged the discipline of integration architecture.

The discipline of integration architecture essentially involves the touch points that exist between different components, whether they are software to software, hardware to hardware, or software to hardware. Integration architecture (aka middleware) is

---

[2]For a more complete list of messaging patterns and subpatterns of architectural subtypes, refer to *Enterprise Integration Patterns: Designing, Building, and Deploying Messaging Solutions* by Gregor Hohpe and Bobby Woolf, 2004, published by Addison-Wesley, ISBN: 0-321-20068-3.

responsible for standards and frameworks pertaining to communications and interfaces between application systems, operating system environments, and technologies.

The original and most simple approach to integrating applications is called a point-to-point architecture, where application systems directly communicate to other application systems as necessary. As the number of application systems increase, so does the complexity of having many interconnections.

The first integration architecture to significantly reduce the number of connections was the hub and spoke architecture where each application system had a connection to a shared hub, which acts as a traffic cop to direct communications between application systems. Due to scalability issues, however, federated architectures and distributed architectures (aka peer to peer) were developed to better load balance.

Fast forward to today, and we have SOAs that have loosely bound applications attached to an ESB with application services exposed as Web services, rules engines, and extract transform and load (ETL) products riding inside the ESB and being scheduled by job schedulers outside the ESB.

The Web services aspect of SOA came when IBM and Microsoft agreed upon a communication standard. Shortly after the emergence of Web services, ESB became the agreed-upon standard for the industry, such as for messaging and BPM technologies mentioned in workflow architecture.

Integration architecture is organized into a number of domains.
They include:

- user integration, which connects a user to applications through networks,
- process integration, which connects workflow processes to other workflow processes,
- application integration (aka service integration), which connects applications to other applications, potentially across disparate technology environments,
- data integration, which performs data movement such as with ESB, ETL or FTP, and
- partner integration, which includes business to business (B2B) and business to customer (B2C) communications.

As such, integration architecture faces a variety of challenges in dealing with communications protocols, which often vary depending upon the type of platform.

3.1.2.7.5 NLP Architecture

Contrary to the expectation of many industry experts, NLP has emerged to demonstrate significant commercial value for a variety of use cases including:

- monitoring social media in real time,
- providing initial or alternative support for customer inquiries,
- accurately identifying structured data from previously unstructured contract files,

- performing language translations of Web-based text messages and company documents,
- scoring essays on exams more consistently and accurately than human experts, and
- providing a hands free voice command interface for smartphones.

NLP provides the ability to monitor countless tweets from Twitter, e-mail messages from customers, Facebook messages, and other electronic social media in real time so that automation can route issues to a human for immediate corrective action.

Significant quantities of structured data can be identified from tens of thousands of unstructured data, such as contracts, in seconds, as opposed to an expensive and time-consuming process to manually determine the answer to simple questions like, "What contracts over $50,000 will be expiring over the next 6 months in the Americas?"

In addition to identifying structured data, NLP can translate documents and text messages from and to any language in real time. When augmented with image recognition, NLP can digitize paper-based schematics, architectural diagrams, maps, and blueprints, into structured content, thereby making their contents machine searchable and usable.

NLP architecture is the discipline responsible for global standards and frameworks pertaining to the capabilities of NLP. At present, there are many commercially available NLP products, utilities, and services that may be incorporated into applications of various types.

As a result, depending upon the characteristics of the component, NLP architecture is a discipline that augments application architecture, application portfolio architecture, and TPM.

3.1.2.8   Life Cycle Architecture

As an architectural discipline, life cycle architecture acts as an accelerator to a variety of activities across the enterprise. It provides one of the most compelling arguments that demonstrate how enterprise architecture is not just about software development, never mind enterprise architecture being just about TPM and APM.

A life cycle is a series of stages or steps through which something passes from its origin to its conclusion. In IT, the first life cycle to emerge was the software development life cycle (SDLC), which oddly enough only addresses the creation or maintenance of an information system and excludes its shutdown.

The easiest way to begin understanding life cycle architecture is to first consider a life cycle that everyone knows, such as the SDLC. Examples of the 10 major life cycles are outlined in the coming sections to provide some ideas as to what to include as life cycles and what their content should be.

However, it is important to note that each enterprise would typically choose which life cycles and which steps are most appropriate to address the priorities of their organization, and that these are offered with the intent to stimulate a constructive conversation.

Once the steps and substeps of a life cycle have been agreed upon, then the various architectural disciplines that support that step and substep can be mapped to it for facilitate deployment of subject matter expertise to assist within the various life cycles of the enterprise.

The life cycles that we will address are the most common ones that are needed, which I have added to over the years which are:

- SDLC,
- data centric life cycle (DCLC),
- data governance life cycle (DGLC),
- architecture governance life cycle (AGLC),
- divestiture life cycle (DLC),
- merger and acquisition life cycle (MALC),
- data center consolidation life cycle (DCCLC),
- corporate restructuring life cycle (CRLC),
- outsourcing life cycle (OSLC),
- insourcing life cycle (ISLC), and
- operations life cycle (OLC).

3.1.2.8.1 Software Development Life Cycle

There are many versions of the SDLC. Perhaps the most exacting is the ISO standard ISO/IEC 12207, which is an international standard comprised of 43 processes, and more than 95 activities, and 325 tasks.

At its highest level, ISO/IEC 12207 consists of six core processes, which are:

- acquisition,
- supply,
- development,
- operation,
- maintenance, and
- destruction.

One reason we will not review this particular standard is that outside of the defense industry, it would appear that it is generally not in use. The main reason that we will not cover it is that it fails to address the basic activities that are required to support many of the most basic and mainstream business activities.

A basic and useful form of the SDLC can be summarized in nine stages. It consists of:

- *inception*—which includes the scope and business justification,
  - *identify scope*
  - *identify business justification*
- *high-level analysis*—which determines high-level business requirements, pertinent architectural frameworks, conceptual data model, and cost estimates,
  - *identify high-level business requirements*
  - *identify applicable architecture standards and frameworks*
  - *further develop the associated conceptual data model*
  - *gather estimates from SDLC participants/service providers*
  - *evaluate business justification for approval and justification*
- *detail analysis*—which identifies detail business requirements, business data glossary terms in scope, and sources of data to support those business glossary terms,
  - *identify and organize business requirements*
  - *define business data glossary entries that are in scope*
  - *enhance data points in the conceptual data model*
  - *business approves business requirements*
- *logical design*—establishing a logical data model, operational workflow, user interface and report design, and application architecture,
  - *using the conceptual data mode develop the logical data models*
  - *design user interfaces and reports*
  - *develop application design and data flow including interfaces*
  - *conduct logical design review*
- *physical design*—developing the physical data model and data movement code, and specifications for the application, system software and hardware,
  - *develop physical data model and any ETL specifications*
  - *develop application, GUI and report specifications*
  - *develop software and hardware specifications*
  - *develop manual operational workflow*
- *build*—generating the necessary code, software installs, and infrastructure,
  - *develop code and implement DDL and ETL*
  - *implement application*
  - *install software and hardware*
- *validation*—migrating and testing,
  - *migrate to integration environment and test*
  - *migrate to QA environment and test*
- *deployment*—conducting a production readiness test and production cutover, and
  - *conduct production readiness test*
  - *conduct interdisciplinary go/no go evaluation*
- *post-implementation*—which evaluates the production cutover and determines lessons learned
  - *conduct postmortem for lessons learned*

3.1.2.8.2   Data Centric Life Cycle

The next issue that emerges then is what happens if you use the SDLC on something other than developing a software application. The answer is, even though the SDLC is well suited to supporting the development stages of an application system, in contrast it is poorly suited as the life cycle for other major categories of activities that require project teams. The first one we will discuss is the life cycle of data warehouses with their related artifacts, such as ODSs and data marts.

Unlike the development of application systems, which are driven by business requirements that become transformed into business rules that automate business processes, the development of data warehouses is data centric efforts that identify and collect information to support operational reporting, ad hoc reporting, and BI.

The stages to develop data warehouses are referred to as the DCLC. In contrast to the collection of business rules in the SDLC, the DCLC identifies categories of use cases and the categories of data that are necessary to support those use cases.

As such, the categories of use cases may pertain to different forms of risk reporting, general ledger activity, regulatory compliance, or marketing. In response to those categories of use cases, the categories of data and their associated data points are necessary to scope data requirements. The primary architectural artifacts needed to support this step are the LDA and its associated conceptual data models.

To briefly describe it now, the LDA is a business artifact that is an inventory of every business context of data across the enterprise, referred to as business data subject areas (BDSAs). Each BDSA has a corresponding conceptual data model, which is only instantiated for those business areas when the need presents itself.

The LDA is discussed further in the section 4.1.2. However, the point is that there is a least one other life cycle that is required to address the development of data centric systems, such as data warehouses and ODSs.

To summarize in a manner consistent with the SDLC previously outlined, the 11 stages of the DCLC include:

- *data requirements*—determining use cases and the categories of data,
  - *identify business stakeholders*
  - *evaluate scope*
  - *determine business drivers*
  - *identify types of use cases*
- *data analysis*—evaluating the data sources,
  - *evaluate existing and prospective internal data sources*
  - *research free and paid external data feeds*
  - *allocate sources and feeds to type of use cases*
  - *validate allocation with business stakeholders*
- *data profiling*—analyzing the data quality of the data points required,
  - *profile each source*

- *compare profile to logical data model to confirm its appropriate use*
- *apply ontology to intended use*
- *identify global reference data and associated data codes*
- *logical data architecture*—classifying each data point to the business context of the LDA and collecting the business metadata of each data point,
  - *determine business context within the LDA*
  - *identify related data points*
  - *determine business metadata*
  - *publish updated LDA*
- *conceptual data modeling*—allocating each business data glossary item to its associated conceptual data model,
  - *incorporate glossary items into the conceptual data models*
  - *establish any additional similar or related data glossary items*
  - *validate data glossary item business context*
  - *publish updated conceptual data models*
- *logical data modeling*—incorporating conceptual data model updates into the logical data models,
  - *incorporate conceptual data model updates*
  - *support preexisting application views*
  - *conduct peer model review*
  - *publish updated logical data models*
- *physical data modeling*—implementing logical data model updates into physical designs,
  - *implement logical data model updates*
  - *gather transaction path analysis*
  - *incorporate physical design requirements*
  - *conduct peer model review*
  - *publish updated physical data models*
- *data discovery*—locating the sources of the data
  - *identify data origins*
  - *data source assessment*
  - *selection of the best data source(s)*
- *data acquisition*—extraction of the data into a landing zone
  - *extract selected data to landing zone*
- *data cleansing*—(aka data scrubbing) cleansing data based upon data profiling specifications,
  - *profile the extracted data*
  - *develop data cleansing specifications*
  - *cleanse data and retain history*
  - *record data quality metrics*
- *data standardization*—standardize the codes for all data in the landing zone,
  - *develop data standardization specifications*

- *apply code table values from the global reference data master*
- *record standardization metrics*
- *data integration*—standardizing and integrating scrubbed data into the ODS layer,
  - *develop data integration specifications*
  - *create ODS layer databases in development*
  - *integrate data into development while masking sensitive data*
  - *record data integration metrics*
- *user acceptance*—business user testing,
  - *migrate to QA*
  - *business user testing without masking*
- *production*—cutting over to production and monitoring data warehouse metrics
  - *retest and perform a go/no evaluation*

3.1.2.8.3 Data Governance Life Cycle

It was easy to understand the differences between the SDLC and DCLC because there are many instances of application systems and data warehouses within large companies that we already had familiarity with. However, now that we have provided an overview of the SDLC and data centric development life cycle, the life cycle needed to support a data governance program, which we call a DGLC, has yet another focus, even though it shares a number of steps with the DCLC.

As we shall learn in the data governance section, the focus of our DGLC is to shift the business users' dependence upon IT to self-reliance, self-service, and self-control in every aspect that is appropriate to empower business. Therefore, in contrast to the other life cycles we've already discussed, the DGLC has the majority of its participation from business users.

To summarize in a manner consistent with the prior life cycles, the 15 stages of the DGLC include:

- *identifying data points*—determining business usage and industry name,
  - *determine business usage*
  - *determine business industry name*
- *populating business data glossary*—identifying business synonyms, business owner, regulatory controls, external standards mapping, and sample values,
  - *identify business synonyms used by business stakeholders*
  - *determine owing business department and business trustee*
  - *record the proper business definition and business purpose*
  - *identify associated business capabilities*
  - *determine related regulatory requirements*
  - *determine data sensitivity*
  - *identify external standards mapping (e.g., MISMO, ACORD)*
  - *identify sample business values or full set of domain values*

- *logical data architecture*—classifying each data point to the business context of the LDA and collecting the business metadata of each data point,
  - *determine business context within LDA*
  - *identify related business data points*
  - *determine business metadata*
  - *publish updated LDA*
- *conceptual data modeling*—business-driven allocation of each business data glossary item to its associated conceptual data model and developing conceptual data models,
  - *incorporate glossary items into conceptual data models*
  - *create any similar and related data items*
  - *validate data glossary item business context*
  - *publish updated conceptual data models*
- *logical data modeling*—IT incorporating conceptual data model updates into the logical data models,
  - *incorporate conceptual data model updates*
  - *support preexisting application views*
  - *conduct peer model review*
  - *publish updated logical data models*
- *physical data modeling*—IT implementing logical data model updates into physical designs,
  - *implement logical data model updates*
  - *gather transaction path analysis*
  - *incorporate physical design requirements*
  - *conduct peer model review*
  - *publish updated physical data models*
- *data cleansing*—(aka data scrubbing) cleansing data based upon data profiling specifications,
  - *identify origin of data*
  - *extract data to landing zone*
  - *profile the data in the landing zone*
  - *develop data cleansing specifications*
  - *cleanse data content and retain history*
  - *record data quality metrics*
- *data standardization*—standardize the codes for all data in the landing zone,
  - *develop data standardization specifications*
  - *apply code table values from the global reference data master*
  - *record standardization metrics*
- *data integration*—standardizing and integrating scrubbed data into the ODS layer,
  - *develop data integration specifications*

- *create ODS layer databases in development*
- *integrate data into development masking sensitive data*
- *business designated access rights*—designating ad hoc reporting access rights for each department based upon their business need,
    - *designate access rights for departments and roles*
- *legal and compliance oversight*—validating and overriding access rights as necessary,
    - *validate access rights*
    - *designate access rights overrides*
- *user acceptance*—business user testing in a secure environment that resembles production,
    - *migrate to QA*
    - *business user testing*
- *production*—cutting over to production and monitoring data warehouse metrics,
    - *migrate to production*
    - *production use*
- *secure canned reporting data points*—designating business data glossary terms to canned reports,
    - *canned report data point analysis*
    - *ad hoc report data point obfuscation*
- *reporting and querying*—controlling canned report access and distribution, and
    - *canned report dissemination*
- *production to nonproduction data movement*—masking sensitive data departing from the controls of production that safeguard the data
    - *mask sensitive data departing from production through ETL controls*

Needless to say for data governance purposes, these stages may be performed iteratively with collections of data points by business area or individually by data point in any order.

3.1.2.8.4 Architecture Governance Life Cycle

The AGLC (aka foundation architecture) is a life cycle that identifies which architectural disciplines are necessary to instantiate or that are no longer needed at a given point in time. The AGLC accomplishes this by analyzing business direction, business strategy, pain points of the business, initiatives that span the enterprise, and the needs of stakeholders across the company and compares this to the architectural disciplines that are already in existence.

The steps of the AGLC include:

- *analyze business direction*—analyze the hedgehog concept of each line of business and the overall enterprise,
    - *identify business direction*

- *identify pain points*
- *map pain points to their corresponding architectural discipline*
- *analyze business pain points*—inventory the pain points and prioritize them for greatest impact while in alignment with business strategy,
  - *prioritize pain points and evaluation metrics*
  - *construct business case for remediation and financial approval*
- *analyze types of technological issues*—categorize each new technology into an existing architectural discipline or identify the possibility of encountering the need for a new architectural discipline,
  - *categorize new technologies into architectural disciplines for SME evaluation*
- *analyze all business initiative types*—categorize each business initiative to identify the possibility of encountering the need to modify an existing life cycle or create a distinct life cycle,
  - *evaluate initiatives across the enterprise to identify its corresponding life cycle*
  - *modify existing life cycles or develop new life cycles as required*
- *assess business alignment*—periodically analyze each architectural discipline to determine if it is in alignment with the hedgehog concept of each line of business and the overall enterprise
  - *depending upon technology gaps define new architectural discipline*
  - *staff architectural discipline*
  - *define the scope and touch points of the architectural discipline*
  - *identify the hedgehog principle of the architectural discipline*
  - *identify and assess current state*
  - *determine future state*
  - *identify metrics to compare current and future state*
  - *identify stakeholders and identify their interests*
  - *develop standards and frameworks*
  - *develop transition plan*
  - *socialize artifacts of the architectural discipline to solution architects*
- *initial architecture review*—implement the AGLC prior to entering any other life cycle
  - *review the type of initiative*
  - *identify the initial architectural standards and frameworks for the initiative*
- *postmortem architecture review*—assess architecture participation in each initiative
  - *review the results of the initiative*
  - *evaluate the role of architectural artifacts in the initiative*
  - *identify the metrics to be evaluated*
  - *identify ways to improve efficacy*

3.1.2.8.5   Divestiture Life Cycle

Large global enterprises frequently acquire and divest itself of lines of business. The DLC addresses the steps that should be routinely considered when performing a divestiture.

The following illustrates the steps that are important to perform when implementing a divestiture in the USA.

The steps of the DLC include:

- *identify scope of business being divested*—determine which lines of business are being sold and those being decommissioned without transferring to another entity,
  - *identify the impacted departments*
  - *identify the managers of the affected areas*
- *identify divested business capabilities*—determine which specific business capabilities are involved in each sale or business decommissioning,
  - *identify internal business capabilities impacted*
  - *identify external business capabilities impacted*
- *identify shared operations and automation supporting divested capabilities*—determine which areas of operations and automation support will experience decreased volume,
  - *identify tier 0 infrastructure components in use by each business capability*
  - *identify shared applications*
  - *identify shared databases and files*
  - *identify shared software infrastructure*
  - *identify shared hardware infrastructure*
- *identify dedicated operations and automation supporting divested capabilities*—determine which areas of operations and automation will be transferred or decommissioned,
  - *identify dedicated applications*
  - *identify dedicated databases and files*
  - *identify dedicated software infrastructure*
  - *identify dedicated hardware infrastructure*
- *detach general ledger*—remove general ledger feeds from decommissioned applications,
  - *identify general ledger feeds to decommission*
  - *decommission divested application general ledger feeds*
- *identify unstructured data of divested areas*—determine what unstructured data is associated with the business areas, operations and automation being divested,
  - *identify servers and personal devices used by business personnel*
  - *identify document repositories supporting business operations*
  - *identify document repositories supporting business users*

- *identify RIM data*—determine what the RIM requirements are for the business areas, operations and automation being divested,
  - *identify applicable RIM data categories*
  - *map RIM data categories to divested dedicated databases*
  - *map RIM data categories to divested shared databases*
- *define RIM business data*—define the collections of data across the data landscape that are within scope of RIM,
  - *identify required business data glossary capabilities*
  - *implement required business data glossary capabilities*
- *safeguard RIM data*—ensure that RIM data will be retained and protected for the required retention period,
  - *develop plan to safeguard RIM data*
  - *implement plan to safeguard RIM data*
- *validate RIM reporting*—develop and test common use cases for RIM reporting to validate RIM reporting capabilities,
  - *identify common use cases*
  - *identify SLAs from stakeholders*
  - *develop tests for common use cases*
  - *implement tests for common use cases*
- *identify LHs*—facilitate the documentation of and document each legal hold with the identifiers necessary to locate associated files and documentation for Legal,
  - *identify existing LHs*
  - *identify pending LHs*
  - *record legal hold search criteria*
- *safeguard legal hold data*—identify files that contain the identifiers associated with each legal hold and safeguard those files without altering their file metadata,
  - *safeguard pertinent structured data*
  - *safeguard pertinent unstructured data*
- *validate legal hold reporting*—develop and test common use cases for legal hold reporting to validate legal hold reporting capabilities,
  - *identify the common use cases*
  - *identify SLAs from stakeholders*
  - *develop tests for common use cases*
  - *implement tests for common use cases*
- *decommission/downsize business operations*—decommission the operational workflows that provide capabilities being divested of,
  - *decommission dedicated business operations*
  - *downsize shared business operations*
  - *decommission/downsize physical facilities*

- *decommission/downsize automation*—decommission or downsize the automation systems following the standards and procedures for an automation shutdown for automation being divested of, and
  - *decommission applications*
  - *decommission databases*
  - *decommission/downsize software infrastructure*
  - *decommission/downsize hardware infrastructure*
- *decommission/downsize IT operations*—decommission or downsize the IT operations associated with the systems being divested of
  - *decommission dedicated IT operations*
  - *downsize shared IT operations*
  - *downsize tier 0 infrastructure components*
  - *decommission/downsize physical IT operations facilities*

3.1.2.8.6   Mergers and Acquisitions Life Cycle

Companies that make merger and acquisition a core competency demonstrate a competitive advantage to meet the expectations of executive management appropriately without delay.

The steps of the MALC include:

- *identify business scope being acquired*—determine which lines of business are being acquired,
  - *identify business capabilities overlapping with existing capabilities*
  - *identify new business capabilities*
- *identify business organization impact*—determine which acquisitions and mergers will be merged into the acquiring business operation versus into the acquired business operation versus standing up a new business operation,
  - *identify existing departments with existing capabilities adding business volume*
  - *identify existing departments adding new business capabilities*
  - *identify new departments for new business capabilities*
  - *identify business infrastructure and equipment requirements*
  - *identify impact to business continuity capabilities*
  - *identify business facility requirements*
- *identify acquired automation*—determine what automation needs to come with the acquisition,
  - *identify acquired applications*
  - *identify acquired databases*
  - *identify acquired business data glossaries*
  - *identify acquired conceptual data models*
  - *identify acquired logical data models*

- *identify acquired physical data models*
- *identify acquired software infrastructure*
- *identify acquired hardware infrastructure*
- *analyze overlapping automation*—determine what automation overlaps and which ones do not,
  - *evaluate existing versus acquired databases*
  - *evaluate existing versus acquired applications*
  - *evaluate existing versus acquired document repositories*
- *identify LHs*—determine what LHs will be transferred in with the acquired lines of business,
  - *identify existing LHs*
  - *identify pending LHs*
  - *record legal hold search criteria*
- *safeguard legal hold data*—identify files that contain the identifiers associated with each LH and safeguard those files without altering their file metadata,
  - *safeguard pertinent structured data*
  - *safeguard pertinent unstructured data*
  - *safeguard pertinent document repository data*
- *validate legal hold reporting*—develop and test common use cases for legal hold reporting to validate legal hold reporting capabilities,
  - *identify common use cases*
  - *identify SLAs from stakeholders*
  - *develop tests for common use cases*
  - *implement tests for common use cases*
- *compare data landscapes*—evaluate the data landscape of the acquired lines of business and compare it to the data landscape of the enterprise,
  - *identify existing versus acquired data glossaries*
  - *identify existing versus acquired conceptual data models*
  - *identify existing versus acquired logical data models*
  - *identify existing versus acquired physical data models*
- *identify automation impact*—determine the automation integration strategy for each acquired automation system within each line of business acquired,
  - *complete and consolidate business data glossary content*
  - *complete and consolidate conceptual data models*
  - *develop integration strategy*
  - *identify impact to technology portfolio*
  - *identify impact to application portfolio*
  - *identify impact to hardware infrastructure*
  - *identify impact to DR*
- *identify development environment impact*—compare the development and maintenance infrastructure of the acquired automation systems with those already existing within the enterprise,

- *identify impact to development infrastructure*
- *identify impact to integration test infrastructure*
- *identify impact to QA infrastructure*
- *identify impact to production infrastructure*
- *implement automation strategy*—implement the integration strategy of automation systems and stand up any additional automation systems that are not subject to integration,
  - *integrate data into the selected application databases*
  - *negotiate licenses per technology portfolio impacted*
  - *run automation in parallel per integration strategy*
- *identify IT organization impact*—determine skills required and conduct a skills assessment to select the combination of best skills among the acquired and acquiring application development organizations,
  - *right-size departments with added business volume*
  - *instantiate new departments*
  - *instantiate new business capabilities*
- *general ledger integration*—integrate the financials from each new automation system with the general ledger of the enterprise,
  - *identify chart of accounts for new business capabilities*
  - *integrate new data feeds into the general ledger*
  - *test general ledger integration*
- *right-size business operations*—determine skills required and conduct a skills assessment to select the combination of best skills among the acquired and acquiring business organizations,
  - *right-size business operational facilities*
  - *decommission extraneous business operations*
- *right-size automation*—determine skills required and conduct a skills assessment to select the combination of best skills among the acquired and acquiring application development teams, and
  - *right-size application infrastructure*
  - *right-size database services infrastructure*
  - *right-size hardware infrastructure*
- *right-size IT operations*—determine skills required and conduct a skills assessment to select the combination of best skills among the acquired and acquiring IT operations organizations
  - *right-size IT operations*
  - *right-size IT operations facilities*

3.1.2.8.7 Data Center Consolidation Life Cycle
DCCLC is distinct from MALC for a couple of reasons. First, during the merger and/ or acquisition, the business strategy had not included data center consolidation, probably because the lines of business were sufficiently disparate from the existing lines

of business that consolidation did not a significant consideration. Second, there is a strong likelihood that the data centers acquired in the merger and acquisition process are geographically located within 50 miles of the business they support.

After a handful of merger and acquisitions of disparate businesses, it becomes apparent that the economics of consolidating multiple data centers have become worthy of being actionable. The first issue for consolidating the data centers of these disparate businesses is to determine the business strategy that everyone must be mindful of as they plan the consolidation.

While data center consolidations are going to differ significantly from one another, the issues to consider are relatively common to the majority of them.

3.1.2.8.7.1 Primary Strategic Considerations There are a number of basics to consider that will determine the scope of the consolidation.

Some of the ones from a high-level perspective include whether:

- to maintain flexibility to be able to divest of a business unit or line of business without facing a massive effort to separate the automation of that business unit out of a consolidated data center operation,
- to address the maturity level of data center operations across the organization as consolidation is planned,
- to consider capabilities that potentially should be consolidated in an outsourced mode as opposed to in-house consolidation,
- to consider capabilities that potentially should be consolidated in an insourced mode as opposed to continued outsourcing,
- there are services provided by data center operations that should not be delivered by operations, and
- there are services not provided by data center operations that should be delivered by operations.

While the list of strategic considerations is being assembled, there are two additional fundamental activities that can proceed in parallel, which include:

- data center inventory, and
- business capability inventory.

The data center inventory is an inventory of hardware (e.g., number of servers of each type and capacity) and software (e.g., corporate HR systems), including the metrics for their utilization so that a baseline of capabilities and service level can be defined, below which one should not venture without good reason.

The business capability inventory is an inventory of every business capability by business and IT department that identifies what "tools" and "applications" are used to support those business capabilities and the underlying data center infrastructure that supports those "tools" and "applications."

As examples, "tools" include technologies that of themselves are not business specific in that they do not contain business rules, such as Internet connectivity to get to external services, whereas "applications" are business specific in that they do contain business rules, such as the general ledger application that contains the chart of accounts.

Associated with an application are usually a database management system, networks, network servers, application servers, database servers, and security servers, such as the active directory server, which represents high complexity and high risk.

The reason that the data center and business capability inventory are done together is that it is important for these two different perspectives to meet somewhere in the middle to enable the various strategic considerations that the business leaders may elect to act upon.

As one speaks with department heads and their management team to inventory business capabilities, one can usually solicit input from them on opportunities and risks. Ultimately as input into a good plan, all opportunities and risks should be analyzed for ROI and presented for consideration by business leaders.

3.1.2.8.7.2 Secondary Strategic Considerations A variety of secondary considerations should also be evaluated in a data center consolidation.

Some of the ones from a high-level perspective include whether:

- to consider the consolidation of applications on application servers, and databases on database servers to take advantage of excess capacity and leverage potentially expensive software licenses

    When the opportunity presents itself to do this on a large scale, and it often does, one of the steps to consider is to evaluate the transaction path analysis (TAPA) profiles of applications and databases to identify good versus poor "server roommate" applications and databases.

- "what-if-scenarios" should determine the ideal target state and transitional steps to get there to help create awareness of the level of effort and trade-offs of different target states

    At a minimum, it is valuable to float a few different target states with which to solicit feedback that can be most valuable. Using a more robust approach, it is often valuable to model different target states for their ability to support various use cases, such as another merger acquisition and DR scenario.

- opportunities for content management clean-up using a "tiered storage" capability to reposition data that is infrequently accessed to less expensive storage where there are tools to sort and eliminate files and documents that are redundant or no longer relevant to anyone

This is one of the low-hanging fruits scenarios of the Big Data space where data can be off-loaded for analysis and disposal as rapidly as it can be determined that it is not required for regulatory data retention requirements, LHs, or other uses.

■ shared services can be organized into services that require no knowledge of the business, some knowledge, or specific business knowledge

Shared services may require a significant degree of business-specific domain knowledge (e.g., data administrators), including application-specific domain knowledge (e.g., solution architects), or they may require virtually no knowledge of the business domain.

These characteristics participate as business drivers for determining which services should be:

■ *in the data center*
  – *with a business SME*
  – *without a business SME*
■ *in the development organization*
  – *business analysts*
  – *IT Plan organization*
  – *IT Build organization*

Ultimately, if the shared service must be within the physical proximity of business users, whether business user is defined as resources on the manufacturing floor or in office buildings, then it should probably not be located within a centralized or regional data center.

Once a DCCLC has been conducted, it then serves as a template for future data center consolidations that can occur with each new merger and acquisition.

3.1.2.8.8 Corporate Restructuring Life Cycle

Companies that restructure to meet the changing economy and business direction as a core competency demonstrate a competitive advantage for meeting expectations of their investors.

The steps of the CRLC including their substeps are:

■ *identify executive management objectives*—understand the business objectives and hedgehog concept of executive management,
  ■ *identify management's perceptions of the brand*
  ■ *identify management's objectives for each line of business*
  ■ *identify management's objectives for the capital structure of the enterprise*
  ■ *identify management's objectives for the organizational structure of the enterprise*
  ■ *identify management's objectives for the operational cost structure of the enterprise*

- *evaluate executive management objectives*—evaluate the existing assets of the enterprise compared to the assets ideally required to achieve executive management's hedgehog concept,
  - *gather current state metrics*
  - *identify core competencies*
  - *identify hedgehog concept*
  - *identify opportunities*
  - *formulate target state alternatives*
- *evaluate target state alternatives*—develop and evaluate alternative target states and the transition plans for each,
  - *identify business risks*
  - *identify costs*
  - *identify tangible and intangible benefits*
  - *select optimal alternative*
  - *identify target state metrics*
- *develop communications plan*—given the selected target state and transition plan develop the communications plan,
  - *customer relations*
  - *public relations*
  - *employee relations*
  - *regulator relations*
  - *investor relations*
- *implement communications plan*—once approved implement the communications plan to the various constituents such as employees and investors,
  - *conduct communications plans*
  - *gather feedback*
  - *evaluate effectiveness*
- *invoke appropriate life cycles*—identify and deploy teams responsible to execute the required life cycles, such as:
  - *DLC*
  - *mergers and acquisitions life cycle (MALC)*
  - *ISLC*
  - *OSLC*
  - *OLC*
- *develop consolidated plan*—integrate the plans from the various life cycles into one consolidated plan,
  - *collect outputs from each life cycle*
  - *determine target state to achieve the hedgehog concept*
- *develop talent transition plan*—develop the talent transition plan from the consolidated plan of life cycles,
  - *evaluate existing talent*

- *identify target state talent*
- *identify gaps*
- *develop plan to bridge the gap*
- *develop facilities transition plan*—develop the facilities transition plan from the consolidated plan of life cycles,
  - *evaluate existing facilities*
  - *identify target state facilities*
- *develop automation transition plan*—develop the automation transition plan from the consolidated plan of life cycles,
  - *evaluate existing automation*
  - *identify target state automation*
  - *identify gaps and overages*
  - *develop plan to achieve target state automation*
- *develop consolidated implementation plan*—develop a consolidated implementation plan of talent, facilities, and automation,
  - *consolidate life cycle outputs*
  - *consolidate plans*
  - *identify metrics for target state over time*
- *execute consolidated transition plan*—execute the consolidated implementation plan and monitor actuals to the consolidated implementation plan,
  - *execute consolidated plan*
  - *collect metrics for target state over time*
- *evaluate actual versus target metrics*—assess the metrics collected before and after implementation to determine if target metrics were met, and
  - *assess metrics for target state over time*
  - *identify success targets met, target shortfalls, and target overages*
- *postmortem*—evaluate why metrics were not met, met, or exceeded
  - *conduct post mortem*
  - *record lessons learned*

3.1.2.8.9   Outsourcing Life Cycle

Companies outsource in the belief that they will save money, which makes sense when demand for the areas outsourced fluctuate significantly, when skills are located elsewhere geographically, or when additional time zone coverage can be readily attained.

The steps of the OSLC including their substeps are:

- *determine intended business value of outsourcing*—understand the specific motivations for outsourcing and begin assessing its business value,
  - *list the expected benefits*
  - *identify reasons to expect each*

- *identify expected value to be derived*
- *scope outsourcing initiative*—understand the intended scope of outsourcing including identification of which business capabilities from among which lines of business,
  - *identify the potential scope of the outsourcing initiative*
  - *identify the applicable business strategy*
  - *determine degree of alignment to business strategy*
  - *define the scope that best aligns with the business strategy*
- *define metrics-driven business objectives*—determine business metrics of the future state,
  - *list the business objectives*
  - *identify the metrics that most reliably measure each*
- *define metrics-driven IT objectives*—determine IT metrics of the future state,
  - *list the IT objectives*
  - *identify the metrics that most reliably measure each*
- *identify sources of increased cost for outsourcing*—determine areas of increased cost and coordination overhead that would result from outsourcing,
  - *list additional communications costs*
  - *list redundant oversight costs*
  - *list transition costs*
  - *list vendor personnel training costs*
  - *list process refinement costs*
  - *list knowledge loss costs*
  - *list personnel reduction costs*
  - *list facility right-sizing costs*
  - *list temporary parallel operating costs*
  - *list stranded infrastructure costs*
- *estimate increased costs and timing*—estimate the increased costs and timing associated with each area of increased cost,
  - *identify budgets impacted by outsourcing*
  - *determine amount of each budget impact*
  - *determine timing of each budget impact*
- *assess current state*—determine the business and IT metrics of the current state,
  - *collect metrics preoutsourcing*
  - *analyze current state metrics*
  - *assess technical debt owed to automation for quick and dirty maintenance*
  - *assess nonextensible IT architectures*
  - *assess overall complexity of IT landscape*
- *compare current state versus intended future state*—compare and evaluate the assumptions of current and future states,
  - *estimate expected metrics of future state*

- *estimate timing of expected metrics in the future state*
- *identify risks in achieving the future state*
- *develop realistic projections of current and future state*
- *identify competing vendor interests*—identify the competing interests and potential conflicts of interest between outsourcing vendors and the enterprise,
    - *identify leading vendors*
    - *evaluate frameworks of each vendor*
    - *identify vendor interests with regard to each framework*
    - *identify vendor interests conflicting with your own*
- *conduct risk mitigation planning*—conduct risk mitigation planning for each competing interest and potential conflicts of interest between outsourcing vendors and the enterprise,
    - *assess risks in achieving future state*
    - *assess risks in managing competing vendor interests*
    - *develop an incremental outsourcing plan*
    - *determine degree of staff augmentation*
    - *determine degree of project outsourcing*
    - *determine degree of function outsourcing*
- *vendor selection*—select the best vendor based upon their ability to meet required terms and conditions within the outsourcing agreement,
    - *select top three vendors*
    - *add internal team as an additional credible vendor*
    - *negotiate to start slow and build slowly*
    - *negotiate insourcing terms for each item to be outsourced*
    - *determine critical SLAs*
    - *evaluate vendors for their ability and willingness to meet your objectives*
    - *identify vendor agreement with the most favorable terms and conditions*
- *compare internal versus negotiated outsourcing options*—compare the option of an internal solution to the best outsourcing option based upon terms and conditions and cost,
    - *reevaluate total cost of outsourcing*
    - *evaluate ability of negotiated terms to meet objectives*
    - *evaluate comparable investments using an internal solution*
    - *determine whether to execute outsourcing agreement*
- *implement outsourcing agreement*—implement the best agreement for the enterprise, and
    - *organize to implement the provisions of the agreement*
    - *measure and track costs and savings*
    - *identify lessons learned of favorable and unfavorable lessons*
- *remedy outsourcing issues/process improvement*—remedy both anticipated and unforeseen issues with the agreement or implementation of the agreement

- *identify outsourcing issues*
- *determine if SLAs on both sides are being adhered to*
- *enforce the agreement where possible*
- *plan for a balanced renegotiation for both sides*
- *evaluate insourcing options*
- *renegotiate and implement an improved agreement*

3.1.2.8.10 Insourcing Life Cycle

Companies elect to insource in the belief that they will improve service or save money, such as when an outsourcing provider fails to deliver a sufficient level of service.

The steps of the ISLC including their substeps are:

- *determine intended business value of insourcing*—understand the specific motivations for insourcing and begin assessing its business value,
  - *list the expected benefits*
  - *identify reasons to expect each benefit*
  - *identify expected value to be derived*
- *scope insourcing initiative*—understand the intended scope of insourcing including identification of the specific business capabilities,
  - *identify the potential scope of insourcing*
  - *identify the applicable business strategy*
  - *determine the degree of alignment to business strategy*
  - *redefine scope to fully agree with business strategy*
- *define metrics-driven business objectives*—determine business metrics of the future state,
  - *list the business objectives*
  - *identify the metrics that most reliably measure each*
- *define metrics-driven IT objectives*—determine IT metrics of the future state,
  - *list the IT objectives*
  - *identify the metrics that most reliably measure each*
- *assess prior state prior to insourcing*—evaluate the current state prior to insourcing and collect pertinent metrics,
  - *collect metrics pre-insourcing*
  - *analyze current state metrics*
  - *assess technical debt owed to automation for quick and dirty maintenance*
  - *assess nonextensible IT architectures*
  - *assess overall complexity of IT landscape*
- *identify sources of increased costs for insourcing*—determine areas of increased cost and coordination overhead that would result from insourcing,
  - *list facility costs*

- *list staffing costs*
- *list training costs*
- *list equipment acquisition costs*
- *list transition costs*
- *list process refinement costs*
- *list parallel operating costs*
- *estimate increased costs and timing*—estimate the increased costs and timing associated with each area of increased cost,
  - *identify budgets impacted by insourcing*
  - *determine amount of each budget impact*
  - *determine timing of each budget impact*
- *identify sources of insourcing benefits*—determine the source for each insourcing benefit anticipated by management,
  - *list of vendor payments*
  - *list of personnel managing the vendor*
  - *list of communications costs involving the vendor*
- *refine business and IT objectives*—refine the business and IT objectives based upon the metrics of the detailed cost-benefit analysis,
  - *refine metrics-driven business objectives*
  - *refine metrics-driven IT objectives*
- *compare current state to future state*—using a metrics-driven approach compare the current state to the proposed future state,
  - *estimate expected metrics of future state*
  - *estimate timing of expected metrics of future state*
- *estimate value of benefits and timing*—estimate the value of the benefits and the timing associated with each area of benefit,
  - *determine amount of each expected benefit*
  - *determine timing of each expected benefit*
- *conduct risk mitigation planning*—assess and mitigate the risks associated with the insourcing plan,
  - *assess risks in achieving future state*
  - *develop risk mitigation plan*
- *develop insourcing plan*—develop the consolidated plan to in source the targeted business capabilities,
  - *determine degree of staff augmentation reduction*
  - *determine degree of project insourcing*
  - *determine degree of function insourcing*
- *determine internal support services and vendor transition costs*—estimate the necessary internal support services and vendor transition costs associated with the plan,
  - *identify transition components from vendor*
  - *negotiate transition support costs with vendor*
  - *identify internal support costs*

- *compare negotiated insourcing to existing outsourcing option*—compare the terms and conditions of the negotiated insourcing plan with those of the existing outsourcing plan and any other negotiated agreements for outsourcing plans,
  - *reevaluate total cost of insourcing*
  - *evaluate ability of negotiated terms to meet objectives*
  - *evaluate a comparable investment using another external solution*
  - *determine whether to execute the insourcing agreement*
- *implement insourcing agreement*—implement the desired insourcing agreement, and
  - *organize to implement the provisions of the agreement*
  - *measure and track costs and savings*
  - *identify lessons learned whether favorable or unfavorable*
- *remedy insourcing issues/process improvement*—remedy both anticipated and unforeseen issues with the agreement or implementation of the agreement
  - *identify insourcing issues*
  - *determine that SLAs of service providers and consumers are being adhered to*
  - *enforce SLAs where possible*
  - *plan for a balanced negotiation for the internal department supporting the business capabilities that have undergone insourcing*
  - *reevaluate insourcing and outsourcing options*
  - *renegotiate and implement an improved internal agreement*

3.1.2.8.11 Operations Life Cycle

Companies elect to establish new data centers as primary or secondary centers to support their primary and backup site requirements to support the business needs of the enterprise for the automation they rely upon.

The steps of the OLC including their substeps are:

- *evaluate business requirements*—identify the near and long-term requirements of data center capabilities,
  - *determine internal user logistical profile*
  - *determine external vendor logistical profile*
  - *determine regulator logistical profile*
  - *determine B2B logistical profile*
  - *determine customer logistical profile*
  - *determine logistical profile of additional data centers*
  - *determine network and communications profile*
- *determine candidate data center location risks*—identify the various location risks that should be taken into consideration for each candidate data center,
  - *evaluate environmental threat profiles*
  - *evaluate local industrial hazards*
  - *evaluate geopolitical threat profiles*

- *evaluate availability of skilled resources*
- *evaluate availability of land, facilities, and business services*
- *evaluate availability of communications services and providers*
- *evaluate power reliability*
- *evaluate availability of local resources and services (e.g., fire department)*
- *evaluate weather profile*
- *determine candidate data center risk mitigation costs*—determine the mitigation costs associated with each candidate data center,
  - *determine cost to protect against environmental threats*
  - *determine cost to protect against industrial hazards*
  - *determine cost to protect against geopolitical threats*
  - *determine cost of addressing skilled resource availability*
  - *determine cost of addressing availability of land, facilities, and business services*
  - *determine cost of addressing availability of communications services*
  - *determine cost of addressing power reliability*
  - *determine cost of rendering resources and local services deficiencies*
  - *estimate climate control costs*
- *evaluate surroundings*—evaluate the specifics of the immediate surroundings of each candidate data center,
  - *determine nearest flood plain details*
  - *determine nearest flight path details*
  - *determine nearest hazardous shipping lane details*
  - *determine nearest water main details*
  - *determine nearest well water details*
- *determine preferred site*—select the most beneficial data center site,
  - *evaluate purchase costs*
  - *evaluate improvement costs*
  - *evaluate cost of taxes, fees, and permits*
  - *evaluate potential tax relief*
  - *project development of the local area over time*
  - *estimate future value*
- *determine compliance requirements*—determine any business or regulatory compliance issues,
  - *determine compliance requirements*
  - *determine SAS 70 Type II solution and cost*
  - *determine LEED solution and cost*
  - *determine PCI solution and cost*
  - *determine HIPPA solution and cost*
  - *determine SCIF solution and cost*
- *determine environmental controls*—identify the required environmental controls associated with the particular site,

- *determine programmable logic controller requirements*
- *determine redundant equipment requirements*
- *determine high sensitivity (HSSD) requirements*
- *determine gas fire suppression requirements*
- *determine single grounding system requirements*
- *determine support service requirements*—identify the necessary support services that must be developed,
  - *determine remote hands service requirements*
  - *determine rack and stack requirements*
  - *determine cabling requirements*
  - *determine technical assistance command center requirements*
  - *determine on-site operations staff requirements*
- *determine access controls*—identify the access controls that must be developed,
  - *determine defensible perimeter requirements*
  - *determine traffic bollard/car trap requirements*
  - *determine gated entry requirements*
  - *determine guard service requirements*
  - *determine digital video surveillance requirements*
  - *determine customer access list requirements*
  - *determine building compartment requirements*
  - *determine visitor tracking requirements*
  - *determine mantrap system requirements*
  - *determine biometric screening requirements*
  - *determine equipment cage and fence requirements*
- *determine infrastructure architecture*—develop the standards and frameworks that must be adhered to for the infrastructure,
  - *determine storage architecture*
  - *determine telephony video architecture*
  - *determine desktop architecture*
  - *determine mobile device architecture*
  - *determine application server architecture*
  - *determine database server architecture*
  - *determine operational utilities architecture*
  - *determine database operational utilities architecture*
  - *determine virtualization architecture*
- *determine network architecture*—develop the standards and frameworks that must be adhered to for networking and communications,
  - *determine local area network architecture*
  - *determine wide area network architecture*
  - *determine firewall architecture*
  - *determine file transfer architecture*

- *determine security architecture*—develop the standards and frameworks that must be adhered to for security,
  - *determine physical security architecture*
  - *determine application security architecture*
  - *determine database security architecture*
  - *determine server security architecture*
  - *determine NAS security architecture*
  - *determine network security architecture*
  - *determine directory services architecture*
- *determine job scheduling architecture*—develop the standards and frameworks that must be adhered to for job scheduling,
  - *determine job scheduling software architecture*
  - *determine job scheduling testing and simulation architecture*
  - *determine job scheduling production architecture*
- *determine system recovery architecture*—identify the backup and recovery services standards and frameworks that should be adhered to,
  - *determine failover architecture*
  - *determine DR architecture*
- *determine technical services architecture*—identify the necessary technical services standards and frameworks that should be adhered to,
  - *determine problem management architecture*
  - *determine release management architecture*
  - *determine service-level agreement architecture*
  - *determine alerts monitoring architecture*
  - *determine change management architecture*
  - *determine configuration management architecture*
  - *determine testing architecture*
  - *determine deployment architecture*
  - *determine help desk architecture*
- *determine infrastructure applications architecture*—identify the necessary infrastructure applications architecture standards and frameworks that should be adhered to, and
  - *identify infrastructure categories*
  - *determine requirements for each infrastructure category*
  - *determine applications to support required capabilities*
- *determine systems performance architecture*—identify the necessary system performance standards and frameworks that should be adhered to
  - *identify system performance categories*
  - *determine requirements for each performance category*
  - *determine systems performance architecture*

Part IV

Information Architecture

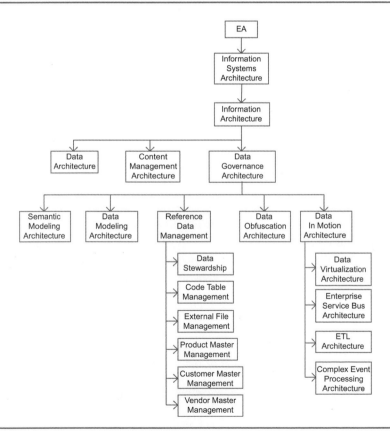

Diagram   Information architecture overview.

4.1 Information Architecture

Information architecture is the foundation of information systems architecture that also represents a significant number of the architectural disciplines of information systems architecture.

To begin, every enterprise has assets. As examples, it has employees, customers, IT facilities, business facilities, and financial assets. However, the most significant asset of most large enterprises is its data.

The reason for this is that the data asset of each and every company defines its individuality. A company's data reflects its particular marketing efforts, business activities, customer interactions, product sets, employees, and financial history.

An enterprise can have its:

- employees lured to other firms,
- customers attracted away by competitors,
- data centers demolished by meteors,
- buildings lost in storms and fires, or
- capital consumed in a single catastrophic event.

An enterprise can also:

- hire new employees,
- build a new customer base,
- construct a new data center,
- acquire new buildings with leases, and
- raise new capital through investors or by borrowing.

However, if an enterprise loses or destroys its information in every location it is kept, then there is no external source from which it can be reacquired.

Information architecture is responsible for knowing everything about the data assets of the enterprise. Due to the extensive breadth and depth of information, information architecture has the greatest breadth and depth of any set of frameworks within any of the architectural disciplines.

The first contributing factor is that the number of business data points within businesses. These are the number distinct items of data that each have their own business definition that for a large enterprise can number in the millions, such as the following sample from a small segment of the employee onboarding process:

- prospective employment candidate resume received date,
- prospective employee interview date,
- prospective employee reference check date,
- prospective employee former employer verification date,
- prospective letter rejection letter date,

- prospective employee offer letter date,
- prospective employee offer letter acceptance date,
- prospective employee intended start date,
- prospective employee pre-hire medical date,
- prospective employee background check date, and
- employee start date.

The above data points are a sampling of dates that do not begin to address the hundreds of data points involved in the other types of data point involving that segment of onboarding and the many hundreds of data points involved in the following onboarding activities:

- assigned work space,
- assigned HR representative,
- assigned furniture,
- assigned equipment,
- assigned telephone number,
- assigned conference calling number,
- employee badge,
- supervisor,
- assigned fire drill station assembly area,
- benefit options,
- associated budgets,
- travel expense reimbursement,
- relocation,
- job training,
- compliance training,
- access to physical compartments,
- access to software applications,
- access to servers, and
- access to network components.

The architectural disciplines that are part of information architecture include:

- data architecture,
- data governance,
- business data glossary architecture,
- data ownership architecture,
- data access rights architecture,
- ETL data masking architecture,
- canned report access architecture,
- data stewardship,

- data discovery,
- semantic modeling,
- architecture governance component registry,
- data governance dashboard,
- data obfuscation architecture,
- data modeling architecture,
- reference data management (RDM)—product master,
- RDM—code tables,
- RDM—external files,
- data in motion (DIM) architecture,
- data virtualization architecture,
- ETL architecture,
- ESB architecture,
- CEP architecture, and
- content management architecture.

Within each of these disciplines, there are a variety of technologies that for the most part are far from inexpensive. These require subject matter experts to match the needs of the organization with the most appropriate technologies, standards, and frameworks.

Within information architecture also exists data life cycle management (DLM) (aka information life cycle management (ILM)). This is a policy-based approach to managing the flow of an information system's data through its life cycle from creation to the time it becomes obsolete and must be properly disposed of.

As such, information architecture must ensure the inclusion of DLM policies into the appropriate information architecture frameworks, namely, data governance standards and frameworks. It should be noted that policy-based approaches are generally not successful unless their content is incorporated into the appropriate data governance standards and frameworks. DLM must also be coordinated with records information management (RIM) and legal hold (LH) in collaboration with areas such as content management architecture.

4.1.1 MASTER DATA MANAGEMENT

In this section, we see that there are over 20 distinct architectural disciplines that comprise information architecture. As you probably noticed, these architectural disciplines were neither named master data management (MDM) nor had MDM participating in any part of their name.

MDM is a term that has been given a variety of different meanings and varying scope that as a term it has become relatively ineffective for communicating clearly.

As examples of what may be found within the scope of MDM:

- some variations on logical data architecture (LDA) (i.e., part of data architecture),
- all aspects of data governance,
- data glossaries of all types,
- occasionally data ownership,
- occasionally data access rights (i.e., data security),
- data masking—usually restricted to batch ETL from Production to a test environment,
- aspects of data stewardship,
- aspects of data discovery,
- occasionally semantic modeling,
- occasionally data mining,
- occasionally content management,
- some aspects of metadata—of which there are many,
- RDM—although MDM has numerous definitions for it including party and product master,
- occasionally data resellers, data concentrators, and data enhancement vendors,
- sometimes RIM and data archival,
- sometimes continuity management and disaster recovery (DR),
- sometimes LHs,
- occasionally data virtualization,
- increasingly ESB architecture,
- increasingly CEP architecture,
- all aspects of data quality—including data standardization, and
- most aspects of data profiling—the term "most" was used because there are aspects of data profiling for advanced data compression that MDM does not consider.

The variety of capabilities that participate under the umbrella of MDM is larger than the topics related to data that are not part of MDM (e.g., physical data modeling). Products marketed within the MDM space range between bundled offerings that are "all encompassing" and extremely expensive, both from a licensing and internal cost perspective, to offerings that are clearly focused and well priced for the value they deliver.

Even though a substantial portion of this book addresses topics that belong to MDM, the only reason that this section was added, with the name "MDM," is to address the fact that someone will ask how an entire book about enterprise architecture could have missed the topic of MDM.

MDM is a term that has been given a variety of different meanings and varying scope that as a term it has become relatively ineffective for communicating a particular idea that anyone would immediately understand.

As examples of what may be found within the scope of MDM:

- some variations on LDA (i.e., part of data architecture),
- all aspects of data governance,
- data glossaries of all types,
- occasionally data ownership,
- occasionally data access rights (i.e., data security),
- data masking—usually restricted to batch ETL from production to a test environment,
- aspects of data stewardship,
- aspects of data discovery,
- occasionally semantic modeling,
- occasionally data mining,
- occasionally content management,
- some aspects of metadata—of which there are many,
- RDM—although MDM has numerous definitions for it including party and product master,
- occasionally data resellers, data concentrators, and data enhancement vendors,
- sometimes RIM and data archival,
- sometimes continuity management and DR,
- sometimes LHs,
- occasionally data virtualization,
- increasingly ESB architecture,
- increasingly CEP architecture,
- all aspects of data quality—including data standardization, and
- most aspects of data profiling—the term "most" was used because there are aspects of data profiling for advanced data compression that MDM does not consider.

The variety of capabilities that participate under the umbrella of MDM is larger than the topics related to data that are not part of MDM (e.g., physical data modeling, name and address standardization, and match and merge). Products marketed within the MDM space range between bundled offerings that are "all encompassing" and extremely expensive, both from a licensing and internal cost perspective, to offerings that are clearly focused and well priced for the value they deliver.

Even though a substantial portion of this book addresses topics that belong to MDM, the only reason that this section was added, with the name "MDM," is to address the fact that someone will ask how an entire book about enterprise architecture could have missed the topic of MDM.

My advice on MDM is to first distill out the disciplines related to it and address them one at a time including those processes that support their governance, starting with:

- LDA
- business data glossary

- RDM
  - code tables reference data—(e.g., country codes) including all codes that may be shared across applications or may be useful for business analytics and reporting including all forms of product and customer segmentation
  - files that serve as reference data—(e.g., pricing feed) including all externally acquired files that can be used to support marketing, pricing, or risk analysis
- LDA reference data subject areas—(e.g., chart of accounts, customer, product, vendor, distribution channel) including any data that can be shared across the organization

The goal is to standardize all information with which management may want to analyze the business activity, such that the data representing the same concepts all reference the same names and codes. When done properly, it becomes possible to correctly determine inventory levels, costs, margins, and profitability across what may have previously been disparate collections of data that don't match.

That said, when asked to kick off an MDM initiative, the following information is useful to gather from business and IT resources before one engages the appropriate architectural disciplines.

4.1.1.1 Business Perspective

- Is there a chief customer officer (CCO) role in the organization?
- Is procurement centralized?
- Is product development centralized?
- What is the desired business direction of the organization?
- What is the business strategy for moving the organization in the desired business direction?
- What is necessary for the business strategy to be successful?
- How would you define the concept of "your biggest competitor"?
- What company would you consider to be your biggest competitor(s)?
- What would you say is their core competency?
- What is the core competency of your organization?
- What core competencies are necessary to implement your organization's business strategy?
- What is necessary to hone the necessary core competencies?
- What data informs and drives the necessary core competencies?
- Where does the data that informs and drive these necessary core competencies originate?
- What business capabilities do you have insight into?
- What would are the biggest business pain points in these business capabilities and why?
- Given the desired business direction what pain points are likely to emerge?

- What data enters the organization from your business areas?
- What business capabilities outside your own use data from other business areas?
- What data originates from your business area?
- What business capabilities outside your own use data originated in your business area?
- What data does your area use that enters the organization from a different business area?
- What data does your area use that originates in a different business area?
- What data that originated within your area does your area update?
- What data that originated elsewhere does your area update?
- What is the definition of customer including any classification schemes for customers?
- Is there a customer hierarchy across the organization?
- What is the definition of product including any classification schemes for products?
- Is there a product hierarchy across the organization?
- Are products uniquely and consistently identified across the organization?
- What is the definition of vendor including any classification schemes for vendors?
- Is there a vendor hierarchy across the organization?
- What is the process for handling LHs?
- After customer, product, and vendor what would you say is the next most important data?
- What percent of staff are primarily maintaining or developing new reports?
- What percent of staff are primarily monitoring and maintaining data quality?
- What is the overall budget used for developing new reports for your area of the business?
- What is the overall budget used to maintain data quality within your area of the business?

4.1.1.2 Business IT Perspective

- What infrastructure is used to support each business capability within your area?
- What external software applications are used to support each business capability in your area?
- What internal software applications are used to support each business capability in your area?
- What software products (MS Excel) are used to support each business capability in your area?
- What software products have business rules to support each business capability in your area?
- For each business capability what types of reports, ad hoc queries, and data analysis are used?
- What types of reports, ad hoc queries, and analysis are produced for executive management?

- What types of reports, ad hoc queries, and analysis are produced for internal oversight?
- What types of reports, ad hoc queries, and analysis are produced for regulatory bodies?
- What business metadata exists for report content and who maintains it?
- What is being done to remediate any lack of business metadata?
- What data quality issues if any would you say impede any of these types of reports?
- What efforts are being made to address data quality issues?
- What is the process for decommissioning business automation?
- To what degree (%) do data models have meaningful business definitions?
- To what degree (%) have data model business definitions been validated by business?

4.1.1.3   IT Perspective

- What is an LDA and is there one for the organization?
- What life cycle does the PMO use for data centric data warehouse initiatives?
- What life cycle does the PMO use for data centric data governance initiatives?
- What information architecture disciplines are you aware of within the organization?
- What data governance architecture disciplines are you aware of within the organization?
- What RDM disciplines are you aware of within the organization?
- What reporting architecture disciplines are you aware of within the organization?
- What reporting technologies are you aware of within the organization?
- What data stewardship disciplines are you aware of within the organization?
- Is DIM architecture restricted to ETL, ESB, and CEP, and which brands of each?
- Is there an ETL CASE tool in place?
- Who determines data ownership?
- Who determines ad hoc data access rights?
- Who determines canned report data access rights?
- Who determines cyclical canned report data access rights?
- Which report types use a master data source?
- Which report types do not use a master data source?
- What are the business and IT purposes for content management technologies?
- Which products are used for content management?
- How is content within each content management repository organized?
- What is the content management ontology for content?
- What is the process for managing content?
- What databases/files/content management repositories house each type of data (e.g., customer, product, vendor, distribution channel, employee, contracts)?
- What is the data lineage for each type of data?

- What are the data quality issues for each type of data?
- Is each type of data cleansed uniformly?
- Is each type of data standardized uniformly?
- Is each type of data integrated uniformly?
- What would business metadata characteristics are captured in data models?

In summary, there are absolutely great architectural patterns available to address various MDM-related challenges in cost-effective ways. Before arriving at one, however, it is critical to understand the Web of desktop software and manual processes that have been deployed to compensate for the lack of unique identifiers for data that is shared across the organization, as well as the Web of desktop software tools and manual processes that perform application integration among business systems and reporting platforms.

4.1.2 LOGICAL DATA ARCHITECTURE

When developing an architecture for anything, whether that thing consists of things that are tangible, intangible, or both, it forms a foundation and foundations are clearly best when they are stable.

As mentioned earlier, the most stable foundation upon which one may organize the parts in a control system—software that operates machinery—is the discrete hardware components that one can point to and touch (e.g., anemometer, throttle). The LDA for a simple control system consisting of just these two parts would be one data subject area for the anemometer and one for the throttle.

In contrast, the role of LDA in information systems is somewhat similar to that of hardware architecture in control systems. In information systems, a well-formed framework formed by the business data can be extremely stable. If well formed in accordance with a rigorous LDA approach, the data architecture would be stable not only for the particular line of business in the particular company, but it would be stable for that line of business across all companies, geographic regions, and political jurisdictions operating the same line of business.

This is not to mean that new data points will not be discovered in one company versus another; however, it does mean that the LDA framework will be stable for use in areas such as application architecture, data warehouse architecture, and business data glossary architecture.

To describe an LDA in more detail, the first thing to remember is that it is a business artifact. The LDA diagram is an illustration of all data and information that is related to the enterprise.

For example, this includes any data about the business, whether it can be found in a computer file or database, e-mail, text message, tape-recorded telephone conversation, on an index card or a sheet of paper in a file cabinet, or in someone's head. It also includes data that is sourced externally and brought into the enterprise.

Examples of external data include:

■ code tables—ISO country codes, zip codes, currency codes
■ external files—securities pricing feeds, prospective customer lists, demographic overlays

The purpose of the LDA is to depict clear distinctions of meaning among each and every business term used to represent every piece of data that can be used or referred to across the enterprise. With categories of clear distinction also comes a rigorous taxonomy.

Just as an expert wine taster is empowered with a vocabulary of almost a hundred words to describe several different characteristics of wine and its effects upon the palate and nose, the business vocabulary of a business domain empowers the participants of business, such as a business user and a developer, to communicate ideas more effectively.

Multiple interpretations and/or ambiguities are eliminated when vocabulary is used effectively. As an example, in insurance, the business meaning of something called Policy Payment Date communicates little information in comparison with something called a Policy Payment Due Date, Policy Payment Received Date, Policy Settlement Date, Policy Clearance Date, and Policy Funds Delivery Date.

As in the above example, individuals equipped with a comprehensive vocabulary are better equipped to communicate details about the business better than individuals that are not so prepared; however, the presence of a large vocabulary brings the burden of managing its documentation and disseminating it to others. As such, another important role of an LDA is to organize vocabulary, by creating easy to use categories for locating and managing it.

Such categories of information may differ from one another in one important aspect, their stability. Categories that are unstable can create massive amounts of work when information has to be reorganized to adhere to a new set of categories.

That said, perhaps the most important role of an LDA is to establish stable components of information that can be used as a foundation for other architectures, such as an object-oriented application architecture. The more stable the application architecture's foundation, the more cost-effective maintenance will become.

The LDA is a top-down hierarchy of data-related topics.

For example, if the business were a bagel store, we would start with three major categories of data:

■ initial business setup
■ conducting business
■ analyzing business

For example, there are large amounts of data and information that are collected and generated well before the business is ever ready to make and sell its first bagel. There are business plans, determining the size and location of the store, its design and equipment, its staffing, its operational processes, various permits, and licensing and inspections, and then there is the matter of ownership, management, and the financial details.

The next distinct category of data and information is the data and information that is generated once the doors of the store have opened for business.

For example, using the same store, there are data and information collected and generated while conducting business, entering into transactions with customers, taking one time orders from walk-in customers, taking and supporting reoccurring orders from local convenience stores and restaurants, and performing the various operations of the business that keep supplies in check with the demands of the store's products and services.

The third distinct category of data and information is generated only after the doors of the store are closed.

For example, the same store may wish to analyze which products and promotions were most and least popular and profitable. A trend analysis may reveal that business is cyclical while also growing at a rapid rate, or declining due to a competitor that just opened down the street. This third category of data uses the information generated in the previous category and analyzes it to help make informed management decisions.

Within each distinct category of data, there are additional distinct categories down that are driven down to the business data subject area, which is the lowest level category that is useful to compartmentalize data into.

Let's consider what is typically the largest category of data, which is called "conducting business." It consists of the information that is employed and generated while business is being conducted, as is legally referred to as "books and records" of the business.

This area of data and information embodies the results of each step within each operational process pertaining to customer acquisition, and engagement, as it encompasses all contractual agreements with customers for the products and services of the enterprise in support of revenue generation, and supporting services to the customer.

As defined by the Securities and Exchange Commission, "books and records" information includes purchase and sale documents, customer records, associated person records, customer complaints, and information specifically designed to assist regulators when conducting examinations of business practices and/or specific business transactions, including accessibility of books and records on a timely basis.

Within the major category of "conducting business," the next data categories are:

- operational workflow,
- reference data, and
- activity data.

To define these, the *operational workflow* layer is data that represents the information about each request or event that initiate operational actions within a given operational process, and includes the assignment of resources that participate in the workflow, the steps they perform, the authorizations they receive, and the conclusion of the request. As such, the operations layer represents information about how, when, and by whom each workflow is exercised within the enterprise representing the workload, the resources involved, and the various logistics that describe how the operational processes occurred.

It should be noted that the same operational information is applicable whether the operation was performed in-house, outsourced, off-shored, or using any combination of the aforementioned.

In contrast, the *reference data* layer is the data that must first be established prior to a specific business transaction. To best understand this, let's consider a simple sale transaction to purchase some number of bagels. Prior to the actual sale, the reference data that we would need to effect the purchase would include:

- product reference data—which would include the product characteristics, its unit price, and its volume discounted pricing,
- tax rate reference data—which would include the tax rates for the various possible jurisdictions within which the transaction to purchase bagels is being conducted, and
- customer reference data—which would include information about the customer, particularly institutional customers that may be purchasing significant quantities of product for delivery each morning.

The *activity data* layer is the data that records the all of the information about the sale, which may include orders that are made well in advance, and well as spot contracts of bagel transactions that are effected for immediate pickup or delivery.

In a large enterprise, the data subcategories of operational, reference, and activity data often include several data categories, such as:

- *front office*—the books and record data associated with the front office includes the business dealings that are the primary sources for generating revenue for the enterprise from sales and sometimes includes corporate finance.

  As such, the front office represents the greatest profit center of the enterprise, which must fund all of the cost centers of the enterprise, which include middle office and back office areas.

  Examples of front office business areas include the various sales, marketing, and distribution channels of the enterprise.
- *corporate actions*—the data and information of corporate actions include the business matters that affect shareholders, which may or may not require shareholders to weigh in by voting at a shareholder meeting or by mail in voting proxy

  Examples of corporate actions include shareholder registration, payments of dividends, payment of debt on bonds, forward and reverse stock splits, mergers, acquisitions, and divestitures.
- *board of directors*—the data and information of board of directors include the business matters that are addressed by the board of directors, who are selected by the shareholders and governed by the company bylaws to provide guidance

to the enterprise in the marketplace and who are accountable to ensure that the company conducts business in accordance to law.

The members of the board of directors are legally charged with the responsibility to govern the corporation and are accountable to the shareholders. The board of directors usually consists of a board chair, vice chair, secretary and treasurer, and one or more committee chairs, and board members.

The board is responsible for establishing and maintaining the corporation in the legal jurisdictions required, for selecting and appointing a chief executive, for governing the company with principles and objectives, for acquiring resources for the operation of the company, and for accounting to the public and regulators for the funds and resources of the company. The board of directors must also agree to corporate actions before shareholder voting takes place.

- *corporate finance*—the data and information of the corporate finance include the financial decisions of the corporation for managing investments, working capital, cash-on-hand, tax remittances, and the securities inventory to maximize the long-term value of the corporation as well as support the daily cash requirements of the operation.

    Examples of corporate finance business dealings include the various activities with contra-parties and large corporations to support primary and secondary market transactions to maintain the appropriate cash balances and reserves, such as a repurchase resale agreement to raise overnight cash reserves.

The lowest level grouping within these is called subject areas of data.

A sampling of data subject areas that would typically be located within the data subcategories of operational, reference, and activity for *corporate actions* includes:

- corporate actions operational workflow
    - shareholder registration operations
    - dividend payment operations
    - stock split issuance operations
    - shareholder voting operations
    - merger and acquisition operations
    - divestiture operations
- corporate actions reference data
    - investors/shareholders reference data
    - corporate initiatives reference data
    - market participants reference data
- corporate actions activity data
    - shareholder registration
    - dividend payment
    - stock split issuance
    - shareholder voting

- mergers and acquisitions
- divestitures

The properties of data subject areas are:

- stability of structure,
- encompasses all business information specifically within its scope,
- based upon business terminology and business concepts,
- manageable size for business stakeholders and IT staff,
- well-defined to achieve clear and unambiguous boundaries,
- creates distinctions among terms that could otherwise have multiple meanings,
- abstractions never obfuscate the true business meaning,
- organized to optimize ease of use,
- names and definitions demonstrate a consistent use of terminology, and
- compliant with the business data glossary.

The LDA has many use cases.
   As examples, let's consider the following:

- provides business context to all data,
- provides a rigorous taxonomy (aka business vocabulary) across all data,
- accelerates communication across business areas and with and across IT,
- acts as an accelerator to the majority of life cycles of the enterprise,
- software development life cycle,
- data centric life cycle,
- data governance life cycle,
- insourcing life cycle,
- outsourcing life cycle,
- merger and acquisition life cycle,
- divestiture life cycle,
- provides a business-oriented view into data governance,
- business data glossary,
- data ownership,
- business administered data access rights,
- organizes the conceptual data models as one per data subject area,
- drives database architectures,
- provides a framework for data warehousing,
- acts as an accelerator to object-oriented application architecture,
- forms the basis for a physical data architecture that identifies the physical location and ownership of data belonging to each category of data,
- maps to the business capability model, and
- teaches vast amounts of business knowledge to newly hired staff.

As a rough gauge to estimate the number of data subject areas to expect, a large enterprise, particularly a large financial conglomerate, may have an excess of 600 distinct subject areas of data. Of the total number of data subject areas, it is common for less than half to have automation associated with them.

Since the LDA is a business artifact, the best approach we have experienced is to train business users how to maintain and manage the LDA.

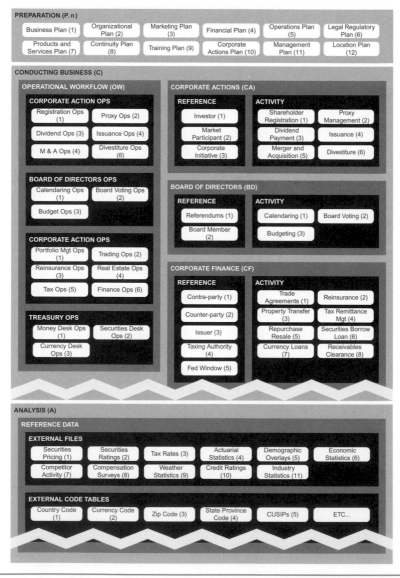

Diagram Logical data architecture sample. (For color version of this figure, the reader is referred to the online version of this chapter.)

There will be departments that are the sole location across the enterprise that originate data for a given subject area of data. For these, data ownership and maintenance of the model are clear.

However, there will also be situations where multiple departments originate data for a given subject area of data. These situations will require information architecture to broker changes to data subject areas across the affected lines of business.

We live in a knowledge economy within which information is the currency. Having information with a clear understanding of its meaning allows us to operate more effectively across a large enterprise to facilitate informed decision making.

4.1.3 DATA GOVERNANCE

If you ask 10 different experts to define data governance, you are likely to get 11 different definitions.

Consider the following definitions:

- Data governance is a committee that convenes to prioritize what data-related initiatives should be funded, to make policies and rules, and to resolve issues among stakeholders.
- Data governance is an IT process that deploys technology to conduct data discovery and data quality initiatives.
- Data governance is a process that determines who can take what actions with what data, when, under what circumstances, using what methods.
- Data governance is the convergence of data management, data quality, data stewardship, data policies, and data security.
- Data governance is cultural shift away from thinking about data as a commodity toward thinking about data as a valuable asset class.
- Data governance is a cultural shift that treats data as an asset class realized through a data stewardship process that acts as a liaise between business and IT to define and organize business data from a business perspective standardizing the business vocabulary to facilitate communication and addressing the data-related needs of stakeholders across the enterprise.

While some of these definitions are notably better than others, none of these definitions can be held up as being completely accurate.

However, to begin to understand what data governance is more accurately, let's first discuss what data governance is not and what it should not become for the well-being of the organization.

They are as follows:

- committee approach—organizations tend to form committees when they do not have a subject matter expert at a senior enough level to look out for the business interests of the enterprise.

Committees too frequently slow down the various data-related activities of the organization with bureaucracy in a struggle to establish the scope of their authority.

■ IT owned process to determine authority over data—data must be governed by the business that is closest to where the particular subject of data originates.

Governing data from IT places those who understand the data and its business value the least in charge of it.

■ process that determines data accountability—every category of data has a source, which is the only place that true data custodianship can pragmatically occur.

If we start by recognizing the natural areas of accountability that originate each category of data and then address the challenges that present themselves, we are on the correct path.

■ convergence of many disciplines— data governance is responsible to determine the framework of architectural disciplines that comprise it and then integrate them in a manner that provides maximum business benefit.

The architectural disciplines that comprise data governance each require subject matter expertise associated with them.

■ cultural shift—wholeheartedly data governance does require a cultural shift, although this is just part of what data governance is

The cultural shift is an important first step that serves to pave the way to achieve data governance within a large enterprise.

■ The last definition listed was our own, and while it is not bad, it is still deficient.

The modern view of data governance is that it is an area of specialization within information architecture that is responsible for a framework of subordinate architectural disciplines to manage data and its associated metadata as an asset of the enterprise in a comprehensive manner.

It begins with understanding the business scope of the entire data landscape of an enterprise and then expands into the following:

■ business data glossary—to provide a taxonomy to uniquely identify each data point in a manner similar to establishing unique identifiers for each financial account, staff member, or unit of property

■ business owner—to identify the organizational unit or units that originate data for each category of data

■ business metadata—to establish a clear understanding of each data point collect the important business information about data assets in a manner similar to that of establishing important information about financial transactions, staff members, and property

■ stakeholders—business owners need to have a 360° view of stakeholders (e.g., legal compliance, financial compliance, HR compliance, auditing, CCO) and what is required to protect their interests

- determining the framework of component architectures—candidate architectural disciplines for a large enterprise include:
  - data stewardship—the stewardship of data begins within the business areas that originate it,
  - RDM—consists of three area of specialization,
    – product master management—a form of code table management that focuses on code tables that are generated internally within the enterprise,
    – code table management—a form of code table management that focuses on code tables that are generated outside the enterprise,
    – external file management—a form of file management that focuses on files that are purchased externally for use across the enterprise,
  - DIM architecture—management of the technologies that transport data,
    – extract transform and load/extract load and transform (ETL/ELT) architecture—management of a class of batch tools that transport data,
    – Enterprise service bus (ESB) architecture—management of a class of real-time tools that transport data,
    – data virtualization architecture—management of a class of technologies that render data from disparate sources while hiding the details of their data types, data formats, and database structures,
    – complex event processing (CEP) architecture—management of a class of rules engine that inspects DIM for patterns that may be useful to detect and act upon,
  - semantic modeling architecture—management of a class of models that either illustrate the relationships data values have among themselves or more advanced models, such as those that depict the usage, sources, and destinations of data,
  - data modeling architecture—management of a class of models that depict conceptual, logical, or physical characteristics for classes of data, and
  - data obfuscation architecture—management of the technologies that mask and/or encrypt data as it is transported.

As we can see, the modern view of data governance shifts the role of data governance from IT to the business taking the lead utilizing IT to support its automation requirements, which are focused on empowering the business to govern one of its most valuable business assets.

Now that we have established a good appreciate of what data governance is and is not, let's look briefly at the not insignificant path of how to get there, or at least some high-level milestones.

The *first* step toward achieving this modern view of data governance begins when IT finally recognizes that it lacks expert knowledge about the data they manage.

To business users who observe the condition of their data, data is lots of database columns with definitions that are systematically missing, incomplete, misleading, or ambiguous. When IT eventually understands what a real business definition is, then they have taken the first step.

Some of the distinctions about "customer" that IT will eventually understand include:

■ customer—any individual or legal entity that has one or more agreements or contracts with the enterprise or has amounts on deposit with the enterprise, including any of its domestic or international affiliates, or for whose person, family members, or property, the enterprise or affiliate otherwise provides protection, or an administrative or other service.

 A legal definition of "customer" was established by the US Congress within the Gramm-Leach-Bliley Act (GLBA) in 1999 for financial companies as it relates to the treatment of individual persons. Although insurance companies are state regulated, they must minimally comply with federal legislation, such as the GLBA.

 First, the GLBA defines a "consumer" as "an individual who obtains, from a financial institution, financial products or services which are to be used primarily for personal, family, or household purposes, and also means the legal representative of such an individual."

 A "customer" is a "consumer" that has developed a relationship with privacy rights protected under the GLBA.

 For example, a "customer" is not someone simply using an automated teller machine or having a check cashed at a cash advance business. These are not ongoing relationships with the "consumer," as compared to when the "consumer" participates in a mortgage loan, tax return preparation, or line of credit.

 Privacy rights protected under the GLBA require financial institutions to provide a privacy notice to customers that explain what information the company gathers about them, where this information is shared, and how the company safeguards that information. An official policy that addresses each of the three areas of information is a legal requirement for financial companies. The privacy notice containing this information must be given to the "consumer" prior to entering into an agreement to do business. Additionally, the GLBA also requires customer notification of their right to "opt-out" under the terms of The Fair Credit Reporting Act.

 The law also requires that companies keep a record of all customer complaints as part of the books and records of the firm, which would be associated with the customer.

■ prospective customer—an individual or legal entity that has never had and/or does not presently have a customer relationship with the enterprise
■ former customer—an individual or legal entity that previously had a customer relationship with the enterprise

- the concept of customer within the confines of a particular database—such as the business concept of customer versus the database containing only customers who are residents of Canada, and
- beneficiary—an individual or legal entity that is designated as the heir, recipient, successor, or payee only within the context of a specific customer contract, policy, or other agreement

The *second* step toward achieving this modern view of data governance begins when IT recognizes that they cannot realistically govern something (i.e., business data) that they lack expert knowledge in. Similarly, it would be like business users thinking that they should be governing the company's firewall architecture.

At this point, IT is then somewhat prepared to adopt the realization that it has an even more important role to play than governing business assets, and that is to transform itself to empower the individuals that have the knowledge to govern.

This means that control shifts away from IT back to business users, which is where it actually all began decades ago. In the beginning, business users sat side by side with IT resources. At that time, many data assets were still not automated and hence were under direct control of the business.

Initially, when IT slowly began to grow into the behemoth that it is today, the separation of business and IT did not manifest itself as a problem immediately as many of the early IT resources was nearly equally as fluent in the business as the result of working so closely with the people in the business. It was only when business knowledgeable IT resources became increasingly scarce as IT continued to grow and become increasingly distant from the business.

Hence, in the modern view, there are 10 basic areas of data governance that belong to the business as opposed to IT.

The 10 areas of business-driven data governance, which can incidentally be consolidated into a data governance portal, include:

- business data glossary,
- business data ownership,
- business administered data access rights,
- business designated data masking templates for data leaving production,
- business designated canned report access and distribution,
- business data stewardship,
- business-driven data discovery,
- business-driven semantic modeling,
- data governance and architecture registry for business and IT artifacts, and
- consolidated business metrics in a data governance dashboard.

The new role of IT for data governance is to render the technologies to support these 10 areas usable to business users.

4.1.3.1 Business Data Glossary Architecture

Prior to written language, there was only spoken language. Spoken language only ever occurred one individual time, that is, unless there was the rare experience of an echo, where the same words could be heard exactly as spoken a second time. During this extensive historical period prior to written language, story tellers roamed the land to tell their stories of historical events. When the Greek myths and legends were told by these story tellers, there would invariably be subtle differences in the stories. It was not until Homer wrote down a version of each Greek myth and legend, he encountered that the variances found in the telling of myths and legends could be brought under relative control.

When written language first emerged using the alphabet as we know it, terms were not controlled by their spelling. Instead, terms were phonetically spelled, and within the same documents, the spelling of the same phonetically spelled words could and often did vary.

Plato, when reflecting upon the oral culture that surrounded him, recognized that the preliterate masses lacked the ability to truly think in a structured way when he wrote, "They have no vivid in their souls." Without written words to capture ideas in a firm medium, how could anyone understand the numerous and complex ideas of others to ponder and weigh in ones' mind? This was not just the discovery of the self, but the thinking self.

Eventually, when Newton developed his theories involving force, time, and mass, there were no formal definitions of these terms available to him at that time. Newton used these terms with new purpose and gave them new and precise definition for the first time. Without precise definitions for the terms we use, there is little ability to communicate to others the exact meaning of what we think.

Today, the notion of thinking and the recorded word are hardly separable. The recorded word is the prerequisite to conscious thought as we understand it. We know the exact spelling or usage of most words we employ, we can look up their meaning, we know there are reference books that use these words from which we can gather information, and we can put our thoughts about that information into a recorded form using those words to share ideas with others, using books, articles, e-mails, film, or online videos.

Once recorded, thoughts are able to become detached from the speaker speaking them. Instead, the thoughts become attached to the words so that they may be shared with others to learn and understand, and share with still other individuals. Transitioning from the oral culture to the written one is a journey that begins with the notion of things represented by sounds to the written word where language can further develop. The journey then continues from words to taxonomies with specific meaning and from taxonomies to logic.

Also from writing came mathematics. Derived data is the result of mathematics where the sentences or formulas that define derived data must be recorded to convey their derivation and meaning. If we look at the progression it starts with the emergence of the first written language around 3200 BC, then money around 2500 BC, with the emergence of numbers necessarily having to be somewhere between those time periods.

> *Note: The origin of numbers is debated to be well after the emergence of money which seems to be an unsupportable argument no matter how many pints of mead (i.e., fermented honey beverage predating both wine and beer) one consumes.*

Regardless of the type of industry or commerce, at the core of all business and commerce is data, consisting mostly of numbers. As an example, modern energy companies analyze streams of data using distributed sensors and high-speed communications to determine where it should drill for natural gas or oil. The data points of these sensors however have precise definitions that anyone who would use them needs to understand.

While the breadth of data can vary significantly in organizations, the larger the business, generally the more data there is. However, the most interesting fact is that most data within these large enterprises is not even being recorded though it can hold the key to significantly higher productivity and profitability. As an example, large amounts of data about operational workflow in large organizations are routinely not collected.

That said many organizations spend large sums of money managing what are perceived as their other valuable assets. People assets are well managed with a vast array of HR policies and processes, and similarly, financial and property assets have meticulous oversight and management, and are even insured where possible.

However, when it comes to arguably the most valuable asset of all, data, often just the basics are collected and then few of the protections that exist for people, finance, and property assets have analogous counterparts to manage it as a company asset.

Data can be found in many locations. It can be found in computers of various types, on paper in file cabinets, index cards in boxes, in smartphones, and in people's heads. Regardless of where it is, it is the life blood of almost every enterprise. However, for it to be useful, someone has to know where to find it and they have to be able to understand what it means.

In a way, what is needed is for business management to take ownership and responsibility of data assets the same way that corporate officers take ownership and responsibility for financial assets. But what does this mean?

Consider a bank manager who must account for every penny of his branch's transactions. While resources are dedicated to ensure that every financial account is completely accurate to the penny, comparatively few resources are spent to ensure the underlying data collected from each transaction is equally valid.

For example, the customer's name, address, phone number, tax ID number, birth date, nationality, mother's maiden name, and occupation are data that are collected for a purpose. Yet no matter how well the data services organization of the enterprise secures and protects the data, the concern for the validity of its content is of less importance.

While many business users generally believe that the ownership of data and information is the responsibility of IT, others have correctly zeroed in on the fact that responsibility for data cannot reside with those who do not originate the data. IT is simply responsible for the safekeeping of the data across the many files, databases, disks, tapes, and other storage media, and the technology that supports them.

In a comparable analogy, accountants are responsible for organizing and reporting financial data that have been provided to them. Even so, they are not responsible for the business decisions and activities that generated those financial numbers. Whether it involves financial accounting or data accounting, the responsibility for the accuracy and completeness of the finances and the data must reside with the business.

As such, when someone in the business buys or sells an asset, the accountant tracks the financial asset, its cost basis, depreciation, appreciation, accretion, and so on. The accountant is not responsible for the transaction or the gain or loss of assets that resulted. The accountant's responsibility is to organize these calculations and tabulations, and then accurately report on these figures to management and the necessary regulatory bodies.

Similarly, IT reports on the data that it organizes and safeguards for the business. Like the accountants, IT is responsible for reporting on the data, although it is not responsible for the accuracy and completeness of the data provided them.

The primary focus of data that is collected in an enterprise is usually to support the particular business operation within the particular line of business. However, the usefulness of that data across various other parts of the organization can extend well beyond that particular line of business.

As examples, it could be useful for:

- opportunities to cross sell products and services to customers,
- new product development decisions,
- merger and acquisition decisions,
- divestiture decisions,
- marketing decisions,
- expansion decisions,
- corporate restructuring decisions, and
- budgeting decisions.

Hence, to be useful across these different areas, the parts of the organization that collect data need to be aware of the impact of capturing data in a nonchalant manner.

This includes eliminating a few bad habits, such as typing any characters as values into required fields just to get to their next activity faster.

These types of habits create and support entire industries, such as the development of data quality products. In the end, however, the only ones that have a chance at figuring out the correct data is the business.

Let's also consider the usefulness of business areas managing the business metadata for data that they originate.

If we consider the alternative, which is usually having a team of data modelers in IT enter hundreds and thousands of definitions for data points for which they are not the subject matter experts, we find that the usefulness of the resulting definitions can range significantly.

For example, a small portion of data modelers research each data point with business users or industry reference materials, while a larger portion of data modelers leave the definition blank or they simply repeat the name of the data point as part of its definition.

I can't speak to how other people react, but when I see a data point name like "Coupon Rate," it disturbs me to see a definition the likes of "A coupon rate is the rate of a coupon."

In contrast, a data steward or other individual that has a thorough understanding of the business would provide a somewhat more useful definition.

4.1.3.1.1   Coupon Rate

Definition: A coupon rate of a financial instrument (e.g., bond, note or other fixed income security) is the amount of interest paid by the issuer of the financial instrument per year expressed as a percentage of the "principal amount" or "face value" of the security, to the holder of the security, which is usually paid twice per year.

Purpose: The coupon rate of a financial instrument participates in calculations that determine the market price and the rate of return of the financial instrument that bears the coupon.

Data format: Coupon rates are represented or quoted in either fractions of 32nds or decimal.

Data sensitivity: Coupon rates are not considered sensitive data as there are neither external regulatory restrictions nor internal policies that restrict its disclosure for competitive or proprietary reasons.

Business synonyms: "fixed income interest," "coupon yield."

Subject area of data: This data point is based within the business context of the data subject area named, "PRODUCT."

The difference in usefulness to other business stakeholders and IT is simply remarkable. One approach actually costs the enterprise money to have a high-priced IT resource to perform data entry of content that is of no use to anyone, while another approach takes a less expensive subject matter expert to record knowledge that will be useful to mentor new staff and to convey the true business meaning of the data point to every stakeholder across the enterprise.

In fact, if we were to disclose a more complete set of useful business metadata that a business subject matter expert could record, we would consider recording the following business metadata characteristics:

- LDA data subject area,
- unique business data glossary name,
- business trustee for the data glossary field,
- business definition,
- business purpose and usage,
- format of the data,
- data sensitivity, such as confidential for customer privacy,
- specific regulatory or compliance rules that are deemed applicable,
- synonyms used in the industry,
- labels typically used in applications, forms, and reports,
- business processes that originate the data content,
- business area(s) and business processes that typically use, report, or analyze the data content,
- related business data glossary fields,
- source of the data in the business where the data point originates, or if calculated, what is the formula for its derivation,
- basic business data class (e.g., date, amount, quantity, rate) and required level of precision,
- whether the data point is sent to the general ledger (GL),
- whether the data point is sent to external organizations, such as regulatory bodies,
- mapping to external standards, such as ACORD and MISMO,
- complete or sample business values or domain values, and
- global variances in definition, such as with "personally identifying information" (PII) where the European Union includes small businesses as those that have an income under ten million Euros and less than 50 employees.

4.1.3.1.2 Identifying the Source of Data

Once the business has thoroughly defined a business data point, then it is the role of IT to work with the data steward to locate its sources from across the various production databases of the company. Each source will have its own profile for data quality (e.g., data sparseness, accuracy, numerical precision versus rounding, standardization of format and values, and segment of the business, such as pertaining only to Canadian business)

4.1.3.1.3 Extracting Data to a Landing Zone

Once the sources of data have been confirmed, it can be extracted into a landing zone, either a conventional landing zone or a low cost big data landing zone. The considerations here will involve the appropriate frequency with which data extracts to the landing zone need to occur, or whether a real-time feed from the production database will be required to stream data as it is written, or updated.

The answer to this will depend upon the real-time requirements, and to an extent, it will depend upon the degree of data cleansing, standardization, and integration that may ultimately be required before the data can be useful to a real-time business capability.

What's important here is that the extraction stage provides valuable metadata to the business data glossary to communicate to the user which applications the data is available from, and the business assessment of the degree of reliability of the data from each source being reliable.

These types of metrics can provide guidance to stakeholders that may need the data to request additional services from IT to improve the quality of the data by enhancing the application software, provide monitoring and alerts on data quality, assist business users in viewing and correcting data, or request additional services from data stewards to develop training for business users to capture the information more reliably.

4.1.3.1.4 Data Profiling

Data profiling is mostly a consideration during the development process, but in some cases can continue into production. Once landed, the data can be analyzed so that specifications can be developed to perform data cleansing (aka scrubbing) on the data.

As data cleansing occurs, the original data should be retained partially for historical purposes and partially for the possibility of needing to reprocess the data if issues arose downstream that required corrections at this early stage of processing.

Once cleansed, the data is placed in the next layer of the landing zone, with statistics and metrics about the cleansing process being stored for display into the business data glossary.

4.1.3.1.5 Data Standardization

When even the same business data is sourced from different application databases, a number of issues tend to arise. The first issue that becomes apparent is that each application tends to use different codes and/or different data types for the same things, which is easy to remedy with a good RDM code tables initiative. The additional issues tend to demonstrate somewhat greater complexity, such as:

- values of a data point not having a one to one relationship with the corresponding data point in another system,

- values of a data point corresponding to domain values that are outside the domain values of the same data point in another system,
- values of a data point containing values that correspond to something that should have been a separate data point, but was incorrectly combined together.

As in each previous phase, the standardized data is placed in yet the next layer of the landing zone, with statistics and metrics about the standardization process being stored for display into the business data glossary.

4.1.3.1.6 Data Integration

Once standardized data is available, it is possible to prepare specifications for data integration. The ideal target state for data integration is one that closely resembles the conceptual data model that data stewards and business users develop for the particular data subject areas involved.

As in each previous phase, the integrated data is placed in yet the next layer of the landing zone, with statistics and metrics about the integration process being stored for display into the business data glossary.

These metrics can be far more comprehensive and can include for each data point the following:

- sparseness,
- reliability,
- mean,
- median,
- standard deviation,
- skew, and
- any other standard or proprietary calculation.

As for the usefulness of metrics such as sparseness and reliability, if a metric for a business data glossary entry indicates that data values are missing 30% of the time or have invalid values 10% of the time, then using that business data glossary data point to organize totals or subtotals may not be practical.

At this point, the integrated data can be stored within an operational data store (ODS) layer that mirrors the data subject areas of the LDA.

If the resulting ODS layer is too large and complex to support ad hoc joins using a standard relational database management system (DBMS), then one more step should be undertaken to migrate it into a high-performance analytical data base that can support real-time joins and analytics pertaining to one or more technologies associated with big data architecture.

The result has far reaching implications for the many stakeholders of business and IT. For the first time since automation, business will have taken back control of their data asset. In addition, the data with the highest priority to the business has meaningful definitions that can be communicated across the company.

4.1.3.1.7 Shopping Cart

The next step for the business data glossary is to make it go somewhere. In other words, let's suppose the business data glossary was also a business data catalog for business users. A business user or stakeholder can look up the data points that they need to see in a report, confirm that the data points are in fact the correct ones based upon their business metadata, and then put them in a shopping basket for reporting.

Once the shopping cart contains everything the particular business user requires, then they can automatically get a list of existing reports that they can run from a mashup technology, or they can easily assemble their own report using a mashup technology.

The benefits from a business perspective are compelling, such as:

- the correct data points required by business can be identified in seconds as opposed to negotiating months with various IT resources,
- from this point forward the analysis to determine what applications to source the data is performed just once,
- from this point forward the development work to land the data from production is performed just once,
- from this point forward the analysis and programming to cleanse the data is performed just once,
- from this point forward reporting results no longer display inconsistencies that resulted from different rounding factors and data cleansing logic,
- from this point forward the analysis and programming to standardize the data is performed just once,
- as additional data points are sourced, cleansed, standardized, and integrated, they become permanently available to stakeholders,
- the speed with which new reports can be developed is a fraction of what it was previously,
- the cost of new reports to be developed is a fraction of what it was previously,
- the development effort that ties up resources to develop duplicate reports is eliminated,
- the costs associated with developing duplicate reports are eliminated,
- the licensing costs associated with a high-end mashup technology is a fraction of the costs associated with non-mashup technologies,
- the ability to gather metrics about data usage across the entire data landscape is facilitated by a high-end mashup technology,
- data masking for ad hoc reporting is automatically facilitated by a high-end mashup technology,
- a high-end mashup technology can source data from an HDFS and/or HBase environment, and
- a high-end mashup technology will support high-speed data streaming for critical real-time reporting, analysis, and alerting.

As is now apparent, a modern business data glossary places a great deal of knowledge about the data assets in the hands of the business. This allows business to make informed decisions about how to prioritize the activities of IT to address data-related issues that are of greatest priority to the business and reveals what data assets are available and their condition for use in business decision making where informed decisions are required.

As such, business data glossary architecture is the architectural discipline responsible for building the foundation for the data assets of the company. Standing on the foundation of an LDA, the business data glossary architecture has synergies with and impacts every area of the business as well as all of the other architectural disciplines within business and information systems architectures.

4.1.3.2   Data Ownership Architecture

The next valuable area associated with data governance is data ownership architecture. The foundation for data ownership is also the LDA. Using the LDA as a source that identifies all subject areas of data across the enterprise, each subject area is designated as being owned by the business department or business departments that originate the data for that topic of data.

The principle at work here is that the most appropriate individuals to act as custodians for a collection of data points are the individuals that are responsible for originating the data for those data points. The department head, or their designated data steward, would therefore act as the person managing responsibility for that portion of the data asset.

In our earlier discussion of LDA, we know that there are many business categories that data may be organized into.

As examples of this:

- when considering the data that is originated during business preparation, the owners are the company founders,
- when considering the data that pertains to any operational workflow while conducting business, this data is originated with the workflow inside the department whose workflow it is,
- when considering the business activity data while conducting business, this data is originated with the business users that perform the activity, such as the board of directors creating conducting corporate action activity, and
- when considering analysis activities, the data originates in the business area that conducts business intelligence.

However, not all data originates within the company, and therefore data ownership is at times external to the company. In fact, there are several situations when data is originated outside the company, such as "reference data."

While not all reference data originates outside the company, such as the reference data of corporate initiatives and company bylaws associated with "corporate actions," there is a considerable amount of information about many reference business subject areas of data that do originate from outside the company.

Examples of data that originates outside an enterprise include:

- customer data—which can be entered through a Web interface by the customer,
- distribution channel data—which can be entered through a Web interface by the distribution channel,
- shareholder data—which is provided via feeds from brokerage firms whose customers have acquired financial instruments in your enterprise,
- issuer data—provided from external feeds,
- vendors—which can be entered through a Web interface by the vendor,
- RDM code tables—which originate from various external authorities, such as the International Organization for Standardization (ISO) which originates many categories of data including country codes and currency codes, and
- RDM external files—which originate from various authorities and may include topics, such as economic data and demographic data.

When data originates externally, it is still important to designate one or more internal departments and data stewards to act as the custodian for those data assets within the enterprise. As an example, information architecture, reference data architecture, or the data governance area of data stewardship and their associated subject matter experts are good candidates to act as data custodians for data that is typically shared across the enterprise.

The role of a data owner should include:

- fiduciary responsibilities of the data assets that are "owned" by the particular department including the proper designation of business metadata,
- mentor department personnel in their role as "owners" of the particular class of data assets,
- liaise with the individuals that are stakeholders in the data "owned" by the department,
- understand the data quality-related issues affecting the data assets "owned" by the department and their impact upon other stakeholders,
- coordinate with IT to prioritize and remedy the business critical issues affecting the data assets "owned" by the department,
- facilitate the reporting needs of the department by coordinating with IT to source, cleanse, standardize, and integrate additional data points from production applications,
- convey to IT any reporting requirements in which their assistance is requested,
- with regard to sensitive data, administer access rights to the other departments across the enterprise based upon their functional need to know,

■ coordinate to acquire from the appropriate authorities the necessary RDM code tables or external files by the enterprise

As such, data ownership architecture is the data governance-related architectural discipline responsible for the frameworks associated with determining data ownership and subsequent fiduciary responsibility over the data assets that are owned by the department.

4.1.3.3 Data Access Rights Architecture

Data access rights architecture, introduced in the data ownership architecture section just prior to this, is associated with data governance and continues the theme of business empowerment, particularly with respect to the data assets of the enterprise.

In the modern view of data governance, data access rights are determined by the data owner. The data owner is best defined as the department head or designated data steward for the department that originates the majority of data within a given data subject area. Once data has been designated as being owned by a particular data owner, then access rights can be administered according to the need for other departments and stakeholders to view sensitive data.

If the subject area of data that is "owned" by a department does not contain sensitive data, then all business departments across the enterprise would be given access to it.

Sensitive data, however, includes any data points that are subject to:

■ regulatory restrictions, such as PII,
■ promises made to customers or vendors regarding the privacy of their information, or
■ company restrictions due to the value of the data from the perspective of a competitive advantage or generally held as confidential across the enterprise.

Once data has been restricted to a given set of departments that do not have a general need to have access to the data to perform their activities, there may still be an isolated role within a given department that does require access to sensitive data. When this occurs access can be granted to just that role within a given department so that the individual assigned to that role can access the data content to perform their job function.

Although many large companies tend not to administer role-level security within their LDAP security framework, role-level security can usually be provided as an additional layer around LDAP to provide for the few cases where role-level security is crucial.

As an additional layer of protection, data access rights architecture also provides "data access rights overrides" that can be administered by the legal and compliance departments of a company. Using this approach, legal, regulatory compliance, financial compliance, and HR compliance departments are provided the ability to override the access right designations of a data owner to further restrict access.

This is particularly important if one or more business owners fail to restrict access to departments that may expose the company unnecessarily to violations of regulatory requirements. In such circumstances, legal and compliance may focus on the categories of data that are deemed most sensitive from the perspective of either regulations or proprietary competitive concerns to provide a safety net for data accessibility.

Once access rights have been determined by business "owners," it is useful for the architecture to render that information to any data virtualization layer that could mask data that a particular user is not permitted to access in an ad hoc or canned report.

It is also useful for architecture to render access right information to an ETL CASE tool to automatically identify sensitive data that should be routinely obfuscated when it leaves the safety of a production environment (see Section 4.1.3.4).

In our final example, it is also useful for the architecture to render access right information to either the file access layer or report dissemination layer of a document repository for controlling which individuals an already existing report may be retrieved by or disseminated to by another individual or automation system (see Section 4.1.3.5).

As such, data access rights architecture is the architectural discipline responsible for the frameworks associated with determining accessibility of business data in ad hoc reports, canned reports, or already existing cyclical reports, such as end of quarter or year-end reports. In contrast, access to the source databases themselves is controlled through a completely separate set of processes that control application access to production data, where user access is managed in the form of controlling access to the applications that in turn have access to data.

4.1.3.4   ETL Data Masking Architecture

ETL data masking architecture, a discipline associated with DIM architecture, was introduced in the data access rights architecture section just prior to this and is associated with data governance and continues the theme of business empowerment, particularly with respect to the data assets of the enterprise. Data masking is pertinent to ETL more than say other forms of DIM, such as ESB movement of data, because ETL is typically used to transport data out of a production environment, whereas ESBs and CEPs are almost never used to transport data past the production boundary.

ETL data masking architecture addresses the standards and frameworks associated with identifying and protecting sensitive data points that are within a production environment that are being transferred out of production into an less controlled environment.

Examples of less controlled environments of varying degrees include:

- QA test environments—which house business users for preproduction testing of applications,
- integration test—which houses IT and business personnel for the testing of various application or system components that have been brought together for testing,
- unit test—which houses IT developers for the testing of their individual software components.

One approach to automating ETL data masking is to leverage the business data glossary with its record of business metadata that includes data sensitivity with the mapping of the production sources of those data points, which should be recorded when data is extracted from production into the landing zone.

As control of the business definition of data transfers from IT to business, business analysts and IT should be busy identifying the sources of physical data that corresponds with the business view. It is then the responsibility of IT to record the database column names associated with the physical side of sourcing the data to support the business view.

Once these production data sources, which are comprised of production database table names and column names, have been linked to a sensitive data point in the business glossary, it is then reasonable to conclude that the production database table names and column names that provide that data contain sensitive data.

These database table names and column names are generally useful for all architectural disciplines associated with DIM architecture, as they all operate at the physical level with the names associated with the physical files and databases.

This is true for the following sources and DIM techniques:

- conventional database technologies,
- conventional file technologies,
- big data file technologies,
- big data database technologies,
- cloud data transfers,
- ESB data transmissions,
- FTP data transfers,
- XML and XBRL file transfers, and
- ETL data transmissions.

Essentially, if the data is leaving the protections of a secure production environment, sensitive data must be either masked or encrypted.

4.1.3.5   *Canned Report Access Architecture*

There are two general types of canned reports.

4.1.3.5.1   Canned Report with Variable Data

The first type of canned reports is standard reports that are run on demand. In this case, the format of the report is fixed and the data changes potentially up to the point in time when it is generated.

For example, if the user is running a canned report to list all staff members of the enterprise organized by department one day, they will get all of the staff members that were with the enterprise on that particular day. If they rerun the same report the next day, it will use the exact same queries and formatting, but it will include the new hires and will exclude the retirees, and all former employees.

The access rights for these reports are usually administered at the application level when the report is requested. If someone has access to the reporting application, then they can often run any report, such as any HR-related reports.

4.1.3.5.2   Canned Report with Fixed Data

The second type of canned reports is standard reports that are cyclical in nature, such as end of month, quarterly, or annual reports, where both their format and data content are frozen in time. When these reports are generated their output is typically stored as a PDF file in a document repository. These types of canned reports have access controls at the document repository level where access to a report is requested.

The first objective of canned report architecture is to facilitate a framework that makes it easy for any stakeholder across the enterprise to locate the canned report of interest.

The next objective of canned report access architecture is to develop the necessary standards and frameworks to centrally organize canned reports and map their content to the business data glossary so that requests for their subsequent access may be evaluated based upon the access rights as determined by the business owners of the content.

When access requests are denied, the framework may allow for either access to a redacted form of the same report or the creation of a request to either the business owner or business compliance to override a denial of access.

Depending upon the industry that an enterprise is in and the regulatory climate of that industry, canned report access architecture may additionally make use of technologies that can prevent attachment of documents to e-mails, or track the dissemination of canned reports across the IT landscape. This is typically accomplished by incorporating a traceable tag within the PDF file of the canned report.

4.1.3.6 Data Stewardship

Data stewardship in the modern view of data governance is also in line with the theme of business empowerment and data being managed as an asset class. There are many stakeholders that must be across the business with data quality as well as regulatory needs, especially for a global business.

With the volume and volatility of rules about data from regulatory requirements in every country and treaty zone, one of the most useful technologies for the data steward is clearly the "data governance" rules engine. A data governance rules engine focuses on the data quality of information being originated and passed to downstream consumers of that data.

The first advantage of a "data governance" rules engine is its ability to organize the numerous rules into a useful business ontology that begins with jurisdictions.

The jurisdictional level organization of rules consists of a flexible hierarchy of (1) Treaty Zone (e.g., European Union (EU), North America Free Trade Agreement (NAFTA), South Asian Free Trade Agreement (SAFTA), CommonMarket of the Southern Cone (Mercosur), and Andean Community (CAN)); (2) Country (e.g., South Korea, China); and (3) Administrative Levels, which in some situations may be further subdivided into increasingly local municipalities (e.g., US States, Counties, and Cities/Townships).

Note: The term "flexible hierarchy" refers to the fact that the hierarchy permits a parent of "None" or "All," such as a country not associated with a Treaty Zone, or a Treaty Zone without a specific Country or Administrative Level being applicable.

The next level of organization is an authority document level, which embodies the conceptual requirement. The authority document organization of rules consists of a *flexible hierarchy* of:

- authority document name and authority document legislative identifier;
- authority document section name and authority document section identifier; and
- citation, which is the phrase within the section that cites the regulatory requirement in written language.

The level of organization following an authority document level is the data steward level, which embodies the logical requirement. The data steward level organization of rules consists of a *flexible hierarchy* of:

- business data glossary data points,
- business capabilities, and
- application systems.

The final level of organization is the business analyst level of organization, which embodies the physical requirement. The business analyst level of organization of rules consists of a *flexible hierarchy* of:

- database names/file names,
- database tables/file record types, and
- database columns/file field names from across the IT landscape.

Then there are the physical rules, which should be associated with these various levels of organization so that they may be traceable to the jurisdiction, authority document, data steward, and business analyst levels. The physical rules would generate alerts to the data stewards for the areas of the business in which they have responsibility. The data stewards would then work with their respective areas to address the violations detected by the physical rules.

The following approach recognizes the fact that the costs of addressing application-related issues are extremely high. These include the analysis, design, and implementation phases, followed by unit testing, integration testing, QA testing, and production turnover. The full life cycle engages quite a variety of technical services and a large number of individuals.

As a result, data stewardship should seriously consider the following five steps to capture and assess the alternatives for addressing the data governance issues identified to the data steward.

These steps include:

- identify potential manual and automated solutions for each data violation,
- capture estimates for the cost of implementing each,
- select the best solution based upon ROI,
- capture implementation lessons learned, and
- periodically review manually implemented solutions.

Identification of potential manual and automated solutions accepts proposals associated with the outstanding data governance issue. There is no particular limit to the number of proposals that may be associated with a data governance issue, but in general, the more ideas the better.

The capture of estimated resources required for each identifies the various parts of the organization that would have to participate to implement a specific proposal. Once identified, the proposal would be routed to these participants in the same sequence that implementation would have to occur. Once each participant reviews the proposal and records their estimates for the activities that they are responsible for, the proposal is routed to the next participant.

In the end, IT will have identified the applications and components that would require maintenance and the estimated costs associated with each. This approach helps to provide management and data stewards the type of business information that they will need to make an informed decision.

The selection of the solution based upon ROI consists of an automated workflow that illustrates the estimates provided by the participants of each proposed solution.

At this point, the business can identify the business value associated with addressing the specific data governance issue, along with the level of perceived risk associated with each of the proposed solutions.

Once business value has been associated with the data governance issue and a level of risk has been associated with each proposed solution, the evaluation of ROI may be determined for each proposed solution.

This allows the business to select the particular proposal for implementation, which may simply consist of selecting one of the manual proposals, or it may consist of selecting an automated approach. However, regardless of whether a manual operational approach is selected, the automated approaches proposed should be evaluated and the most desirable of the automated proposals should be identified for future consideration.

If the business selects an automated approach, the selection of the proposed solution should include the evaluation of all pending automated proposals that are associated with the same applications and application components. If it is determined that several automated proposals should be combined within the life cycle of this implementation, then an additional round of estimates for a combined solution should be considered.

A new hybrid proposal requiring a combined round of estimates should consist of the identification of the various manual operational alternatives being decommissioned by the automated proposals being included within the life cycle of this implementation. The total cost of the combined implementation to be considered will be the new round of estimates from the various stakeholders for the implementation of the combined automated solution proposals with one pass of the life cycle, and the costs of removing the manual operational alternatives that have been implemented.

In simple terms, the total risk of the combined implementation to be considered will be the risks associated with the selected automation proposals versus the risks associated with the already implemented manual operational alternatives.

In the circumstance when application enhancements are being planned for reasons unrelated to addressing data governance issues, the data governance issues that have been implemented with manual operational alternatives should be considered for inclusion into the specifications of the application enhancements.

The capture of lessons learned from the implementation should consist of an assessment of the cost savings associated with:

- diverting automation to manual operational costs and
- subsequent batching of automation implementations into one pass of the software development life cycle (SDLC) to maintain applications and their associated components.

The uniqueness of the modern approach rests completely with the fact that it recognizes that the entire life cycle of application maintenance costs is extremely high and that manual operational alternatives should always be considered as an alternative either permanently or temporary. This should be considered at least until the particular area of the application would be undergoing maintenance for additional reasons so that requirements may be batched together.

The notion of a manual solution is one where the costs involved are for creating user training with periodic retraining built into the assumptions.

Also unique to the modern approach is the notion that solutions considered and adopted be recorded for future staff members if the same or similar data governance issue emerges in the future. Often the analysis performed is lost causing the resources to perform the same analysis over again without the advantage of learning the lessons from the past, as is what generally happens to those who ignore history.

One key aspect to the modern approach is the notion that automation change may be temporarily postponed until requirements may be batched into a more comprehensive set of requirements, thereby incurring the costs of the full life cycle only once as opposed to several times for smaller units of change.

As such, the role of a data steward requires a broad combination of knowledge and cumulative experience about the business of their area and its associated data quality and regulatory requirements.

4.1.3.7   Data Discovery Architecture

The data landscape of an enterprise consists of every file, database, document repository, and Big Data repository residing on every production server within every data center. As one can imagine, the inventory of database columns and fields that exist across these files and databases can easily number in the millions. In addition, the number of unstructured files and documents that exist on file servers, document repositories, and Big Data repositories can also number in the millions, consisting of hundreds of terabytes to petabytes and exabytes.

As we begin to appreciate the magnitude of our data landscape, it is important to consider the informational needs of business stakeholders, as well as regulatory responsibilities across the various jurisdictions, (e.g., treaty zones, countries, and the sub-country administrative levels) and LH requirements across these jurisdictions.

Considering that the only effective way to understand what each database column or field may be is to inspect the values of the data content for each, to approach this manually would be anything except cost effective. Therefore, the activity to develop a map to illustrate the company's global data landscape requires a significant degree of automation beginning with data discovery capabilities.

Basic data discovery capabilities start by learning to recognize the parts of the data landscape that are well understood, and then they compare the data content of these understood parts of the data landscape with the many parts of the data landscape that are understood less or not understood at all. These data discovery capabilities then propose a map of related columns and fields from across the globe, saving countless man years of effort to conduct this first level of data analysis. The next step is to profile the data and inspect the data points that are related to it.

Data profiling capabilities help determine the qualities of the data content, including the qualities of the data content of the database columns and fields that are related to the columns and fields that are undergoing discovery. The complexity here cannot be overstated, as the data points undergoing discovery may contain data values corresponding to different business definitions.

As an example, if the database column undergoing discovery in some database contains the given name or surname of individuals, the appropriate business glossary field name for one database column could be employee name, employee spouse name, vendor contact name, customer name, conservator name, regulatory agency contact name, and beneficiary name depending upon the row or record number.

Under such circumstances, the only way to decipher the business meaning of a database column undergoing discovery is to analyze the data that is related to it. Depending upon the database design, there will be situations where the information necessary to decipher the business meaning will not be present in the database. Instead, the key to deciphering the information will be buried within application code that must be used to decode the meaning of the information contained within the database.

When this occurs, the effort is a lengthy manual effort requiring analysis of the application programs that access the data. That said, the process of data discovery is still greatly enhanced by data discovery and data automation.

As data is discovered and profiled, it is then classified based upon its usefulness for business intelligence, regulatory, and LH uses.

4.1.3.8   Semantic Modeling Architecture

There are many types of use cases for semantic modeling. Distinct from conceptual, logical, and physical data modeling, and process modeling, the conventions for semantic modeling can vary widely depending upon the particular use case and the objectives that are desired from each use case.

But first, let's discuss what semantic modeling is. Some models illustrate the relationships that classes of data have with one another, such as this example where business concepts are hidden.

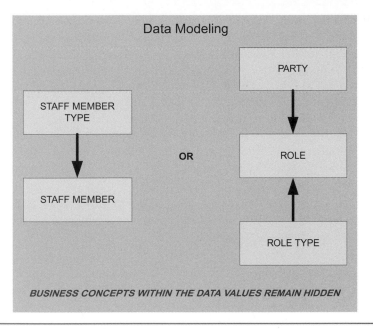

Diagram   Data modeling depicts entity relationships. (For color version of this figure, the reader is referred to the online version of this chapter.)

At its most basic, semantic modeling is used to depict the relationships that exist among specific values of data, such as the example below that models the same topic as the data modeling diagram above, but now focused on the values of the data and the relationship they have.

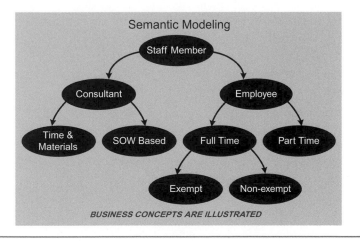

Diagram   Semantic modeling can depict data content relationships. (For color version of this figure, the reader is referred to the online version of this chapter.)

For example, a derivative security can have its various underlying securities graphically depicted in a semantic model to illustrate how the derivative was constructed and the constituent cash flows that determines its return.

Another example that may be applicable to a broader audience would be the distinction between social security numbers and tax ID numbers.

A complete semantic model in this domain would depict:

- *social security number (SSN)* as issued for an individual by the Social Security Administration,
- *employer identification number (EIN)* as issued for a business by the Internal Revenue Service,
- *individual taxpayer identification number (ITIN)* as issued for an individual that does not have, and is not eligible to obtain, a social security number, and is issued by the Internal Revenue Service,
- *adoption taxpayer identification number (ATIN)* as issued for a minor as a taxpayer identification number for pending U.S. adoptions by the Internal Revenue Service to allow the minor to be claimed as a legal deduction, but is not appropriate to have income reported against it; and
- *preparer taxpayer identification number (PTIN)* as issued for a tax preparer by the Internal Revenue Service to safeguard their true SSN or EIN, but is not appropriate to have income reported against it.

Similarly, examples of basic semantic models can be found in online thesaurus portals, where synonyms and their related terms are depicted with linkages to their other synonyms and related terms, which are themselves connected to their other synonyms and related terms.

Such basic use cases do not require much in the way of diagramming standards or procedural workflows. When semantic models are simple like this, it is easy to avoid creating unintended outcomes that can make diagrams overly complex and unusable.

At the other end of the spectrum are the advanced use cases, which typically have different categories of participants with particular roles that follow a customized set of modeling conventions consisting of diagramming techniques and naming conventions, with a well-defined operational workflow.

For example, the diagram below illustrates the life cycle of a country, the ISO standards organization process, and its associated metadata view. The ISO standard that identifies country is ISO 3166-1.

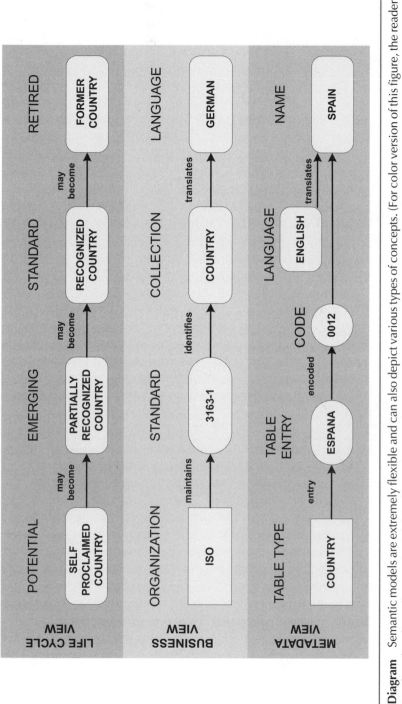

Diagram   Semantic models are extremely flexible and can also depict various types of concepts. (For color version of this figure, the reader is referred to the online version of this chapter.)

An example of an advanced use case would be business users depicting semantic models for business data points present on reports, relating them to business data glossary entries, with IT staff depicting semantic models of the physical data sources used to generate the data points on the same reports as a method to satisfy regulatory reporting requirements that mandate identification of data sources and their business meaning (e.g., pillars two and three of Solvency II).

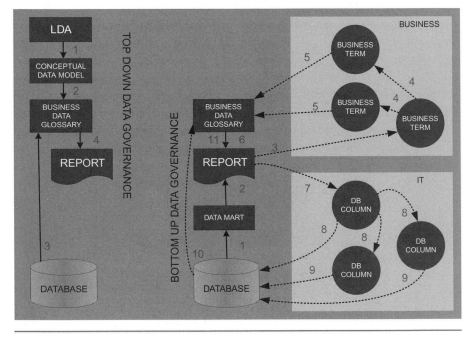

Diagram   Semantic models can depict workflows for data governance. (For color version of this figure, the reader is referred to the online version of this chapter.)

A semantic modeling architect requires a broad combination of knowledge and cumulative experience about business and data, as well as the use cases to be addressed with the aid of a semantic modeling approach. Perhaps most important, the semantic model must be a subject matter expert able to develop semantic modeling standards that are able to take advantage of the diagramming and reporting capabilities of the particular semantic technology to be chosen.

4.1.3.9   Architecture Governance Component Registry

A large global enterprise has architectural subject matter experts that span various architectural disciplines and solution architects that work with application development teams located in various countries around the world. The standards and frameworks created by the various enterprise architects must be accessible by the various solution architects without anyone knowing the name of the directory or document, and as we learn over and over again, there is no good way for anyone to organize documents into directories within document repositories that everyone will understand.

As many of us have seen, directory structures and naming conventions are simply not suitable for stakeholders that may have alternate terms for and ways of viewing the subject matter being stored, especially when considering the use of alternative languages.

To avoid the mass confusion so often caused by directory structures, the first place to start is to have just one place to store all documents. While this may seem odd at first, by eliminating the need to organize content into a confusing directory structure and then hope that stakeholders can guess the correct directory, we will have removed the first obstacle toward achieving a practical approach to document management.

Now we need to avoid the mass confusion so often caused by naming conventions that we have relied on in the past. Instead, let's decide to rely upon a well-developed ontology that addresses the needs of the various stakeholders, which include:

- architects,
- project managers,
- application developers,
- legal,
- financial compliance,
- regulatory compliance,
- HR compliance,
- IT compliance,
- auditors,
- CFO,
- CIO,
- COO, and
- CEO.

The ontology of architecture standards and frameworks is relatively finite. It consists of a number of hierarchical taxonomies that include:

- architectural disciplines,
- business capabilities,
- departments that are accountable to adhere to standards,
- stakeholders across the organization whose interests that standards and frameworks protect,
- legislative jurisdictions and their associated legislation, and
- pertinent regulatory agencies.

As examples, the taxonomy of legislative jurisdictions consists of a top-down hierarchy of:

- treaty zone,
- country,
- subordinated municipalities,
- legislative acts,
- their sections, and
- citations.

However, a taxonomy of architectural disciplines may consist of a hierarchy as defined by the sections and subsections of this book.

Once the taxonomies of the architecture standards and frameworks ontology have been defined, the modern view of an architecture repository consists of handful of major capabilities, starting with an administrative capability to manage the taxonomies and their translation into a set of languages.

4.1.3.9.1 Administration
The objective of the administration function is to identify the various stakeholders and the taxonomies that can be applicable to an architectural standard or framework. The tags associated with each of the taxonomies must be carefully managed to include an easy to understand hierarchy of tags that can be associated with pertinent documents and then subsequently used to search with.

4.1.3.9.2 Document Development
The second major capability supports the document development. One of the objectives of standards and frameworks is to represent the interests of stakeholders from across the company by incorporating their interests into the standard and/or framework. By the time the standard or framework is to go through the approval process, the tags associated with the taxonomies will be incorporated into the document corresponding to the interests of each of its stakeholders.

For example, if the company is required to report customer applications for credit by a set of ethnic categories, then the collection of such ethnic categories becomes part of the standards and frameworks for credit application specifications uniformly across the particular jurisdiction.

4.1.3.9.3 Approval Process
The third major capability is the approval process. Here, the subject matter experts of related architectural disciplines would evaluate the document for completeness and accuracy. The final approval would come from the Chief Enterprise Architect.

4.1.3.9.4   Production Use

The fourth major capability supports locating the desired standards and/or frameworks document by using the tags that the particular stakeholder can relate to best. These tags may be viewed in the language of the stakeholder's choice and will be translated into the tags associated with appropriate documents that have been stored in the architecture repository rendering those documents with an overlapping set of tags.

For example, a stakeholder knows that the document they are searching for belongs to a particular business capability within the company, and it must represent the interests of IT security and business compliance. Selection of these tags will render a list of all documents that have these tags associated with them, and then the stakeholder can either figure out which document is required by reading their descriptions or by providing a few more tags to further reduce the size of the returned set of standards and frameworks.

As such, the role of an architecture repository architect requires subject matter expertise in ontology and taxonomies, Big Data repository architecture, as well as the usage of standards and frameworks within and across a large organization.

4.1.3.10   Data Governance Dashboard

Given that data is a critical asset class of the company, data about the data and data about data governance can only contribute to better comprehending its condition and determine the priorities for improving it, protecting it, and managing it. The data governance dashboard is the focal point for determining and housing the metrics that help guide business decisions about data and data governance.

Useful metrics can be collected for better managing the capabilities associated with a business data glossary, data ownership, data access right administration, ETL data masking, canned report access, data stewardship, global data landscape data discovery, semantic modeling use cases, architecture component registry, and the sourcing of data from production, data scrubbing, data standardization, data integration, and rendering a useful ODS layer for business intelligence, data analytics, and management and regulatory reporting.

Within each of the abovementioned areas of data governance metrics can be used to continually improve upon the areas of data that are a priority to the business to better support its business strategy.

For example, data stewardship metrics can illustrate which applications and/or databases have the most numerous data quality and/or regulatory exceptions, and the trend that is associated with their remediation, such as the rate of increase or decrease of alerts being generated for the data steward.

4.1.4 DATA OBFUSCATION ARCHITECTURE

The scope of data obfuscation architecture includes business operations and nonproduction and production systems to protect business confidential and restricted data. This includes information about data subjects, such as customer and employee, and the ease with which access can be attained by unauthorized individuals.

This includes data obfuscation topics, such as:

- data access restrictions,
- data masking *(mentioned previously with regard to ETL)*,
- data encryption,
- data at rest (DAR), and
- DIM, as well as
- protection of business communications.

This also includes third-party partners and vendors, who must contractually agree to provide the same level of compliancy and security that the company must adhere to.

Data obfuscation architecture ensures that all unnecessary copies of data will be purged, controls and processes must support separation of duties, and access rights require maintenance by the appropriate resources with oversight from:

- legal,
- financial compliance,
- regulatory compliance,
- HR compliance,
- IT compliance, and
- Auditing.

Data obfuscation architecture works to protect the interests of various business stakeholders and regulatory bodies by conducting internal audits across IT, as well as mentoring and coordinating other architectural disciplines to incorporate the standards and frameworks that address the needs of various stakeholders.

For example, with regard to the appropriate use of social security numbers, the following information can be viewed on the US Government GAO Web site (*Use of Social Security Number is Widespread*, GAO document number: GAO/T-HEHS-00-111, p. 7).

> Federal laws, specifically the Internal Revenue Code and regulations governing the administration of the personal income tax system, require social security number to be disclosed in all reporting to the IRS. As a result, customers who receive income from corporations, and employees of corporations that are residents or maintain citizenship in the U.S., must disclose their social security number to facilitate compliance with federal law.

Federal laws that require their use for the statutory purposes regarding income reporting also place limitations on the use of social security number. Specifically, they stipulate that social security numbers are to be confidential with both civil and criminal penalties for unauthorized disclosure.

Although States are permitted by federal law to use social security numbers for broader purposes, such as for public assistance, owning a vehicle, or operating a vehicle, they are not permitted to disclose social security numbers without proper authorization from the individual, and some States have legislated that public assistance cannot be restricted to individuals that fail to provide a valid social security number.

Within the nongovernment sector, there are a few forms of external disclosure of social security numbers that are sanctioned, such as when sharing or requesting information with credit bureaus, or buying and/or selling social security numbers when those social security numbers were acquired legally from either public and nonpublic sources.

The entities that currently make use of social security numbers for purposes other than income reporting include: lawyers, debt collectors, private investigators, and automobile insurers, and placing additional restrictions on social security number use may reasonably hamper their ability to function.

In addition, the following information can be viewed on the US Government Web site (*Social Security Online*, SSA Publication No. 05-10093, October 2006, p. 1). Victims of identity theft, domestic abuse, or other specified crimes can get new social security numbers, resulting in an individual having two social security numbers associated with them. As a result of this condition, a decision has to be made whether to support the possibility of a second social security number retiring the first number. Advice from experts indicates that while it may be important to support a second SSN, it is equally important to never link the first and second SSN together in any form that may be disseminated outside the organization, particularly over the phone by customer service.

The general challenges with social security number are that: SSN lacks checksum/ check digit validation; with a billion possible numbers and a population of 300 million, the chance of entering someone else's SSN is one in three; and an SSN is difficult to validate when it is not provided for employment purposes.

There are also additional restrictions regarding the appropriate use of social security numbers at the state level.

For example, California has the most restrictive legislation regarding the use of social security numbers. The following information can be viewed on the California State Government Web site (*California Law Governing Use of the Social Security Number*, The Law: Civil Code Section 1798.85, p. 1).

The State of California prohibits any public display or communication of an individual's social security number, in any manner; use of SSN on any card that is required to access any products or services; transmission of SSN over the Internet without a secure connection or encryption; SSN to access an Internet Web site, unless also accompanied by another password or device; printing an individual's SSN on any material mailed unless required by State or Federal law; and encoding SSN on any card or document, whether visual or otherwise.

The same legislation identifies the allowable uses of SSN as follows: permits SSN to be collected, used, or released as required by state or federal law; permits SSN to be used for internal verification or administrative purposes.

The role of data obfuscation architect requires subject matter expertise in data governance, data masking, data encryption, DAR and DIM, legal requirements, and the stakeholders across the company including the regulatory bodies whose interests must be represented.

4.1.5 DATA MODELING ARCHITECTURE

The traditional view of data modeling begins with logical data modeling. Logical data modeling is a part of the SDLC for application development and was intended to minimize data redundancy with a database design process known as normalization. *It should not be confused with LDA which is a business artifact for organizing all data of the enterprise, regardless of whether it will participate in a database for automation.*

The intended benefit of achieving minimal redundancy was that it would simplify application logic by only having to maintain the business values of a given database column in one database table, as opposed to having to write application code to maintain its values across multiple database tables.

4.1.5.1 Conceptual Data Models

The somewhat less traditional view of data modeling begins with conceptual data modeling. Conceptual data models utilize a standard system of symbols that form a formal, although uncomplicated language that communicates an abundance of knowledge about the information being modeled. This uncomplicated visual language is effective for communicating the business users' view of the data they work with.

The system of symbols employed in conceptual data model borrows a number of the basic modeling constructs found in entity relationship diagrams (ERDs), containing entities, attributes, and relationships.

The characteristics of conceptual data models that are specific to it include the following:

- *The objective of the model* is to communicate business knowledge to any individuals who are unfamiliar to the business.
- *The scope of the model* is from the perspective of a business subject area of data, as opposed to the scope of an automation project, automation application, automation database, or automation interface.
- *The names of the objects in the model* are strictly restricted to language used within the business, excluding any and all technical terminology related to automation jargon.
- *Diagramming conventions* are that which emphasize what an individual can comfortably view and comprehend on an individual page.
- *Business data points* are simply associated with the data objects they would belong to and are not taken through the data engineering process called "normalization" to separate attributes into code tables.
- *Data abstractions,* such as referring to business objects in a more generic and general way, are not performed as they often lose the business intent and then become less recognizable to the business.
- *Technical details,* frequently found within ERDs, such as optionality and specific numerical cardinalities, are omitted.

The modern approach to conceptual data models is to incorporate them as a natural extension of the LDA. In fact, each conceptual data model should correspond to one business subject area of data and should be developed by business users who have been mentored by information architects to assist in the upkeep of the LDA.

4.1.5.2 Logical Data Models

Logical data models are more technical in nature and often represent the scope of the data for a particular automation effort or project. Logical data modeling belongs to the logical design phase as a data engineering step within the SDLC.

Logical data models also utilize a standard system of symbols that form a formal and rather uncomplicated language that communicates knowledge. That said, unlike an easy to read conceptual data model diagram, logical data models can look like the electronic schematics of your flat screen television and surround system.

The logical data model is effective however for communicating the designers' view of the information to business analysts on application development teams and to database administrators who will perform the physical database design phase.

Once the business analysts confirm that the logical data model meets all of the data requirements, the database administrator is then free to perform the physical design phase.

The characteristics of logical data models that are specific to it include the following:

■ *objective of the model*—to communicate to software developers a detailed form of data requirements to drive the database design,
■ *scope*—is typically from the perspective of an automation project, automation application, automation database, or automation interface,
■ *names of the objects in the model*—include technical terminology related to automation jargon, such as the use of the words (e.g., type, batch file, interface, and system control record),
■ *diagramming conventions*—often require technical specialists that have been trained to work with "bill-of-material" structures and "subtypes,"
■ *business data points*—are taken through the data engineering process called "normalization,"
■ *data abstractions*—such as referring to business objects in a more generic and general way is a frequent practice,
■ *technical details*—frequently found within ERDs, such as optionality and specific numerical cardinalities are required.

4.1.5.3 Normalization

Logical database design requires an engineering step called normalization. Normalization is a set of rules that, when represented in their original form as developed and presented by Ted Codd, are highly technical from a mathematical and engineering perspective. To spare the readers and author alike, we will simplify the presentation without losing the basic idea of each rule.

The starting point for data modeling is said to be a list of data points, often described as atomic data. The term "atomic" simply refers to the fact that each data point is an individual data item not consisting of any combination of data items.

As an example, address is not atomic because it consists of several component data items, whereas "address street name" is atomic.

The most important aspect about these atomic data points is that they must have accurate business definitions so that each of them may be well understood. Sample data and business rules should be analyzed during normalization to ensure that the data are understood. Hence, both the business meaning of the data and sample data values should be considered.

First Normal Form (1NF) identifies atomic data that must conform to the following: The atomic data points in a collection of data points must:

■ be associated with a single set of values that one would expect to encounter as only one occurrence of a thing.

For example, an occurrence of a bank account would have one "account open date," "account number," "account officer approval given name," "account officer approval surname," and "primary tax ID number." It could not have two or more "account open date," "account number," "account officer approval given name," "account officer approval surname," and "primary tax ID number."

- have no particular order or sequence for the data points in the collection.

    Whatever order the atomic data items are specified in, there must be no business meaning or importance associated with that order.

- have no business meaning based on the sequence of the records that occur.

    For example, the first three bank accounts that may exist have no business meaning relative to one another, as all three bank accounts are simply occurrences of three distinct bank accounts.

- have a set of business data points whose values identify a unique occurrence of said collection.

    For example, "account number" will uniquely identify the collection of atomic data point values associated with it, such as the "account open date" and "account officer approval surname" are associated with the unique account occurrence.

    The same "account number" cannot reappear as the unique identifier for the same or any other collection of data points about an account.

Second Normal Form (2NF) identifies data that is already in 1NF and additionally, the following:

The atomic data points in a collection of data points must:

- have no dependency on just part of the business data points that uniquely identify each record occurrence.

    If only one business data point uniquely identifies a record occurrence, then the collection is automatically in 2NF. If multiple atomic data points are needed to uniquely identify a record, then every atomic data point that is not among the unique identifiers must be dependent upon all of the business data points that uniquely identify a record.

    When dependencies exist on a subset of the data points that uniquely identify a record, then those data points must be separated into their own collection of data points with the subset of data points that uniquely identify a record to be in 2NF.

    For example, a product price cannot be in 2NF with the data points of "account number" and "product code" as their unique business identifiers because "product price" is only dependent on "product code."

Third Normal Form (3NF) identifies data that are already in 2NF and additionally, the following:

The atomic data points in a collection of data points must:

- have no dependency on any other data point that is not among the data points that uniquely identify a record.

When dependencies exist on any other nonidentifying data point, then those data points must be separated into their own collection of data points with the subset of data points that uniquely identify a record to be in 3NF.

For example, a product price cannot be in 3NF if it has a dependency on another data point, such as "repricing date" and be in 3NF. If the dependency exists, then the "product price" and the "repricing date" must be separated into its own collection to be in 3NF.

Often just the first three rules of normalization are performed, and very few people know that there are more than four rules of normalization. However, just to provide an easy way to remember all seven rules of normalization, they are as follows:

- 1NF Remove Repeating Fields or Groups
- 2NF Remove Non-Key Fields Dependent Upon Any Part of the Prime Key
- 3NF Remove Non-Key Fields Dependent Upon Other Non-Key Fields
- 4NF Remove Independent Multi-Valued Fields (i.e., multiple hobbies from a student record)
- 5NF Remove Associated Multi-Valued Fields (i.e., a teacher and student from a class record)
- 6NF Remove Fields Associated With Different Contexts (i.e., process, business)
- 7NF Remove Fields With Differing Security Levels

Additional Notes:

- Domain Key Normal Form (DKNF) a competing 6th NF
- Boyce Codd (BCNF) is a stricter 3rd NF

We should mention that 7NF is our personal favorite, probably because it is so obscure. In 7NF, data points that are associated with different security levels must be separated out into distinct sets such that there is uniformity of security levels within a given collection.

Seventh normal form is generally no longer required with the emergence of advanced data encryption technologies that are available in modern DBMSs and data communications hardware and software. It was developed out of a concern that someone would be able to access data points that were unclassified, but which were commingled with data points that were classified within the same collection. Even though the application program could have prevented the display or reporting of the classified data points, the concern was that someone could crash the machine and then the classified data points could be found within the dump of core memory from the crash.

4.1.5.4 Weaknesses of Normalization

There are *two* significant flaws of the normalization process. An easy way to understand these two flaws is through the following true story, where one of the most prominent Wall Street firms sent me to an excellent vendor administered course:

A class of 20 students had just completed a 4-day course in logical data modeling, where they learned the rules of normalization and the fact that these rules were part of a software engineering process that was based upon a sound mathematical foundation developed by Ted Codd—*someone I would become friends with a decade later*.

After having taken the same 4-day course in data modeling and normalization, 20 newly and rather well-trained data modelers sat at separate desks in the same classroom with ample space between each student.

In the afternoon of the final day, each student was given the same single page of "business requirements" describing an area of the business that needed automation and it needed a database for its data. All students were uniformly given the same number of hours to develop the logical data model that would support the requirements provided.

During the exercise, the students were allowed to ask questions of the instructor, but they did not have many questions as the exercise was so simple.

At the conclusion of the 2-hour exercise, the data models of all 20 students were collected and 20 copies were made of each of the data models collected from the students. Each student was then provided a copy of the data model developed by each student.

Upon reviewing the 20 data models, it was discovered that 20 different data models were developed from the same business requirements from 20 individuals that were uniformly trained.

The data model diagrams were simply not the same with merely synonyms of the terms, but instead, the models themselves, including the number of business objects, could not be made to match no matter how the entities were rearranged on the page.

We don't know what the reader thinks, but this doesn't sound like an "engineering process" to this author. Given this true story, it becomes readily understandable why so many people consider data modeling an art form as opposed to a science. However, they are wrong; data modeling is not an art form and we will explain why.

First, let's list all of the explanations that the students gave for their data models being different from one another.

The reasons offered included:

- each logical data model hypothetically supported the data needs to different degrees at the onset when the application would be initially developed,
- each logical data model hypothetically supported the data needs to different degrees into the future,
- each student interpreted the requirements differently,
- each student had different definitions of the data points provided,

- each student incorporated their varying degrees of knowledge about the business domain into the logical data model, and
- none of the students could follow instructions (this one was offered by the instructor).

If you were paying close attention you already know one of the two flaws of normalization. The first issue is that we already know that it is critical for data fields to have accurate business definitions so that each of them could be well understood. If the definition of a data field differs from one individual to the next, then its relationship to other data fields is likely to be different as well.

The students got this correct on their fourth point, "each student had different definitions of the data points provided."

What they didn't see, and what the instructor did not see, was that if the students were also provided a business data glossary complete with business metadata, they still would have had different logical data models, although the degree of variability would have been less, and from logical data modeling courses that we've taught, some of the models will come out identical or near identical.

However, there is one additional contributing factor that fundamentally plagues the normalization process, and it is called abstraction (aka generalization), where we have to consider how the brain works and how we learn.

4.1.5.5   Abstraction

Abstraction is the process by which we simplify the world around us. We take a collection of concepts and we chunk them together into a single concept, which makes it easier for us to think about things.

For a basic example, when we learn to drive, we learn to stop at the specific stop signs and red traffic lights along the route that the driving instructor takes us. We automatically abstract these stop signs and traffic lights into a single concept, so that we don't have to learn to stop at stop signs and traffic lights every time we encounter a new one.

In any form of modeling, such as logical data modeling, we encounter a variety of objects.

As examples, these may include:

- the company that owns a chain of sandwich shops, whose CEO is John, and President is Bob,
- its investors, including Joe and Rajiv,
- its customers, including Jean and Ted,
- its staff, such as Malcolm the sales clerk and Jim the sandwich maker, and
- Hank the driver of the truck that delivers bagels from the local bakery and Frank the driver that delivers milk from the dairy farm.

Depending upon the individual, these objects can be abstracted in several ways, such as the following:

- John, Bob, Joe, Rajiv, Jean, Ted, Malcolm, Jim, Hank, and Frank—representing the least abstraction possible,
- franchise owner, vendor, investor, staff, customer, and vendor contact—
- franchise owner, vendor, investor, customer, and staff—"vendor" representing the person from the vendor that represents a point of contact,
- franchise owner, vendor, and individual—"individual" representing investors, customers, and staff,
- company and individual—all companies can be abstracted together and all individuals can be abstracted together,
- party—all companies and individuals can simply be referred to as one concept.

We find through various sessions with logical data modelers, and anyone doing modeling, that the way in which concepts are abstracted or generalized contributes to significant differences in the way models are conceptualized in people's minds.

This does not mean that the rules of normalization are wrong, and it does not mean that they are an art form. What it does mean, however, is that the rules of normalization by themselves are incomplete.

As a result, to avoid the inconsistency found among data models, the rules of normalization must be preceded by the rules of data abstraction.

4.1.5.6   Rules of Data Abstraction

The rules of abstraction completely invalidate the arbitrary grouping of data points into collections based upon an individual's way of viewing the world. As such, the first step of normalization does not make any sense until after the rules of abstraction have been applied.

For ease of use, we will refer to the data points whose combination forms a unique identifier for a record as the "primary key" and collections of data points as "business objects."

The rules of abstraction are as follows:

- First Abstract Form (1AF) [*synonyms*] identifies business concepts for collections of data points (aka business objects) that must conform to the following constraints:

    Business object synonyms that share the same business definition should be abstracted together into the term that is most commonly used by business.

    For example, if the business definitions for "client" and "customer" are identical, then they can be combined into the business object referred to as "customer." If however the definitions differ, then the individual concepts cannot be merged together.

Second Abstract Form (2AF) [*time dependence*] identifies a business object that is already in 1AF and additionally the following constraints:

Business objects that represent the same underlying business object at different points in time, such as business objects that follow a life cycle, when sharing the same primary key data points should be combined.

For example, "applicant," "customer," and "deceased customer" share the same primary key data points and should be combined into the business object referred to as "customer."

If however they do not share the same primary key, such as "direct mailing prospect" and "customer," where "direct mailing prospect" has a primary key of name and address, and "customer" has a primary key of home telephone number, then the concept of "prospect" and "customer" cannot be combined.

- Third Abstract Form (3AF) [*essential dependence*] identifies a business object that is already in 2AF and additionally the following constraints:

Business objects that have different business definitions that are uniquely identified by the same primary key data points should be combined into the term that is most common for the joint collection of business objects.

For example, a long-term treasury and a common stock have different business definitions but both uniquely identify their occurrences by a CUSIP number. Therefore, these two business objects should be combined into the business object referred to as "financial security" or "financial product."

- Fourth Abstract Form (4AF) [*accidental dependence*] identifies a business object that is already in 3AF and additionally, the following constraints:

Business objects that combine other concepts that do not share the same set of business data points to uniquely identify them must be separated into their discrete individual business objects.

For example, "vendor contact" and "customer" cannot be combined into "party" as they do not represent an appropriate abstraction. The primary key data points for a vendor contact involve the contact's work address, work phone number, and business tax ID, while the primary key data points for the customer involve the customer's home address, home phone number, and social security number. These are clearly not the same business identifier.

4.1.5.7 Class Words

Another important note about abstraction applies to class words in logical data modeling. Class words are the terms added onto the end of the name of a data point (aka attribute) to indicate the type of data point it is, such as:

- quantity
- amount,

- price,
- frequency,
- percent,
- indicator,
- date,
- rate,
- rank,
- score,
- grade,
- name,
- code and
- description.

Some logical data modeling engineers choose to abstract class words into a simple set of class words, such as:

- number,
- text,
- alphanumeric,
- date, and
- code.

It should be noted, however, that like any vocabulary, the greater the number of distinct class words, the more useful it is for understanding what the data point actually is.

For example, the class word number reveals very little about a data point, whereas the following numerical class words reveal much:

- quantity—the number of things there are of a particular unit,
- amount—the number of things there are in a particular currency,
- price—the exchange rate of a thing as stated in a particular currency for trade,
- frequency—the number of events of something over a specific period of time,
- percent—the ratio of a thing relative to a hundred,
- dateyyyymmdd—the full year, month, day,
- dateyymm—the year and month,
- datetime—the full year, month, day, and time potentially to thousandths of a second,
- rate—the velocity of a thing in quantity per unit of time,
- rank—a number indicating the relative standing within a finite set of occurrences,
- score—the result of an assessment, usually regarding performance, or proficiency in a discipline of knowledge, which may be raw, weighted, and/or scaled to a mathematical function or model, and

■ grade—an assessment based upon one or more scores and type of scores that may precede an assigned grade indicating a level of overall performance and proficiency.

4.1.5.8 Logical Data Modeling Summary

Hence, the modern approach to data modeling differs in four important ways:

■ **First, a business data glossary establishes the appropriate business definitions for data points before data modeling activities can begin.**
■ **This includes business metadata that is defined by business users stated earlier so that a consistent and accurate definition can be understood by all "parties" involved.**
■ **Second, the use of the LDA.**
■ **The LDA provides the necessary business context within which to understand any given data point. Additionally, the conceptual data models that depict the data subject areas in more detail can provide a valuable source of related data points and any already known business object names.**
■ **Third, rules of abstraction provide a necessary method that transforms data modeling into an engineering discipline.**
■ **Although many enterprises have assembled teams of artists, it is important that they instead assemble teams of information engineers so that models contain properly abstracted business objects that create logical data models that have a high degree of consistency and stability over time.**
■ **The more representative and well formed a logical data model is, the less complex an application has to be in order to interpret and maintain the business data.**
■ **Fourth, class words are employed to convey the most information possible as opposed to being employed to require the least amount of effort possible to assign.**

4.1.5.9 Physical Data Models

Physical data models are the most technical of all the data models, and of the various entrance criteria that is associated with it before it can begin, the most important is the *transaction path analysis* (TAPA).

Physical database design is a set of tasks performed by the data base administrator (DBA) that requires an in-depth knowledge of the specific DBMS product and the physical environment of the database to determine the appropriate physical database structures and parameters that can best satisfy database performance requirements for one or more applications.

A DBA knowledge of the DBMS is analogous of a doctor's knowledge of medicine, and hence the patient that the DBA must analyze is the application programming.

The TAPA is analogous to the patient. The information that the DBA requires is information about the application because that is what will suffer if the physical database design is inappropriate.

The role of each of TAPA workbook is to concisely consolidate the various aspects of an application that the DBA needs to understand in order to competently perform their responsibilities.

The first two TAPA workbooks, "TAPA 01 Significant Transactions" and "TAPA 02 SQL Data Services," support the first step of the physical design process called "denormalization," which is an approach that trades improved performance for additional storage by replicating information in strategic ways.

> *Denormalization*—can only be performed after "normalization," which is a step performed during the logical design. "Normalization" is a set of rules, where the completion of each rule reduces the presence of data redundancy to save space, while "denormalization" is a set of techniques that cautiously increase data redundancy to meet performance-related service-level agreements.
>
> The valid types of denormalization are: (a) column denormalization, (b) table collapsing, (c) horizontal partitioning, and (d) vertical partitioning. All forms of denormalization share a common characteristic, in that each one causes the further redundancy of data in a calculated manner to improve performance for those transactions that require their performance to be enhanced.
>
> The transactions usually evaluated are those that are performed most frequently, for both retrieval and update, as updates are always impacted adversely by denormalization, while retrievals are sometimes impacted favorably. Hence, denormalization cannot be performed without knowledge of how selected transactions act upon the data, any more than one can realistically provide an answer, without first knowing the question.
>
> To truly appreciate what denormalization is, it is equally important to appreciate what it is not. As such, the goal of denormalization is not to enhance the clarity of a database design; foster an understanding of complex data structures; or reorganize, redesign, restructure, or reabstract a poorly designed data model. In contrast, these abovementioned activities are the indicators of a poor database design.

The "TAPA 03 SIGNIFICANT TRANSACTION DB TABLE USE" workbook identifies the sequence of lock placement and escalation, which is used to alert the DBA to the possibility and likelihood of potential deadlocking problems.

> *Deadlocks*—when two transactions place or escalate locks on resources they share and acquire in opposing sequences, they inadvertently create a condition

where each waits on one other to release their locks. When the DBMS detects that a deadlock has occurred, the only course of action available to it is to terminate one of the waiting transactions.

When deadlocks occur in rare or isolated circumstances, the approach of automatic termination and restart may go virtually unnoticed. However, when the circumstances for deadlocks are not so rare or isolated, as the number of users increase the DBMS can become surprisingly preoccupied with the overhead of terminating and restarting an ever-increasing number of transactions that never seem to complete, eventually overwhelming the available resources.

Although deadlocks can also stem from within transactions that are not high volume, complex, long running, or memory intensive, these deadlocks will occur in rare and isolated circumstances such that the automatic detection mechanisms of the DBMS can manage them.

The fourth TAPA workbook, "TAPA 04 DATABASE TABLES," helps the DBA determine database sizing and archiving requirements by identifying average row sizes, initial data volume, growth rates, data retention periods, and other aspects that have a "table" focus.

"TAPA 05 DATABASE USER AVAILABILITY" identifies the database availability profile for the users' online and batch business processing, "TAPA 06 DATABASE PROCESSING VOLUME PROFILE" identifies the processing profile for the time of day and periods of the calendar, and "TAPA 07 DATABASE PERFORMANCE SLA" identifies the service-level requirements of the application. Together, these three TAPA forms help the DBA determine the databases that can be colocated on a server or load balanced cluster.

The last TAPA workbook, "TAPA 08 DATABASE INSTANCES," identifies the various requirements for database instances in development, test, quality assurance, production, and production failover environments, such as size, access privileges, and firewall ports, and identifies databases that must share availability, high-level ETL requirements, and database backup and maintenance windows.

In order to provide the DBA the opportunity to perform their responsibilities, the DBA will need to understand the information that is organized into these TAPA workbooks. Each TAPA workbook encompasses its particular aspect of physical database design that helps ensure a high-quality product to support the various needs of the organization.

Each TAPA workbook is an integral part of the documentation capturing the physical database design requirements of the database used by the DBA to effectively support the various service-level agreements of the application.

To maintain the database SLA over the longer term, changes in the application and database will be routinely reflected in the corresponding TAPA as a part of the approval process for migration of each production release.

The data modeling department(s) of a large enterprise are at the heart of an organization IT automation capabilities. It is the single most critical function in any organization, as it can do the most damage long term to an enterprise's ability to understand its data assets.

That said, many large enterprises still operate under the old view of architecture and do not manage their logical and physical data modeling activities to the engineering level commensurate with treated data as a valuable asset class. In fact, the majority of large organizations neither adhere to rules of abstraction in their logical data modeling activities nor adhere to performing TAPAs in their physical data modeling activities.

The role of the data modeling architecture subject matter expert is to ensure that the appropriate standards and frameworks are addressed across the enterprise that treat data in its proper place as a valuable asset class across the enterprise.

4.1.6   RDM—Product Master Management

Given the growth strategy of corporate acquisition, it can be surprising how many products and services a large enterprise can accumulate, even from an individual acquisition. It is even common for large conglomerates to have a number of acquisitions and divestitures through the course of each year across the various countries in which they operate.

Additionally, it is also relatively common for a large enterprise to introduce new products and services through their new product development process, as well as to decommission products and services as a normal activity. As a result, it is often difficult to determine to accurately know at any point in time the products and services that are offered in each jurisdiction globally.

The compilation of an accurate inventory of the products and services offered by the company within each jurisdiction has business value to a number of stakeholders, such as sales and marketing, legal and compliance, accounting, product development, merger and acquisitions, executive management, as well as enterprise architecture.

The RDM subject matter expert coordinates the collection of product master management across the enterprise. They establish the relationships to the various stakeholders that have business needs for the information about products and services, and they frequently have access to every department of the company globally through data stewards and the application development teams within every country supporting them.

As examples, the business metadata for a product or service should include:

- jurisdictions where the product is being offered,
- original date when the product or service was offered within each jurisdiction,

- date when the product or service was no longer offered within each jurisdiction,
- product name within each jurisdiction,
- global product name,
- product description,
- the merger or acquisition that the product or service stems from, or the product development team that created the product,
- jurisdictions where the product was offered prior to a merger or acquisition,
- regulatory bodies that govern the sale and distribution of the product or service,
- distribution channels that are permitted to offer the product or service, and
- GL account that the product or service rolls up into.

The modern approach to enterprise architecture recognizes that each stakeholder of product and service master data most likely has a product hierarchy distinct to their business perspective to support their business needs. Once the business metadata has been determined, the RDM subject matter expert should record the product or service within the various product type hierarchies.

Examples of stakeholders with distinct product type hierarchies include:

- sales and marketing,
- accounting,
- auditing,
- financial business compliance,
- legal business compliance, and
- product servicing organizations.

4.1.7   RDM—CODE TABLES MANAGEMENT

The automation associated with various lines of business and the various business capabilities across a large enterprise frequently makes use of different codes that are intended to mean the same things, such as country codes, local jurisdiction codes, currency codes, language codes, and identifiers of legislation and regulator directives.

For example, country codes across different applications may use:

- two character International Organization for Standardization (ISO) codes,
- three character ISO codes,
- World Intellectual Property Organization (WIPO) two character country codes,
- telephone international country codes, or
- internally grown set of country codes.

Centralized code table management is an approach to improve the accuracy and consistency of codes across application systems and business stakeholders globally, and its business value is high.

In the absence of centralized code table management, applications frequently have code tables that are out of date creating adverse downstream effects on reporting that cause the organization to perform the same work over and over again.

BI reporting seeks to organize business activity from across many applications. Depending on where these applications were originally developed, and when they were developed, the codes used for their code tables will undoubtedly be a good degree of inconsistency across the application landscape. As data moves, however, from its origins to the various stages through its life cycle, its codes must sometimes be adjusted to match the target systems that serve as stops along the journey.

Data often moves from front office systems to back office systems as well as to reporting systems often referred to as middle office systems. When data moves into an ODS or data warehouse (DW), its codes are typically standardized to those being used in the particular ODS or data warehouse. As additional operational data stores and data warehouses are developed, the same types of standardization processes are conducted to comply with the code standards of the particular target database.

An RDM subject matter expert focused on codes tables in a large enterprise can easily identify well over a hundred externally acquired code tables that are purchased frequently redundantly across the enterprise. Once inventoried and coordinated, code table purchases can be centralized and notices of their updates can be passed to the areas that consume them for timely deployment. In fact, each code table has a life cycle.

For example, an emerging country may declare itself to the global community, and then gradually other countries begin to observe the new country until the country in which your company is headquartered recognizes it. Likewise, the former country becomes decommissioned.

The business capabilities of code table management include:

- adopting support for newly identified code tables being used in applications,
- adding support for a new code table,
- management of the contents associated with each code table,
- notification of code table changes to stakeholders,
- coordinating the adoption of new code tables and code table contents with stakeholders,
- dissemination of code tables and their corresponding updates to the various stakeholders, and
- the collection of metrics associated with the code table management process as well as with the adoption of code table updates across the data landscape.

The primary difference between the discipline of code table management and product master management is that code table management's first priority are the code tables that associated with external authorities outside the enterprise as well as internal codes for many organizations, especially those involved in manufacturing.

A more advanced form of code table management would seek to deliver analytical software that would scan application databases and application code to estimate and facilitate the adoption of a standard code table.

4.1.8 RDM—External Files Management

The discipline of RDM with regard to external files is similar to that of code tables in that there are files that may be routinely purchased by the enterprise from various external organizations.

These types of authorities are far greater in number than authorities for code tables, which is often limited to standards organizations, and often include:

- treaty zones—(e.g., EU),
- federal governments and associated state governments—national governments and their subdivisions,
- quasi-government agencies,
- industry groups,
- company that originates and sells its data,
- data reseller that gathers data external to itself and then resells it,
- international organizations,
- nonprofit organizations.

A small portion of examples of authorities include:

- A.M. Best,
- Bank of Canada,
- Bank of England,
- Dun & Bradstreet,
- Equifax,
- Experian,
- Fitch,
- Moody's,
- Morningstar, and
- United Nations.

External files RDM are distinct in the following ways:
They generally have a much greater:

- frequency of files,
- number of data points per record, and
- number of records per file.

The external files portion of RDM primarily supports business departments such as marketing, investments, and risk management.

4.1.9 DATA IN MOTION ARCHITECTURE

DIM architecture encompasses a handful of disciplines pertaining to the movement of data, including:

- data virtualization architecture,
- high-speed data streaming,
- ETL architecture—ETL and ELT,
- ESB architecture—enterprise service bus,
- CEP architecture—complex event architecture, and
- technologies such as rules engines, FTP, and XML.

The DIM architecture discipline is interactive with a variety of other architectural disciplines, such as data governance, data architecture, data obfuscation architecture, compliance architecture, data warehouse architecture, system recovery failover architecture, and DR architecture.

4.1.9.1 Data Virtualization Architecture

Not to be confused with virtualization within operations architecture, data virtualization is an architectural discipline that has been slowly expanding in functional capabilities and its frequency of use within large companies. While these technologies are often marketed as a having numerous use cases, such as a means to create a virtual ODS or data warehouse, there are actually few use cases that are practical when large amounts of data are involved, high velocity, or significant levels of data cleansing required. That said, they still offer a good deal of business value.

A valuable use case for data virtualization is for the rendering of data from a physical ODS layer or data warehouse to a mashup reporting platform (see Section 3.1.2.5). The data virtualization capabilities that are particularly valuable for this use case are the ability to perform LDAP lookups of users, correlate the individual's access rights with data access rights that have been designated to the individual's role or department, and then to automatically mask data as it is passed to the visualization component of the mashup technology to prevent unauthorized viewing.

Another use case that offers considerable value is that of handling database stored procedures in a data virtualization layer, as opposed to embedding them within the particular brand of DBMS. Placing data base stored procedures in the data virtualization layer provides complete flexibility to transition from one brand of DBMS to another.

4.1.9.2 ETL Architecture

ETL is a type of technology that is used to move data from one place to another with data manipulation capabilities that can convert the data into the format of the target location.

In fact, ETL effectively integrates systems that have different:

- DBMSs,
- data types,
- data values for code tables,
- data formats,
- data structures,
- operating systems,
- hardware types, and
- communication protocols.

Conventional ETL architectures encounter the problem of becoming overwhelmed with transformation overhead (see the below diagram).

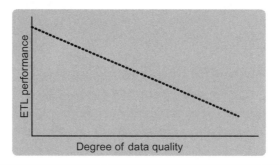

Diagram ETL performance with transformation overhead. (For color version of this figure, the reader is referred to the online version of this chapter.)

The modern ETL architectures provide approaches that facilitate sharding, where additional nodes can be added on to facilitate increased transformation overhead and volume.

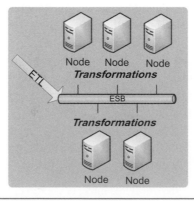

Diagram Modern ETL architecture and sharding. (For color version of this figure, the reader is referred to the online version of this chapter.)

Automation systems in large companies move massive numbers of records and data points from and to hundreds of databases daily using a variety of means, often including vast numbers of programs that have been written in many programming languages, file transfer utilities from various vendors, database product exports and imports, database utilities, XML, and ETL.

However, as the variety of tools moving data increases, the greater the complexity that results. It doesn't even take much complexity before all reasonable attempts to understand data movement across the data landscape of the enterprise is severely compromised.

A more modern view of ETL architecture eliminates this problem as well by standardizing the tooling used to manage all data movement across the data landscape to strictly ETL technologies with the key proviso that all ETL be centrally administered from the same ETL CASE tool.

The advantages of central administration are considerable. Use of an ETL CASE tool facilitates reuse of transformation specifications that have been recorded within the ETL CASE tool, thereby making it possible to generate consistent ETL code across an environment consisting of several different ETL products. Thus, ETL tools can be commoditized in a manner as effectively as with DBMS products that the industry has experienced with the use of database CASE technologies that can generate DDL associated with most any major brand of a DBMS.

These types of architectural decisions can significantly reduce the costs associated with data scrubbing by not incurring the costs associated with developing data transformation logic redundantly across the environment. Consistent transformation logic also provides business with more consistent results in reports by ensuring that conversions and numerical rounding factors are identical across each instance of ETL.

For information architecture, understanding data lineage is an essential first step toward simplifying the automation landscape of any environment. The modern approach involving central administration within an ETL CASE tool is one of the few approaches that can make data lineage reporting practical across the entire data landscape even when multiple ETL products are deployed.

The alternative suggested by the vendors still trapped in the past is to manually document data lineage in a tool that is separate from the technologies moving the data. This approach is not only redundant, but it is more costly to implement and maintain, not to mention impractical to expect that the informational content, never mind the constant flow of updates, could be reliably recorded to any meaning extent.

Intelligent standards and frameworks for ETL tool use are an integral part of a successful ETL architecture.

For example, a corporate standard that disallows ETL use when there are no data transformation requirements will create gaps in the reporting capabilities of data lineage across the data landscape.

Instead, not only should ETL be permitted, but it should also be encouraged and within a reasonable cost structure.

High-priced ETL products and high-priced administration of such products only serve to thwart their adoption across the enterprise. The key architectural characteristics are "distributed" and "open source" where possible. Paid versions will always be necessary when high volume and high data velocity are involved, but there are open source versions of ETL software for conventional databases as well as for Hadoop and HBase, as well as their paid full feature counterparts.

Examples of architectural touch points for ETL architecture include code table management, where nonstandardized code values bound for an ODS layer or data warehouse may be dynamically substituted with standard code table values, and data obfuscation, where data masking may be performed dynamically when production data is leaving the safety of the more rigorously controlled production environment.

4.1.9.3   ESB Architecture

ESB architecture is a discipline that facilitates uniform, flexible, and asynchronous communications across applications potentially residing on disparate operating system environments.

Although opinions of ESB services differ, the basic set of communications services provided by an ESB includes:

- routing, to identify the environment of the recipient application,
- transformation, for potential message format conversion,
- adaption, when the message must be transformed to or from the format of a non-standard service-oriented architecture protocol (SOAP) (e.g., standard protocols are SOAP/HTTP or SOAP/JMS),
- messaging, to transport the message to the environment identified,
- orchestration, to manage the flow of control from one ESB service to another,
- service registration, to inventory the ESB services available to applications,
- security, protecting the bus from intruders,
- consumer integration, allowing message consumers the ability to tell ESB services where to find them,
- service request validation, to enforce policies enabling secure service invocation,
- metrics monitoring, to measure performance variables, and
- B2B support, to allow communication services with external applications over a firewall.

The discipline of ESB architecture deals with the:

- application architectures that need to communicate through the ESB,
- environments upon which these applications depend upon,

- software and hardware infrastructures required to support the high-availability needs of the service bus, such as clustering and failover, storage requirements, and power and racking requirements, and
- appropriate testing and deployment procedures.

ESB architecture also has close cooperation with a variety of other architectural disciplines, such as directory services architecture, for identity management and LDAP registries; ETL architecture, for deploying ETL within the ESB; network architecture, for SSL certificate management; and IT compliance architecture.

4.1.9.4   CEP Architecture

CEP architecture involves a type of real-time business analytics based on event pattern detection techniques and event abstraction that is well suited for use cases requiring rapid situational awareness. From an artificial intelligence perspective, the information interpreted from the patterns of numerous event data is referred to as an event cloud. At any given moment, the event cloud contains business situations that have been inferred to exist at the moment that may warrant action.

The components of CEP include:

- use case discovery,
- event pattern determination,
- event hierarchy models,
- relationships between event hierarchy models,
- abstraction of business situations, and
- determination of a rapid response.

For example, the earliest use cases for CEP in the financial services industry included program trading when particular trading behaviors were detected.

CEP engines can:

- filter which events to pay attention to,
- store events in memory (aka windows) or databases,
- determine if new events are related to events that have been stored,
- identify missing events within time periods, and
- can perform database lookups and joins.

The CEP architect determines the appropriate standards and frameworks for managing the CEP life cycle and inventory of each of these components with traceability to their associated use cases. The modern approach to CEP architecture involves recording from a variety of systems the events detected and/or their abstractions over time so that real-time events may be observed simultaneously with historical time series data as a technique for learning from previous event patterns.

The role of information architecture in CEP is to manage the metadata associated with CEP rules and frameworks.

As such, the role of a CEP architect requires a broad combination of knowledge and cumulative experience in business and business applicable use cases, pertinent areas of artificial intelligence, application development, DR, and CEP standards and frameworks.

4.1.10   CONTENT MANAGEMENT ARCHITECTURE

Content management architecture encompasses the standards, frameworks, strategies, methods, and tools to capture, manage, store, preserve, and deliver content and documents related to organizational processes in both business and IT operations.

The types of documents involved are often unstructured, although they are actually semistructured. These include documents that have structured data, such as within their document properties.

As mentioned earlier, unstructured data refers to the types of data that do not have discrete data points within the data that can be designed to map the stream of data such that anyone would know where one data point begins and ends after which the next data point would begin.

Similar to the requirements of an architecture component repository for standards and frameworks, an ontology that supports the needs of stakeholders must be developed on a case-by-case basis so that the pitfalls of directory structures and naming conventions can be similarly avoided where possible.

Content management architecture subject matter experts tend to focus on the separation of capabilities to be handled by the appropriate technologies. For example, if the backend that stores the documents is IBM's FileNet or a Big Data repository of some type, then the front-end GUI can be Microsoft's SharePoint product or other GUI.

4.1.11   INFORMATION ARCHITECTURE—SUMMARY

Information architecture is a highly specialized area that is frequently inadequately addressed among large enterprises. We believe that part of the explanation lies with the fact that the scope of information architecture is frequently confused as being related to reporting architecture, which consists of a vast area of visualization, database, and data virtualization technologies for developing BI applications.

It not only contains many disciplines, but it is also an area that requires support from a variety of other architectural disciplines across enterprise architecture.

A lone information architect is certainly not a good thing to be unless you can systematically educate and inform the executive leadership team what a functional ecosystem looks like. I suggest you start by making analogies that illustrate a lone doctor, when what is needed are the many supporting disciplines of an inner city medical center.

The way we look at it, if information architecture was easy, then everyone would be doing it.

Part V

Control Systems

5.1 "Control Systems" Architecture and Governance

Few individuals get the opportunity in their career to work with both, information systems and control systems, never mind succeed in understanding both.

Information systems started when businesses needed to cut the manpower costs associated with doing intellectual tasks, such as bookkeeping and accounting. Essentially, information systems could perform most any tasks that could be performed by people using a paper and a pencil.

Although information systems have software drivers that operate hardware peripherals, those peripherals are always standard devices, such as printers, monitors, or an interface to an I/O substructure loaded with disk drives.

Control systems, on the other hand, started as a way for software to replace people to operate machinery. Today, control systems range from the simplicity of operating a beverage machine to operating a cruise missile, a B-2 stealth bomber aircraft, or even a human-like robot.

5.1.1 KEY DEVELOPMENT ISSUES

Through their development process, control systems necessarily have an emphasis on hardware. The events that they react to are environmentally driven within the physical world, their processing is real time, they are more often computationally intensive, they have few lines of software code, there have few data points, and the development environment of a control system is almost always radically different than their production target environment.

In contrast, information systems have an emphasis on software, their events originate with a man-machine interface, they have online and batch processing, they are more often I/O intensive, there is usually large quantities of software in terms of lines of code and layers of software architecture, they have large numbers of data points, and their development environments are similar or identical to their target production environment.

5.1.2 ANALYSIS ISSUES

Regarding the analysis portion of their respective system development life cycles, control systems require modeling of the entire system including hardware. They have a process-oriented focus with heavy process modeling and control modeling component, and they have little or no man-machine interface.

Information systems analysis focuses upon modeling just the software containing the business rules that are built into the application components, thereby excluding analysis functional analysis of hardware and infrastructure software, such as operating system, database management system, and network and security software. There is a preponderance of data architecture and data modeling, and they have a significant man-machine interface.

5.1.3 SYSTEM DESIGN ISSUES

Regarding the system design portion of the systems development life cycle, control system responses are always time critical. Any degradation that must be tolerated must be graceful (i.e., control systems do not roll back transactions, roll forward transactions, or dump system memory to a file or a printer). They usually do not have the notion of a transaction, and their error handling is all about keeping the system operational. The system environment is physically centralized and is typically equipped with a variety of sensor devices that generate streams of I/O.

Information systems in contrast focus upon data integrity as the single most important priority. Rollback and recovery are required to protect data integrity. Transactions and logical units of work are essential concepts. They require error handling to protect each unit of work. Information systems are often distributed, and the I/O devices range between man-machine interfaces or databases with large assortments of data points.

5.1.4 IMPLEMENTATION ISSUES

Regarding implementation issues, control systems have custom designed and developed operating systems and I/O drivers, with an emphasis on algorithmic solutions that are sometimes instantiated within hardware.

Information systems employ commercial off the shelf (COTS) operating systems, sometimes open source operating systems (e.g., Linux), middleware (e.g., JBOSS), COTS database management system software, sometimes open source database management system software (e.g., Hadoop, HBase), security software, network operating systems, programming languages, and Web-based infrastructure.

5.1.5   TEST ISSUES

Regarding test issues, control systems have a variety of program-specific integration and test environments including host-based test beds, real-time closed loop test beds, real-time open loop test beds, and operational testing in a simulated environment.

Information systems often have program-independent unit test, integration test, user acceptance, and stress testing environments, as well as occasional additional environments, such as an emergency test environment to troubleshoot production without directly impacting the software development life cycle environments.

5.1.6   COST ISSUES

Regarding cost factors, control systems employ product-specific materials, extensive labor requirements for development, and test deployment, development of program-specific integration and test environments, and manufacturing units of the system.

Information systems, on the other hand, have for each release systems analysis and design costs, software development labor, testing labor, and labor to maintain and support the application.

5.1.7   PROFIT AREAS

The profit area for control systems is hardware unit production with breakeven usually 3 years after deployment.

Information system profit areas are numerous including profits generated for services rendered for the systems development life cycle, user support agreements, software support, maintenance, and software licensing potentially involving participation in the business profits.

5.1.8   ARCHITECTURAL ISSUES

The architectural artifacts and architectural disciplines of control systems and information systems are significantly different than one another. Even though objects in control systems are from the tangible physical world and information system objects are from the intangible intellectual world, the one thing they can share is an object-oriented approach to analysis, design, and implementation.

The application architecture for error handling is perhaps the most unsettling aspect to developers from the other system paradigm. On one hand, you don't want a billion dollar aircraft falling out of the sky because it decided to perform a memory dump, but on the other hand, you also don't want zero divide errors gracefully handled by explicitly being ignored in a global money transfer system.

We've only briefly covered the differences of controls systems and information systems mostly because this book would double in size if we addressed the architectural disciplines of control systems in the manner that we have done so for information systems.

Operations
Architecture

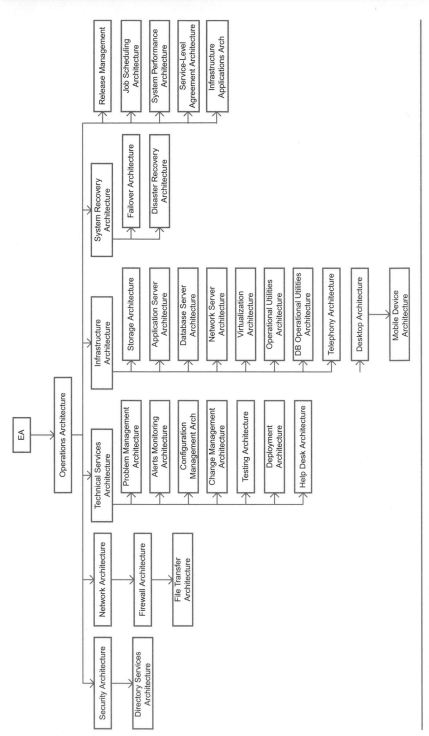

Part VI

Diagram Operations architecture overview.

■ 6.1   Operations Architecture and Governance

A common global operating model for operations systems architecture and governance is one where there are three major regions each with a regional data center supporting an associated federation of local country data centers that must be maintained due to regulatory prohibitions on transmitting customer information outside the jurisdictional borders of those countries.

As of the publication of this book, the countries with restrictions already implemented include:

- Albania,
- Andorra,
- Argentina,
- Australia,
- Bosnia and Herzegovina,
- Canada,
- Chile,
- Croatia,
- all European Union (EU) member states,
- Hong Kong,
- Iceland,
- Israel,
- Japan,
- Liechtenstein,
- Macau,
- Macedonia,
- Mauritius,
- New Zealand,
- Norway,
- Paraguay,
- Peru,
- the Russian Federation,
- South Korea,
- Switzerland,
- Taiwan,
- Tunisia,
- United Arab Emirates (UAE),
- United States, and
- Uruguay.

The trend is abundantly clear as many other countries are also pursuing privacy legislation with many already in their legislative process, with none considering relaxation of their customer privacy restrictions.

As a result, going forward the frameworks for regional data centers will necessarily need to accommodate the need to support many in country data centers, with transfers of data that mask the categories of data that are restricted by each jurisdiction.

That said, regional data centers still play an important role that supports the enterprise. In fact, having regional data centers helps:

■ provides support for shared services,
■ addresses the different time zones,
■ it mitigates a considerable part of the language differences and geographic differences, and
■ lends itself to a general familiarity with cultural differences and sensitivities.

When regional and in country data centers are coordinated, they may make better use of global purchases, licensing, and services, although some services, such as power and communications, will always be dependent upon local providers and their associated in country infrastructures, and the many challenges associated with them.

The opportunities for standards and frameworks for operations architecture are applicable to in country data centers. If anything, the emergence of additional in country data centers increases the need for operations architecture standards and frameworks to help avoid doing things differently in each country across the globe.

The products, licenses, and services that generally do not have a local dependency, and can be standardized globally, include:

■ directory services architecture,
■ job scheduling architecture,
■ infrastructure applications architecture,
■ infrastructure architecture,
■ telephone video architecture,
■ desktop architecture,
■ application server architecture,
■ database server architecture,
■ operational utilities architecture,
■ virtualization architecture,
■ release management architecture,
■ system recovery architecture,
■ failover architecture,
■ disaster recovery architecture,
■ system performance architecture,

- technical services architecture,
- problem management architecture,
- monitoring alerts architecture,
- configuration management architecture,
- change management architecture,
- help desk architecture,
- service-level agreement (SLA) architecture,
- network architecture,
- firewall architecture, and
- file transfer architecture.

As such, the role of an operations architecture subject matter expert requires a broad combination of knowledge and cumulative experience in operations and governance disciplines involving various degrees of the above mentioned areas of architecture.

We will now briefly touch upon a collection of operations architecture disciplines mostly just to define the scope of their responsibility.

6.1.1   DIRECTORY SERVICES ARCHITECTURE

Directory services architecture is a discipline that develops the standards and frameworks for the capabilities used to organize and manage access rights of business users and IT resources to the applications, files printers, networks, and servers of the enterprise.

Unlike the traditional approach which is department centric, the objective of the modern framework is to optimize maintainability of LDAP with the level of granularity to manage the groups of individuals and resources at the business capability level, as well as within specific roles within those business capabilities.

A well-architected directory services business capability is able to effect additions, removals, and changes in access rights across the organization in minutes with a centralized workflow without error, as opposed to weeks with unforeseen complications and errors.

To achieve this, standards and frameworks must be made consistent across the enterprise, often requiring a transition plan that begins by gaining an understanding of the blend of architectures and cultures of administration that exist across the various directory services repositories.

Similar to disaster recovery architecture, the items that must be inventoried include:

- business capabilities,
- applications,
- technologies,
- equipment that support those business capabilities,

- use cases for directory services, and
- services offered by directory services with their related request types.

As such, the role of a directory services architect requires a broad combination of knowledge and cumulative experience in developing standards and frameworks of a directory services capability in a large conglomerate; the challenges of directory services; common traditional architectures and cultures of administration; and the business capabilities, applications, and technologies of the company.

6.1.2   JOB SCHEDULING ARCHITECTURE

Job scheduling architecture is an architectural discipline within operations architecture and governance that is responsible for the standards and frameworks to support a unified, centrally administered job scheduling capability across all computing platforms within a data center.

It is also a discipline that assesses, plans for, and monitors the implementation of a uniform job scheduling framework that illustrates the health of operational activities and provides simulation capabilities for changes being introduced into the job stream and run book.

When evaluating the current state of a large enterprise, one may find that there are several disparate methods being used to schedule the execution of a job.

As examples, job can be started:

- manually, or
- automatically by job scheduling capabilities provided in
  - applications,
  - database management systems (i.e., a number of which are mini operating systems),
  - online transaction processing systems (e.g., OLTPs, a number of which are mini operating systems),
  - operating systems, or
  - standalone job schedulers.

The use of more than one job scheduling product or more than one method of scheduling jobs creates additional complexity, cost, and risk. Operations staff and their backup staff must possess knowledge and experience for each brand of job scheduler, causing more redundancy in staff than is typically required, with additional challenges in rotating personnel.

In contrast, a centralized job scheduler is the only approach that provides an ability to coordinate activities across all platforms using automation. The high-end job schedulers have a number of advanced features, such as facilitating simulations to test the impact of proposed job scheduling changes and impact analysis for what-if scenarios.

The common architectural features that should be evaluated across job schedulers include the ability to support:

- the full set of operating system environment required for your company,
- workload planning,
- modeling,
- forecasting,
- a high degree of fault tolerance,
- Web-based consoles,
- storing and transferring scripts to target platforms,
- event driven scheduling to eliminate wait times as opposed to clock based,
- install agents on every platform to communicate back to the scheduler,
- flexible user operating system accounts to avoid having excessive access rights and privileges than is necessary,
- file events to be able to initiate a job at the creation of a file as opposed to polling,
- file transfer capability to retain control when a file transfer fails,
- role based security administration, and
- full development life cycle support to:
  - develop,
  - test,
  - approve, and
  - deploy changes.

6.1.3 INFRASTRUCTURE APPLICATIONS ARCHITECTURE

Data center operations are so different than typical business applications and IT management applications that infrastructure applications architecture is best as a separate architectural discipline within operations architecture responsible for technology portfolio management, application portfolio management and application architecture for technologies, and applications that are specifically for the use within an operations environment. As a matter of fact, data center staff usually has a completely different culture. From what I've experienced, it is perhaps closer to the culture found working in a firehouse of a major city with a much higher degree of camaraderie and a detectably lower level of political correctness. These are real people that get right to the point without delay because they need to in order to keep their data center running. If you are thin skinned and intolerant of stress, OPS may not be the ideal career choice.

Unlike information systems applications, operations applications neither access business data nor support legal or regulatory reporting requirements, and as such, are best overseen by an individual with an extensive operations background.

As a result, applications that are operations based tend to be major technology purchases or applications that address gaps in operations automation to support any given operations capability.

While it is generally not acceptable for an operations area to have a software development capability, it should be noted that operations applications would not have access to business databases and business files, nor should they.

6.1.3.1 Infrastructure Architecture

Infrastructure architecture is responsible for the standards and frameworks for infrastructure specifications for automation systems and their components across all regional and in country data centers of the enterprise, including:

- production,
- failover,
- disaster recovery, and
- nonproduction environments to optimize the delivery of services for the best cost structure with flexibility and maintainability.

Many large companies outsource their data center's hardware deployment and maintenance, while still retaining control over platform configurations to ensure the appropriate computing capacity to support the needs of the application systems in the various parts of their life cycle.

> *Note that you should always negotiate to retain control over the design of platform configurations. Of course the vendor will make sure that you will have to pay for whatever you select, but that is what will keep your folks from building computing platforms that will outperform HAL 9000.*

Also, the fact that hardware deployment and maintenance may be outsourced does not in itself negate the need to manage infrastructure applications architecture. The vendor is your partner and improving the operational capabilities is just another role that must be negotiated in your outsourcing agreement.

The best outsourcing agreements are those that reward the vendor for implementing improvements in your operations. Just note that the only reasonable method to ensure verifiability of improvements is the appropriate identification and collection of metrics before and after.

6.1.3.2 Telephony Video Architecture

Telephony video architecture is responsible for the standards and frameworks involving the infrastructure and components across the globe involving:

- teleconferencing,
- video conferencing,

- internal and external company telephone systems, and
- multimedia technologies.

Deployment of telephony equipment for new hires is an ongoing process in every large organization. This architectural discipline has synergies with compliance architecture, particularly with regard to the records of telephony equipment and its potential for being involved in legal matters.

6.1.3.3   Desktop Architecture

Desktop architecture is responsible for the standards and frameworks involving the infrastructural components for desktop and portable computing across the globe involving:

- hardware,
- software, and
- accessories, including:
    - virtualization components that may be required to support capabilities.

This includes the processes that establish, maintain, and decommission components efficiently across the enterprise, particularly while maintaining an accurate inventory of deployed components, their versions, and any applicable metadata.

Deployment of desktop equipment and the required refreshes for aging equipment is an ongoing process in every large company. This architectural discipline has synergies with data obfuscation architecture, particularly for the encryption of data held on the hard drives, and compliance architecture, particularly with regard to the decommissioning of equipment and its potential for being involved in records information management and legal holds.

6.1.3.4   Operational Utilities Architecture

Operational utilities architecture is an architectural discipline within infrastructure architecture that specializes in the standards and frameworks involving utility components, such as adapters, drivers, DLLs, and print utilities.

The role of an operational utilities subject matter expert requires a broad combination of knowledge and cumulative experience in developing the standards and frameworks to support operational utilities, including their selection, testing, upgrades, decommissioning, and their appropriate participation in configuration management for use in disaster recovery and system decommissioning.

6.1.3.5   Virtualization Architecture

Distinct from "data virtualization architecture" within information systems architecture, "virtualization architecture" is responsible for the standards and frameworks associated with operation-related technologies that can be virtualized, including software, such as VMware and Citrix, or hardware, such as storage virtualization (e.g., block virtualization, file virtualization, and disk virtualization), virtual desktop, and virtual memory.

With the advent of cloud computing, entire data center virtualization is a viable option for many organizations to consider.

6.1.4 RELEASE MANAGEMENT ARCHITECTURE

Once application systems are deployed into production, they can be functionally stable with few maintenance or enhancement requests, or they can be dynamic, rapidly evolving application systems potentially using agile development.

Release management architecture is responsible for the standards, frameworks, principles, and policies for planning the implementation of new versions, integration testing, user training, help desk training, user acceptance testing, defect management, and production deployment.

Release management architecture cooperates closely with the disciplines of life cycle architecture, configuration management architecture, change management architecture, and disaster recovery architecture.

6.1.5 SYSTEM RECOVERY ARCHITECTURE

System recovery architecture is responsible for the standards and frameworks for system recovery involving each type of technology across each type of operating system environment, typically including:

- z/OS,
- Windows,
- Novell, and
- UNIX.

As well as each type of platform, such as:

- tablet,
- smart phone,
- desktop/portable,
- Intel box, or
- mainframe.

This architectural discipline serves to assess, plan for, and monitor the design of standard recovery capabilities, failover and disaster recovery for the various types of environments deployed globally across an organization. Its specialization and scope is such that it is comprised of failover architecture and disaster recovery architecture.

6.1.5.1   *Failover Architecture*

Failover architecture is responsible for the standards and frameworks associated with failover of applications and infrastructure technologies involving the various types of components that comprise automated capabilities.

At a high level, there are a number of options for the recovery of an application system or technology.

First is the option of "no failover," which is appropriate for business capabilities that can incur an indefinite delay for recovery without significant cost or risk to the company.

Second is the option "cold failover," which is appropriate when the SLA involving the window of recovery fits the time required to restore database and application server from the backups, including the process of applying the transaction journals and rollbacking incomplete units of work.

Often such an environment is not dedicated, but compatible with the environment being recovered, including networking. This option provides failover ranging from days to weeks, depending upon the number of application systems being recovered.

The third option is a "warm failover," where a dedicated environment is ready, backups have already been applied, and the tasks that remain are simply the process of applying transaction journals, rollbacking incomplete units of work, and potentially manually switching the network over to the new environment.

This option provides failover ranging from hours to days, depending upon the number of application systems being recovered.

The fourth option is a "hot failover," also known as high availability (HA) failover, which generally has three levels associated with it. Potentially, a hot failover may use HA clustering and a low latency messaging technology to keep its alternate configuration current with active-active and active-backup, or both.

The three levels associated with "hot failover" are:

- HA hot-cold,
- HA hot-warm, and
- HA hot-hot.

6.1.5.1.1   HA hot-cold

The first "HA hot-cold" has a dedicated system already synchronized including its application and data, but requires relatively simple manual intervention, such as having a second gateway server running in standby mode that can be turned on when the master fails.

This option provides failover ranging from minutes to hours, depending upon the number of application systems being recovered.

6.1.5.1.2 HA hot-warm

The second "HA hot-warm" has a dedicated system already synchronized including its application and data, but requires the slightest manual intervention, such as having a second gateway server running in standby mode that can be enabled when the master fails.

This option provides failover ranging from seconds to minutes, depending upon the number of application systems being recovered.

6.1.5.1.3 HA hot-hot

The third is "HA hot-hot," which has a dedicated system already synchronized including its application and data, but requiring no manual intervention. This is accomplished by having a second gateway server actively running simultaneously.

This option provides immediate failover regardless of the number of application systems being recovered.

6.1.5.1.4 Fail back

One additional failover strategy that exists is referred to as a "fail back," which is the process of restoring a system to its configuration corresponding to its state prior to the failure.

6.1.5.2 Disaster Recovery Architecture

Disaster recovery (DR) architecture represents the technology side of business continuity architecture. While business continuity is responsible to identify business capabilities, and the applications and technologies upon which they are dependent from a business perspective, disaster recovery takes it to a greater level of detail from an IT perspective.

Behind the scenes of automation, applications and technologies are dependent upon a myriad of application, database, and hardware and software infrastructural components, which only IT would be qualified to identify in its entirety.

The standards and frameworks of disaster recovery extend into standing up a disaster recovery capability, its regular testing, and cooperation with IT compliance to make disaster recovery standards and frameworks available to regulators.

Although it is obvious that the more holistically a company approaches disaster recovery architecture, the better it is actually by having an appropriate set of subject matter experts looking out for their specialized area of interests that makes it holistic.

For example, the disaster recovery architecture must cooperate closely with nearly all of the other enterprise architectural disciplines, including:

- technology portfolio architecture,
- infrastructure architecture,
- network architecture,
- firewall architecture,
- application and database server architectures,
- data in motion architecture,
- operational utilities architecture,
- application architecture,
- reporting architecture,
- workflow architecture,
- failover architecture,
- configuration management architecture,
- release management architecture,
- compliance architecture, and
- SLA architecture.

This will help ensure that the synergies among the architectural disciplines are being appropriately identified and integrated into their corresponding standards and frameworks.

Any operating environment that cannot be virtualized, such as certain technologies that cannot be stood up in a VMware environment, must have dedicated equipment where every last DLL and driver must be replicated in a disaster recovery site before the particular system can successfully be made operational.

The enterprises that look at disaster recovery most holistically realize the tremendous benefit that mainframe applications enjoy by greatly simplifying the majority of disaster recovery issues. In fact, it is easier to recover an entire mainframe in a disaster recovery scenario than it is to just identify the sequence in which hundreds of application systems across a distributed environment must be recovered to optimally support the business priorities for just a single line of business.

Modern enterprise architecture also recognizes that disaster recovery that depends upon the fewest number of individuals, and their knowledge, is far more advantageous in an emergency environment that cannot predict which staff resources will be available.

6.1.6 SYSTEM PERFORMANCE ARCHITECTURE

System performance architecture is responsible for the standards and frameworks for performance monitoring plans, technologies, and procedures for each of the various types of components that comprise:

- an operating environment,
- application system,

- database management system,
- Big Data repository,
- BI reporting tools,
- deep analytics products,
- networks, and
- supporting infrastructure including the I/O substructure and resources of the computing platforms involved.

System performance architecture as a discipline involves a variety of information about hardware specifications, system capacity, system logs from a variety of component types, historical performance measurements, and capacity testing prior to deployment.

From our experience, very few large companies approach system performance correctly. Among the few are leading financial services companies who require that each new application be stress tested to its breaking point to determine in advance the maximum capacity that it can support.

The less effective alternative is to limiting capacity testing to levels that are believed to be the maximum number of users or transactions. When these guesses are wrong, the resulting surprises are rarely pleasant.

6.1.7   TECHNICAL SERVICES ARCHITECTURE

Technical services architecture is comprised of and oversees:

- problem management architecture,
- monitoring alerts architecture,
- configuration management architecture,
- change management architecture, and
- helpdesk architecture.

It develops the standards and frameworks for data center selection and management, data center supply and installation, and data center infrastructure including power, heating, and air conditioning, as well as fire prevention and suppression systems.

6.1.7.1   Problem Management Architecture

Problem management architecture collaborates closely with incident management, which is responsible for resolving incidents reported into a help desk.

In contrast, problem management architecture determines the standards and frameworks associated with retaining history and analyzing causes of incidents, including their trend analysis, to determine if there are patterns and correlated events that are at the root cause of incidents so that solutions may be developed to minimize or eliminate them, both in production and prior to production.

For example, with the proper frameworks in place, problem management in a large enterprise is likely to determine that a greater proportion of resources within their incident management departments are spent on addressing issues with Linux, as compared to UNIX, Windows, and z/OS.

This type of business intelligence should cause mission critical systems to choose UNIX rather than Linux, and it should cause them to factor in a higher level support costs for Linux within infrastructure architecture.

The role of a problem management subject matter expert for a large enterprise requires a broad combination of knowledge and cumulative experience in incident management and problem management, with familiarity across the broad spectrum of automation tools and disciplines to properly identify the architectural disciplines that should be engaged for each type of incident.

Collaboration with numerous other architectural subject matter experts will provide valuable cross training to a problem management architect. Given the quantities of data that can be involved, two areas of close collaboration should be with Big Data and BI reporting architecture.

6.1.7.2 Monitoring Alerts Architecture

Monitoring alerts architecture is responsible for standards and frameworks associated with monitoring business applications and infrastructural systems including policies regarding alert notifications to notify the appropriate operational areas as early as possible.

Monitoring alerts architecture collaborates closely with problem management architecture to centrally record all problems detected through automation and those detected manually that were routed through the help desk.

Early alerts may require support from CEP and artificial intelligence architecture. This discipline also provides direction on tools and technologies that can best support monitoring capabilities, the detection of issues, and the routing of alerts to appropriate stakeholders.

As such, the role of a monitoring alerts architect must understand logs and journals generated automatically by:

- operating systems,
- database management systems, and
- communications software.

Alerts architecture also collaborates closely with Big Data architecture involving technologies, such as Splunk, as one of the first Big Data business intelligence tools specializing in analyzing collections of automatically generated logs.

6.1.7.3 *Configuration Management Architecture*

Configuration management architecture is responsible for the standards and frameworks associated with uniquely identifying the complete set of components associated with a version of a system using an ontology pertinent to the components and their life cycle.

Configuration management is responsible for safekeeping the components that belong to a configuration in a repository, including status reporting of their life cycle, and their migration through environments that participate in that life cycle.

Essentially, configuration management acts as a procedural firewall between development resources and the movement of software assets through the development/deployment life cycle to production.

The one thing that we have observed that has never failed is that when organizations allow developers to migrate fixes into production themselves without following a prudent configuration management process, things happen and they are not always good.

In the modern view, configuration management architecture aims to provide complete transparency of configuration content and their movement through the development life cycle for each iteration, version or release.

Configuration management architecture collaborates closely with:

■ change management, which determines what components and functionality will be developed and in what sequence;
■ quality assurance and user acceptance testing, which determines the appropriate level of testing and whether the components meet the documentation and operational requirements to make it to the next step within their life cycle;
■ migration control, which identifies and manages the migration of a complete configuration to the next environment within its life cycle; and
■ production turnover, which turns over all system components and their associated documentation, deploys the configuration into production, and conducts a go/no go review by all stakeholders to determine whether the production deployment goes live or is backed out.

6.1.7.4 *Change Management Architecture*

For a useful definition of change management, "change management is the coordination of introducing new components, updating existing components, and removing decommissioned components associated with transitioning from one configuration of a system or application to the next iteration" and the impact of that transition.

Change management architecture (aka product management architecture) collaborates closely with configuration management architecture, to manage the components that belong to an iteration of a configuration.

In the modern view, change management architecture aims to provide complete transparency of component changes in each iteration, version or release. Change management is responsible for the standards and frameworks for determining the components of a system that require management, their functionality, and their sequence of development and deployment, which is communicated to configuration management.

Change management is responsible for planning and identifying the functionality and system components of a product, and project management may negotiate to ensure the functional requirements and system components are appropriate for the time and budget that is associated with the agreed to product changes.

6.1.7.5   Help Desk Architecture

Help desk architecture is responsible for the standards and frameworks for all first level support that is provided to assist the following with any type of question, request, or problem related to automation, procedural, or operational topic:

- customers,
- vendors, and
- employees.

In the modern view, help desk architecture aims to provide complete transparency of incidents with BI metrics for all issues being reported from across the globe to provide the various architectural disciplines of enterprise architecture with a view of incidents related to their areas of specialization, regardless of whether the incident was handled by level one support or transferred to level two or three support.

The role of a help desk subject matter expert requires a broad combination of knowledge and cumulative experience in the various stakeholders and use cases that a global help desk capability would provide.

Collaboration with other architectural disciplines will provide valuable cross training to a help desk architect. In modern enterprise architecture, problem management architecture collaborates closely with the Chief Customer Officer, and the various architectural disciplines that are associated with each category of help desk stakeholder and use case.

6.1.8   SLA ARCHITECTURE

SLA architecture is responsible for establishing the standards and frameworks associated with service levels for each business capability, including the capabilities provided by the various areas associated with IT.

This requires that the services offered by each business capability are clearly understood, what their responsibilities and priorities are, as well as any commitments that have been made and must be made relative to them providing their services in compliance with standards within a specified range of time and cost.

The metrics associated with service delivery will vary depending upon the type of service, such as:

- metrics associated with automation services or equipment,
- mean time between failure (MTBF),
- mean time to repair or recovery (MTTR), or
- metrics associated with operational workflows, such as
  - time frame within which personnel will be assigned,
  - time frame within which a status will be provided, and
  - delivery of service completion.

In contrast, an operating level agreement (OLA) defines the relationship, coordination, and SLAs required among the various support groups that often must collaborate to address issues and outages of known and unknown origins.

The role of an SLA subject matter expert requires a broad combination of knowledge and cumulative experience in the business capabilities that are provided across the company globally, including IT, and vendors, especially outsourced IT operations vendors.

For example, it is experience with SLAs that creates awareness in subject matter experts that a percentage uptime SLA for a collection of systems as an aggregate is simply not as valuable as a percentage uptime SLA for each individual system.

This explains why outsourcing vendors only tend to offer SLAs for percentage uptime SLA for a collection of systems as an aggregate, as one problematic critical application can be statistically compensated for by 50 other stable applications.

6.1.9 NETWORK ARCHITECTURE

Network architecture is responsible for standards and frameworks for the various layers of communications networks, such as the seven open systems interconnection model, which includes:

- physical,
- data link,
- network,
- transport,
- session,
- presentation, and
- application layer.

These standards and frameworks address the types of networks, such as:

- local area networks (LAN) (i.e., under a kilometer),
- metropolitan area networks (MAN) (i.e., under a hundred kilometers), and
- wide area networks (WAN) (i.e., long distances over 100 km).

Network architecture includes their associated hardware, software, and connectivity within the facilities of the company and to external communications service providers, as well as plans for monitoring and assessing the various components and touch points to external service providers.

Not to be confused with use of the term "network architecture" when it pertains to the participating nodes of a distributed application and database architecture, this taxonomy of enterprise architecture refers to the application and database usage as "application and database network architecture."

6.1.9.1   Firewall Architecture

Firewall architecture is responsible for the standards and frameworks associated with the architecture of sub-networks (aka subnets), which are a subdivision of an IP or TCP/IP network that exposes the company's services to a larger untrusted network, such as the Internet.

Large companies use TCP/IP (i.e., transmission control protocol/Internet protocol) as the network protocol of choice, which is a protocol maintained by the Internet engineering task force (IETF) that organizes the functionality of the protocol into four layers specifying how data should be:

- formatted,
- addressed,
- transmitted,
- routed, and
- received at its destination.

For example, from highest to lowest, the layers of TCP/IP consist of the following:

- an application layer (e.g., HTTP),
- a transport layer (e.g., TCP),
- an internetworking layer (e.g., IP), and
- a link layer (e.g., Ethernet).

In firewall architecture, the architecture of subnets is used to create a DMZ, a term derived from "demilitarized zone," to create a perimeter of around and between the networks of the enterprise that could be vulnerable to attack from users outside the networks of the company.

The global architecture of these subnets has long-term implications to a company's ability to protect its networks while providing necessary access to support internal communications across data centers, company facilities, and vendors.

6.1.9.2 File Transfer Architecture

Unlike ETL which usually transports parts of databases within the same data center, file transfer architecture is responsible for the standards and frameworks for all methods of file transfer that are transported, such as FTP, SFTP, and AS2 to and from all data centers globally including all aspects of their approval process and security, as well as the use of digital signatures (e.g., PGP), SSL and various data encryption/decryption technologies, and high security certificates.

As a result, file transfer architecture collaborates with firewall architecture, infrastructure architecture, compliance architecture, data obfuscation architecture, and data governance.

6.1.10 OPERATIONS ARCHITECTURE—SUMMARY

Data centers care for and support the core machinery of the organization's automation. Operations architecture ensures that the data centers, and their corresponding IT infrastructures, support systems, and applications are made available to the various users and stakeholders in as consistent a manner as possible.

Some organizations, which require machinery to manufacture their products, truly have a deep appreciation of the role that the data center plays in the day-to-day survival of the organization. Other organizations that rely solely on the movement of data and information to support their financial activity are actually more dependent upon their data center operations than those reliant upon manufacturing, but often demonstrate less appreciation of the health of their data centers, without which they would not be able to conduct a stitch of business.

Cross-Discipline Capabilities

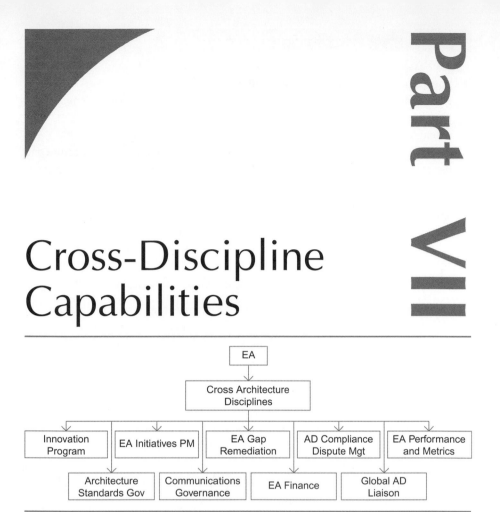

Diagram   Cross architecture discipline overview.

7.1   Cross Discipline Capabilities

Cross discipline capabilities are the collection of architectural disciplines within enterprise architecture that span business architecture, information systems architecture, control systems architecture, and operations architecture.

The business capabilities that span the architectural disciplines of enterprise architecture include the capabilities of:

- supporting an innovation program,
- project management for EA initiatives,
- detecting gaps across architectural disciplines and their remediation,
- management of application development team disputes with architectural disciplines,
- measuring performance of architectural disciplines,

287

- governing standards development and adoption,
- governing the development of architectural artifacts and global dissemination,
- governing global communication,
- managing finance across and within architectural disciplines, and
- providing a liaison as single point of contact between enterprise architecture and the global application development (GAD) team that supports the development needs of the enterprise architecture organization globally.

Essentially, cross-discipline capabilities are simply the shared services across the various architectural disciplines of enterprise architecture.

7.1.1 INNOVATION PROGRAM

The basic premise going into an innovation program is that it will facilitate a free exchange of thought as a marketplace of ideas that is equally fair to all participants. While the definition of fairness is going to vary somewhat among individuals, it should encompass a broad meaning that the overall majority of potential participants would agree with.

For example, some participants know how to communicate their thoughts effectively in an organized manner, while others clearly do not. In cases where the ability to write and express ideas may be a hindrance, the offer to extend the services of a coach or counselor may make the program fair to all potential participants.

This recognizes the simple fact that anyone can have an awesome idea, irrespective of their writing skills in general or writing skills in the language in which business is conducted within the enterprise.

Innovation programs in global companies can be structured many different ways, with different costs and returns on investment. The few that are the most effective are the ones that take full advantage of the beneficial aspects of human nature to contributing ideas.

The subtle yet important note that must always be kept in mind is that ideas must be evaluated while considering the possibility that it will not receive a fair evaluation if individuals affected by the idea are busy protecting their turf. Therefore, complete transparency of the entire process of the program can help significantly.

Although staff awareness of an innovation program may be high, typically a remarkably small percentage of individuals ever tend to participate. Among those that do participate, an even smaller percentage participate multiple times, and usually just a handful on an ongoing basis.

This, however, has much to do with the motivations of the individuals that can participate, the structure of the innovation program, and the outcomes that individuals experience when having participated. The ability to participate anonymously can also be a motivator for some.

As for motivations, there are a number of use cases that may be applicable to an innovation program.

As examples:

- an individual may simply desire to make a simple anonymous suggestion,
- an individual may simply be testing the program to see how it works prior to submitting their intended idea,
- an individual may simply want to get attention,
- a group of individuals may wish to propose a new method for performing a particular business capability,
- an individual may have an idea for a new product, or
- an individual may simply wish to create awareness of a problem that executives may be able to stumble upon if they periodically review submissions.

A good innovation program may want to support all of these use cases in an easy and simple way.

While it can be simple to design an innovation program, it is not simple to design one that is necessarily successful in achieving the objectives of management or in having a beneficial return on investment.

For example, while it may not be worthwhile for large enterprise to institute the approach adopted by Google to allocate 20% of staff time toward innovating a business idea,[1] it may prove worthwhile piloting such an approach with leads of architectural disciplines one month out of the year.

The innovation program architect collaborates with all of the subject matter experts across enterprise architecture, and perhaps most closely with life cycle architecture, workflow architecture, application architecture, and technology portfolio management.

The role of an innovation program subject matter expert requires a broad combination of knowledge and cumulative experience with human factors of stakeholders, potential outcomes of different program approaches, the various use cases of an innovation program, ontologies to support varied categories of innovations, operational workflow design, and developing proposals to present to management.

7.1.2 EA INITIATIVES PROJECT MANAGEMENT

Project management is the discipline of planning, organizing, controlling, and motivating resources of various skills to achieve specific results involving the development or deployment of a system or application. Project management typically

---

[1]*From Good to Great*, Jim Collins.

employs a life cycle to achieve its particular objectives, typically with a finite budget of resources within a specified amount of time.

Within enterprise architecture, the initiatives are typically of modest magnitude focused on discovery to develop a process for a larger project. Although there are numerous project management methodologies for the software development life cycle (SDLC), for small projects, the project management methodology, an increasingly common approach is Kanban and Scrumban, which is simply Kanban with Scrum-like iterations.

Kanban originated in the 1940s and 1950s with developing just in time manufacturing at Toyota in Japan. The method carefully visualizes well-defined steps of the workflow in diagrams that are reviewed by team members to help them understand how to do their work. Understanding the steps of the workflow helps management monitor progress and allows intervention to remove impediments that delay steps in the workflow. Thus, it is manageable to incorporate changes in requirements mid-stream.

In contrast, Scrum focuses on well-defined inputs and well-defined outputs for software built in sprints where the workflow cannot be defined due to complexity of the development process. Another difference is that Scrum requires management to trust the team thereby preventing interference. In Scrum, it is generally not acceptable to introduce changes in requirements mid-stream.

Both Kanban and Scrum take into consideration the fact that multitasking diminishes productivity, and equally important is the notion that switching focus is not the primary driver in diminishing productivity, but that the delay between events actually creates more work. Hence, running lean, in the context of Kanban and Scrum, is not about running fast, but instead, it is about eliminating and better managing delays by optimizing coordination among project activities and resources.

For example, a bug is much more work after it is detected 2 weeks later, and even more work after several weeks as others may have introduced changes in the interim. This requires the creation of product units that can be tested immediately, and coordination to achieve that. As such, more numerous yet smaller units are more efficient than fewer large units.

Larger project management efforts should be handled by an application development team, such as the global AD team to support the application development needs of enterprise architecture.

Other life cycles that require project management architecture, each with their own methodologies, include:

- data centric life cycle,
- data governance life cycle,
- architecture governance life cycle,
- divestiture life cycle,

- merger and acquisition life cycle,
- corporate restructuring life cycle,
- outsourcing life cycle,
- insourcing life cycle, and
- operations life cycle.

7.1.3 EA DISCIPLINE GAP REMEDIATION

Discipline gap remediation attempts to stay abreast of the technologies being reviewed for use across the company to determine if an architectural discipline exists to properly manage that particular area is missing from the inventory of architectural disciplines or if the applicable architectural discipline currently has a subject matter expert for that discipline.

It can be possible that the architectural discipline had been previously well defined with standards and frameworks that a full-time subject matter expert isn't required. Needs for such subject matter expertise may be available from experts on retainer or simply sent to experts on an as-needed basis.

Enterprise architecture discipline gap remediation assesses the relative cost to the company to establish an additional architectural discipline or to acquire coverage for a particular architectural discipline versus the potential cost of providing no active coverage for the particular architectural discipline.

7.1.4 AD COMPLIANCE AND DISPUTE MANAGEMENT

Application development compliance and dispute management is a discipline that determines the process to address potential and actual noncompliance with standards and/or frameworks by an application development team, as well as handle application development team disputes with any of the architectural disciplines within business, information systems, control systems, and operations architecture and governance.

The process requires a method to rapidly resolve issues among the appropriate stakeholders of the standard or framework, and to promptly escalate them to management if unresolved.

7.1.5 EA PERFORMANCE AND RESOURCE MEASUREMENT

Enterprise architecture performance and resource measurement collaborates with the lead of each architectural discipline to review the objectives, principles, future state, and transition plan to determine objective metrics that may be collected nonintrusively to determine the effect of architectural standards, frameworks, and governance.

The intent is to evaluate the efficacy of:

- architectural standards,
- architectural frameworks,
- governance process,
- knowledge level of the subject matter expert, and
- the subject matter expert's ability to successfully manage the specific architectural discipline.

The role of enterprise architecture performance and resource measurement requires a broad combination of knowledge and cumulative experience in:

- application development,
- objectives, principles,
- future state,
- transition plans of each architectural discipline,
- metrics driven principles,
- nonintrusive methods of metrics collection, and
- the broad topic of metrics and measures in operational workflows and work products.

7.1.6 ARCHITECTURE STANDARDS GOVERNANCE

Standards produced in isolation often do not agree with what constitutes a standard. The results are typically the following:

- categories of content are erratic,
- actual standards are capricious,
- objectives of standards are often unclear or omitted,
- stakeholders are not identified,
- interests of stakeholders remain unrepresented, and
- adherence to standards is not uniform or nonexistent.

Modern enterprise architecture recognizes that standards must have:

- a consistent life cycle for their development with the appropriate approvals and periodic reassessments,
- stated purpose as to why the standard is necessary,
- context to facilitate an improved understanding of how the standard fits within an overall framework,
- scope to identify the boundaries of what is to be specifically included and or excluded within the standard,

- the standards themselves with their reason for being (e.g., regulatory compliance, stakeholder interest, or cost reduction) with traceability to the specifics of the reason,
- principles governing the standard in order of priority,
- intended outcomes that can be measured,
- governance to ensure compliance as well as dispute resolution,
- tools and technologies that provide automation for aspects of the standard,
- methodologies and processes that should be adhered to as part of the standard,
- ontology that facilitates classification of and easy identification of the standard,
- and notes supporting the thought process that went into the development of the standard to record the decisions that were made when each section was created.

7.1.7   ARCHITECTURE ARTIFACT GOVERNANCE

Architectural diagrams and models are intended to communicate ideas and concepts efficiently and easily to various stakeholders. Produced in isolation diagrams and models are typically inconsistent and confusing often using symbols and diagramming techniques inconsistently across one another and even within the same diagram.

Modern enterprise architecture recognizes that architectural artifacts must have:

- a consistent life cycle for development with the appropriate approvals and periodic reassessments,
- types of architectural diagrams and their content,
- a proper taxonomy to name the artifact as a framework, blueprint, reference architecture, template, or guideline; templates used for commonly used diagrams and models,
- graphical symbols and colors used within diagrams,
- use of legends to illustrate the usage of graphical symbols and colors; a clear purpose,
- a depiction of the overall context to facilitate an improved understanding of how the artifact fits within an overall framework,
- scope to identify the boundaries of what is to be specifically included and or excluded,
- traceability to the specifics of the reason,
- principles governing the artifact in order of priority,
- intended outcomes that can be measured,
- governance to ensure compliance as well as dispute resolution,
- methodologies and processes used to create the artifact,

- ontology that facilitates classification of and easy identification of the artifact, and
- notes supporting the thought process that went into the development of the standard to record the decisions that were made when the artifact was created.

7.1.8   EA COMMUNICATIONS GOVERNANCE

Communications governance is responsible for developing and implementing a process by which all communications from enterprise architecture will be developed, approved, disseminated, and recorded, including the measurement of feedback.

The standards for communications governance should be leveraged by every architectural discipline, especially the discipline responsible for standards governance.

For example, the use of simple language is required using basic grammatical structure, such that the use of complex or lengthy sentences, metaphors, or colloquialisms should not be permitted in standard documents.

7.1.9   EA FINANCE

The typical enterprise architecture organization is unusually weak with respect to their financial skills. Some may believe that this may be because EA budgets are so small to begin with, or that there their budgets are often treated as management overhead to the organization. Often, EA staff members do not even have to participate in time accounting. This, however, is not a good idea. Accountability begins with time accounting, so management can simply determine where time and effort was spent.

In a modern enterprise architecture department finance is responsible for the standards and frameworks by which each architectural discipline must plan and manage financial resources and financial reporting, with finance being one of many essential metrics.

7.1.10   GAD TEAM LIAISON

Enterprise architecture has reoccurring needs for application development capabilities, including the ability to eventually migrate applications and technologies into production. To accomplish this, there are two basic approaches to consider.

7.1.10.1   Internal Application Development

The first option is to create an application development team within the enterprise architecture organization. The benefit of this approach is that a dedicated team will be more responsive and more specialized.

7.1.10.2 *External Application Development*

The second option is that a large enterprise should have a GAD team that supports development needs that span all regions and countries. The benefit of this approach is that there are likely to be core business capabilities that a GAD team would develop by consolidating multiple application systems into.

Since application consolidation is no simple matter, a GAD team requires a higher level of skills than most application development teams, and this meets the needs of enterprise architecture and its architectural disciples extremely well.

The GAD team liaison provides a single point of contact for coordination, planning, and reporting of application development support needs of enterprise architecture with the global development team of the company.

The role of GAD team liaison requires a broad combination of knowledge and cumulative experience in project management, and the current and near term development needs of enterprise architecture.

7.1.11 ARCHITECTURE STAFFING MODEL

There is a saying in sports that good coaches play the team they have rather than the team they want. IT organizations, including EA, have the same problem. They must be willing to honestly assess their capabilities and make adjustments. Few organizations are "world class" regardless of what their C-suite says (in fact by definition some of them must be among the worst—by whatever yardstick is used).

Simply put, this means that not all organizations are capable of performing all tasks that they dream up. I can imagine winning a Stanley Cup, but do not have the talent to do so.

The number of architectural disciplines necessary to properly manage the automation efforts of a given company can vary significantly depending upon the complexity that has resulted from numerous:

- acquisitions and mergers,
- business lines,
- data centers,
- computing platforms,
- product lines,
- applications,
- technologies,
- databases, and
- IT management.

In general, though, it is fair to say that the number of architectural disciplines in a large enterprise that does not develop control systems is likely to range between

50 and 80, sometimes more, sometimes less. Adding into that the disciplines required to support control systems and it roughly doubles.

When it comes to staffing architectural disciplines, some subject matter experts can cover just one architectural discipline, while others can handle a collection of them. At that point, it is somewhat more a factor of the number of concurrent initiatives that they may be required to support.

Once a company determines the set of architectural disciplines appropriate to control and direct the architectural decision making across the globe, it is time to illustrate the potential staffing levels and organizational structure of resources to deliver these services in a global operating model.

From experience, the process of identifying the candidates that are suitable to lead each architectural discipline is a long and arduous one, although with great rewards once the right team has been developed. Depending upon the background of the individuals, some candidates can easily lead multiple architectural disciplines, whereas some individual disciplines are extremely difficult to staff.

For the most part, educational institutions and vendors do not yet offer studies in most architectural disciplines of enterprise architecture. Therefore, the approach we recommend is simply the approach we used, which is to review large numbers of resumes of senior consultants, interview 1 of 50 by telephone, out of those bring in 1 of 5 for an in-person interview with your team, and onboard 1 of 3 as a consultant.

Once onboarding has been completed, the assessment period to determine if the candidate can appropriately lead the architectural discipline begins. If we are successful in mentoring the individual to appropriately lead the architectural discipline, then we may offer the consultant a senior role to convert to an employee of the enterprise, or potentially provide a part-time consulting position to them eventually to reduce the costs of having full-time coverage for a few of the less active and or demanding architectural disciplines.

I should note that over an 18-month period, we had to onboard a third candidate a handful of times, and in a couple of situations, we had to onboard a fourth candidate until a suitable subject matter expert could be identified.

By starting with consultants, it easily avoids the problem of hiring full-time employees only to find out shortly after they start that they cannot do the job they were hired to perform. If hired as employees from the start, to terminate and replace them could take the remainder of your career—potentially a deservedly short one.

We found that a few requirements were standard across all architectural disciplines, such as:

■ Candidate must be able to articulate the pertinent principles that guide their architectural discipline to executives in business and IT, including to other architects to guide the activities of IT to be in alignment

- Candidate must be able to support the informational needs of business and IT, including architects and application development teams in a mentoring style
- Candidate must be an effective communicator in business and IT at all levels of the organization
- Candidate must be results oriented
- Candidate must consistently demonstrate initiative, constructively engage, and be a strong advocate of the business across IT

The mindset of architectural leads can have a significant effect on their ability to properly protect the interests of the business. It is therefore valuable for subject matter expert to understand the effects of dealing with other staff members, especially when they have multiple degrees of separation from the business, and business concepts.

7.1.12   EA RELATIVE THE PROGRAM MANAGEMENT OFFICE

The primary goal of the program management office (PMO) is to standardize project management processes, policies, methods, and reporting guidelines. Over time, the PMO can provide guidance, documentation, examples, and metrics for managing projects. The PMO will commonly oversee project management and report project management status back to executive management.

The effectiveness of the PMO is typically determined by how well it is staffed and the experience level of the staff. Many large organizations recognize the need for a strong PMO, but fail to position it so that it can deliver the type of value that it is actually capable of delivering.

Although there are often a variety of challenges that a PMO faces in order to become effective, perhaps the most significant is that it is typically only aware of a SDLC and its associated steps, standards, and documentation. This positions the PMO to perform the role of project management oversight with one lens.

In an analogy with a professional photographer, this would limit the photographer to taking photos well when the subject of the photo is just the right distance away under only one ideal type of lighting condition.

One of the most advantageous organizational alignments that we have seen in successful organizations is to include within the organizational structure of enterprise architecture. This alignment allows EA to determine the appropriate set of life cycles for the PMO to become proficient in and causes project management alignment with the right architectural standards for the appropriate life cycle.

To continue the analogy, this would allow the photographer to take professional photographs at a variety of distances under a variety of lighting conditions, day or night, in any direction from the light source, for any distance.

It is important to note that the benefits of this organizational alignment work in the reverse direction as well. When the PMO encounters issues with certain types of life cycles, steps, standards, or documentation, they are now as close as they can be to ideal source to collaborate with to remedy the problem or take advantage of the opportunity.

Miscellaneous

8.1 Special Topics

There are a handful of related topics that simply do not fit neatly in the main sections of this book. One such topic is that of vendors and consulting firms, many of them involving particular big name vendors and big expensive products that come with big expensive consulting engagements. There is a significant difference between vendors providing value to customers versus maximizing their own profits for the quarter.

How many times have we seen vendors delivering software packages that fall out of use, or that place high priced individuals on a project that have little experience, or that deliver presentation decks that instantly became shelf-ware costing hundreds of thousands of dollars?

That said, there are a small number of vendors in the marketplace, some large, some small that do understand the problem, and that possess the knowledge and experience to address the challenges. These few vendors are the ones that have that attitude established by Benjamin Franklin, which is to deliver value to the customer the old fashioned way, which is to under sell and over deliver.

One way to find the great vendors out there and to protect your company from the others is to leverage your first and best line of defense. This would be by using your smart and lean enterprise architecture practice, not major research companies with vendor relationships.

8.1.1 NONFUNCTIONAL REQUIREMENTS

8.1.1.1 Background

The concept of functional versus nonfunctional requirements has been the subject of a debate that began in the 1980s. The notion was that nonfunctional requirements were different than functional requirements because they represented concepts regarding the properties of a system that stemmed from desirable design principles. As such, they were easily separated from functional requirements simply because they were not specific, expressed as general characteristics of a system in nonquantifiable ways that formed qualities of a system that were good to have, such as being secure, reliable, and cost effective.

The tricky part is that these same qualities can be and often are expressed in precise terms, such as:

- Users of the system shall have their user names authenticated by a common framework administered by the business compliance department to determine their access rights to each system capability. This statement would then be decomposed further to the following:
  - The first function to be performed is to acquire the unique user identifier from the logon function and to pass it to the LDAP directory to retrieve the department identifier and the list of user roles.
  - The department and user roles would then be validated against the list of business data glossary data points that the user requested, where data points that the user is unauthorized to view would be masked using the masking template associated with the particular business data glossary data point immediately prior to being rendered to the data visualization layer.
  - The business rules associated with data masking template requirements can be found in the enterprise data security standards document under the section named 'Data Masking Template' requirements.
- Databases of the system shall have physical protection as well as system access protection.
  - Physical protection of databases shall be provided by being placed on servers that are protected physically within a secured area that is fenced in within the data center.
  - System access protection shall be provided by network security to ensure that only database administrators and authorized applications have access to the databases of the application on an as needed basis only for the period required for them to perform previously approved activities.

To many, the specificity of these requirements then caused nonfunctional requirements to suddenly be categorized as functional requirements. However, I think we can agree that there is probably something wrong with a taxonomy for categorizing requirements that causes the categorization to change simply as a result of how much detail was used in stating the requirement. After all, what is the threshold of detail that can be added to a requirement before it changes from a nonfunctional requirement to a functional requirement?

There is a much easier way however to view the topic of functional versus nonfunctional requirements and requirements in general.

To begin, for any requirements to be implementable, as well as traceable for that matter, requirements have to be specific and detailed. Requirements that are vague cannot be implemented; at least they would have to be if the outcome is to be expected and repeatable.

Sometimes, vague requirements are understood to simply be preferences which can be easily lost or ignored as their exact meaning is up to the interpretation of the individual that reads them. Only once they are stated in specific terms involving inputs and outputs can they receive treatment as requirements.

This is not to say that all specifically stated requirements can be implemented, but at least now, you have a chance that there may be a way to implement them and that no matter who reads them each person would interpret them in a consistent manner.

8.1.1.2 Business Rules

Now that we have established what "requirements" are and are not, they must contain business rules, where the business rules can be specific to: the particular line of business (e.g., mortgage origination), industry (e.g., retail financial services), or business in general (e.g., retail business).

If a requirement contains one or more business rules that are particular to the specific line of business, industry, or business in general, then let us declare that it is probably safe to classify such as "functional requirements." However, what constitutes a business rule is worth mentioning.

A business rule can only exist at a detail level where specific data are present and/or specific events have occurred and there are clear activities to be performed based upon the presence or content of data and or events.

Depending upon the type of system, the specific data or event can be associated with the external environment or it can be internal within the system.

8.1.1.3 Nonfunctional Requirements

Nonfunctional requirements also must contain business rules. However, they belong to a different set of categories. Instead of business rules being pertinent to a specific line of business, industry, or business, they belong to a category of nonfunctional requirements or nonbusiness-specific requirement categories.

These nonbusiness-specific requirement categories are not requirements; they are only categories (aka "ilities") within which nonbusiness-specific requirements may be organized.

8.1.1.4 Nonbusiness-Specific Requirement Categories

Nonfunctional requirement categories may include, but are not limited to:

Accessibility—refers to the relative ease with which end users of the system can make contact and get into the system. It can be performed from each stakeholder location and end-user computing platforms. Accessibility testing can be achieved using automation that would reside on each end-user computing platform, which can then ping the system to test its ability to access the system.

Adaptability—refers to the degree to which the system components use open standards that make it easy for its components to be interchangeable. It can be performed by switching out interchangeable components with analogous capabilities.

Affordability—refers to the cost of the system in terms of money, time, and personnel resources relative to the other priorities of the organization. Unless frameworks exist to act as accelerators for incorporating nonbusiness requirements, the inclusion of additional nonbusiness requirements tends to act in direct opposition to affordability.

Architectural compatibility—refers to the degree to which the system is compliant with enterprise architecture standards and frameworks. Unless there are frameworks in place to measure this, it can be performed by engaging a subject matter expert in enterprise architecture to assess the system for its compliance with the pertinent architectural standards.

Audit ability—refers to the degree to which the system can be evaluated for properly performing its activities and the accuracy with which it performed those activities. It can be performed by incorporating metrics within each system capability to provide the appropriate level of record keeping for regular operation or for testing purposes.

Availability—refers to the portion of the time that the entire system can be considered available and functional across all stakeholders and their locations. Testing of availability can be performed from each stakeholder location and end-user computing platforms. Availability testing can be achieved using automation that would track all attempts to invoke capabilities of the system which can be compared with a system log of requests to determine if any requests for capabilities arrived or were not supported to completion.

Backup and restorability—refers to the ability to establish a backup of the entire system and apply it on demand when restoration is required. Testing of back and restorability can be accomplished by data services subject matter experts who would test regular backups and invoking the restoration process.

Capacity—is the knowledge of system limitations to support each use case and combinations given various system workloads. Testing capacity is conducted by applying increased workloads for a given computing configuration to determine the maximum level of work that can be performed before service-level agreements can no longer be met.

Capacity predictability—is the ability to predict system limitations to support each use case and combinations given various system workloads using various computing configurations. It can be performed during system capacity testing usually in the form of a formula involving resource availability and consumption rates of computing platforms.

Certify ability—is the ability to confirm that the system can meet its business-specific and nonbusiness-specific requirements over a period of time through periods of full deployment from the perspective of all stakeholders. Unless there are frameworks in place to measure this, it can be assessed by engaging a competent subject matter expert to confirm that the system can meet the requirements of all stakeholders over a period of time.

Change control ability—is the ability to appropriately manage changes to and versions of each and every component of the system through the life cycle of the system. It can be assessed by engaging a competent subject matter expert to confirm that the scope of change control is appropriate and that the tools and procedures are appropriately managed by the components of the system as they change and move through the life cycle.

Completeness—is the degree to which the capabilities provided each end user fully support their requirements such that additional manual activities or use of other automation systems are no longer required. It can be assessed by engaging a competent subject matter expert to determine the degree to which the scope of capabilities is complete.

Compliance ability—is the degree to which rules and policies from business, legal, regulatory, human resource, and IT compliance are adhered to. Unless there are frameworks in place to measure this, it can be assessed by engaging a competent subject matter expert to review the rules and policies of compliance and then determine the degree to which compliance can be traced through architecture, design, and implementation of the system.

Configurability—is the proportion of the system that is easily configurable from a parameter and data-driven perspective as opposed to requiring custom development and nonconfiguration-type customizations. Unless there are frameworks in place to measure this, it can be assessed by engaging a competent subject matter expert to review the configurable and nonconfigurable aspects of the system, such as involving the adding of application and/or database nodes, business data inputs, business data outputs, reports, and business rules into rules engines.

Configuration management ability—refers to the ability to appropriately manage collections of changes that together form a matched set or version of the system. Unless there are frameworks in place to measure this, it can be assessed by engaging a competent subject matter expert to review the scope and workflow of configuration management scope and tools and procedures through the life cycle of the system.

Cost predictability—refers to the ability to project the total cost of the various areas of system development, maintenance, operations, and eventual decommissioning. It can best be managed through cost models that are developed over time within the organization that are based upon experience involving similar systems.

Data cleanse ability—refers to the ability to cleanse or scrub the data to make it usable to a system or analytical capability.

Data governance alignment—refers to the ability of the system to support a variety of data governance-related capabilities that serve to manage the metadata of the information content of the system. It can be assessed by the end users access to a business data glossary, manage ownership of data categories, administer access rights of owned data, and the ability to identify existing reports, queries, dashboards, and analytics.

Data ingest ability—refers to the ability to ingest a file that has been received for its schema or metadata, ability to unencrypt, ability to locate the correct algorithm to decompress it, or general ability to determine its contents.

Data mask ability—refers to the ability to mask the contents of sensitive data without rendering the file useless for application and or analytical purposes.

Data source ability—refers to the ability to discover viable data sources to supply the informational needs of a system or analytical capability.

Debug ability—is the degree to which error handling is incorporated into each capability of the system to support detection, information tracking and collection, and reporting of abnormal or unexpected conditions across the system. Unless there are frameworks in place to measure this, it can be assessed by subject matter experts for comprehensiveness in error handling, process tracking and data collection for diagnostics, and reporting.

Deliverability—is the ability to supply system capabilities in an operational state to end users and stakeholders on schedule. It can be assessed by comparing scheduled and actual delivery dates of various system capabilities.

Dependability—is the degree to which capabilities delivered by the system meets expectations of the end users when the capabilities are needed. It can be assessed by periodically surveying end-user satisfaction for the system's ability to consistently deliver services.

Dependencies on external systems—is the degree to which capabilities delivered by the system are dependent upon activities of external parties, data sources, and systems. It can be assessed by counting the parties, data sources, and systems that are required for this system to meet its objectives.

Deploy ability—is the degree to which capabilities of the system can be made available to end users across all locations and time zones with minimal additional effort. It can be measured by determining the level of additional effort required to deploy capabilities across geographic locations and time zones.

Documentable—is the degree to which activities of the system within its various areas of capabilities can be supported by documentary evidence. It can be measured using a sampling approach to confirm a set of data instances that are in various normal and abnormal states with documentary evidence from alternative sources to illustrate the accuracy of the normal and abnormal states.

Disaster recoverability—is the degree to which systems components can reside on VMware in a primary and DR data center. Disaster recoverability is enhanced when components of the system can operate in environments that provide virtualization to avoid the need of exactly replicating system DLLs and drivers across nonvirtualized operating systems.

Distribute ability—is the degree to which components of the system can be distributed across more numerous computing platforms that are connected through a network. It can be tested by moving system components across computing platforms over a network.

Efficiency—is the degree to which the system can handle workloads with small increases in resource consumption. Testing increased workloads, while measuring resource consumption using performance monitoring tools can demonstrate efficiency.

Effectiveness—is the delivery of capabilities in relation to the degree of effort where the lesser the effort, the greater the effectiveness. There are several ways to measure effectiveness, where one is to measure the level of effort prior to and after implementation of the system.

Emotional factors—is the degree to which the use of the system provides a stress-free experience to the user for accomplishing their business objectives. End-user experience relative to emotional factors can be surveyed at regular intervals during and after training.

Escrow ability—is the degree to which licensed software components are available on deposit with a third-party escrow agent as a means to protect against default of the software vendor. Confirmation from each vendor can be attained for every software version of source code for those products licensed to your organization.

Exploitability—is the degree to which stakeholders and end users can exploit the system for previously unanticipated capabilities. End-user experience of the ability of the system to provide unanticipated capabilities can be surveyed.

Extensibility—is the degree to which capabilities can be added to the system, thereby taking into consideration the potential future growth of the system which can extend its life. Unless there are frameworks in place to measure this, it can be evaluated by a subject matter expert who can assess system architecture, design, and implementation for business and technology extensibility considerations, such as use of industry standard interfaces and protocols.

Failover ability—is the degree to which the system can automatically switch over away from infrastructure components that have failed to the remaining operational infrastructure components and can be routinely tested.

Fault tolerance—is the degree to which infrastructure components have redundant capabilities that provide a way for hardware failures to be compensated for by using redundant components that are automatically routed to. It can be tested by unplugging and turning off components while they are actively being used.

Flexibility—is the degree to which the system can support additional products, product types, workflows, data sources, reports, and analytics. It can be tested by adding additional products, product types, workflows, data sources, reports, and analytics.

Hardware compatibility—is the degree to which the system can be supported on the intended hardware and operating system environment. It can be tested by installing the system on the intended hardware and operating system environment.

Handle ability—is the degree to which end users of the system can easily employ capabilities of the system without committing user errors. It can be tested by measuring error rates of end users and by conducting user surveys to assess the frequency of rework.

Integration ability—is the ability to bring together systems and subsystems into a cohesive framework that minimizes the replication of data and streamlines the transfer of data from one system to another. Unless there are frameworks in place to measure this, it can be best assessed by a subject matter expert.

Internationalization—is the degree to which the system supports alternate languages through the integration of translation software and Unicode support in limited areas as well as in national differences including compliance and regulatory differences. Unless there are frameworks in place to measure this, it can be assessed by a subject matter expert and can be tested.

Interoperability—is the ease with which the system can interface with other systems of similar and diverse computing platforms, operating system environments, and network protocols. Unless there are frameworks in place to measure this, it can be best assessed by a subject matter expert and can be tested.

Legal, licensing-infringement, patent-infringement avoid ability—is the degree to which legal, license infringement, and patent infringement can be avoided with rigorous procurement and legal standards and talent for vetting vendors and internal procedures for IT compliance. Unless there are frameworks in place to measure this, it can be assessed by engaging subject matter expertise.

Likeability—is the degree to which users like to use and work with the system. End-user experiences of the system for likeability can be surveyed at regular intervals.

Maintainability—is the ease with which defects can be isolated, defects can be corrected, new requirements can be supported, and the life of the system extended with minimal additional difficultly over time due to frameworks that enhance maintainability. Unless there are frameworks in place to measure this, it can be evaluated by a subject matter expert who can assess system architecture, design, and implementation for frameworks that minimize the additional difficulty associated with incorporating change.

Network topology autonomy—is the degree of independence that the system has upon logical and physical network topology and unless there are frameworks in place to measure this, it can be evaluated by a subject matter expert who can assess the system for dependencies.

Open source ability—is the degree to which an open source community would likely take interest in the product or framework to further enhance and support it and can be determined by engaging the process for donating software to the Apache Foundation and vendors who may wish to support it as open source.

Operability—is the degree to which the parts of the system can work together to meet the objectives of the system and can be determined through testing the parts of the system in an integration test environment for business and system requirements and business rules.

Performance—is the ability of the system to complete logical units of work within the necessary period of time for supporting various workloads and can be determined by testing the parts of the system and the system in its entirety while measuring its ability to complete work under various loads using performance monitoring tools and test beds.

Performance predictability—is the degree to which performance of the system can be predicted at various loads and can be determined by developing predictive methods and formulas that can be tested during performance testing.

Platform compatibility—is the degree to which the computing platform (e.g., hardware and operating system environment) can support the system components (e.g., licensed software, acquired software, and custom built/bespoke software). This is routinely tested.

Price negotiability—is the degree to which aspects of the system (e.g., software licenses, hardware, labor, support, and training) can be negotiated down or restructured over time. It is highly dependent upon the vendor ability and willingness to negotiate with procurement subject matter experts.

Privacy—is the degree to which data privacy is architected into the system from the perspective of the workflow of the various roles of individuals and the architecture of the system. Building privacy into the architecture from the beginning is usually the only way to achieve an effective level of privacy.

Portability—is the degree to which a system can be replicated or moved to an alternate hardware and/or operating system environment with as little or no effort in application coding, or simple configuration parameter changes. Some technologies are more portable than others which can be determined through testing.

Quality—in this context refers to faults within the system, including faults discovered prior to delivery, faults delivered, and faults discovered after delivery in relation to the scope of the system. Quality can be many ways, such as based upon the number of faults per functional component, lines of code, data points, and user interfaces. Better architectures and designs will minimize the number of quality related issues.

Recoverability—is the ability to meet recovery time objectives, recovery point objectives, and overall mean time to recovery. Recoverability for Big Data is particularly concerning, as while traditional Big Data products support recoverability, their Hadoop-based counterparts do not. Backups of data, metadata, applications, and configurations are an important part of a Hadoop ecosystem as many have the misconception that Hadoop replication of data automatically protects one from data loss.

In fact, simple human error can wipe out terabytes of data in a matter of seconds (e.g., creating a Hive table in a Hadoop folder that is already populated with production data, only fs shell copies deleted data to the Trash Server, whereas programmatic deletes do not employ the Hadoop Trash Server, HDFS upgrades involving disk layout changes pose a high risk to existing data); backups in Hadoop must also have full consistency by backing up components that form a configuration together (e.g., data and metadata must be backed up in the same flow). Aside from human error, a severe electromagnetic pulse (e.g., from solar activity) can wipe clean petabytes of a Hadoop system above ground.

Reliability—is the degree to which the system remains consistently available providing services to end users without interruptions of any type, such as a failure or denial of service resulting from any unplanned condition, including human error, hardware failure, software failure, vandalism, and attack (e.g., distributed denial of service). Depending upon its criticality, a system can detect, protect against, and capture metrics on most any type of potential failure or attack. Reliability is often measured in terms of mean time between failures.

To cite just one example, most variations of UNIX offer a greater degree of reliability than Linux to such an extent that cost differences and standards should be momentarily considered.

Report ability—is the ability to report business data as well as normal and abnormal conditions to the appropriate system stakeholders, administrators, and support staff in a controlled manner with the appropriate set of corresponding data to diagnose and remediate the condition. Unless there are frameworks in place to measure this, subject matter experts can be used to assess the degree to which the system supports report ability.

Requirements traceability—is the degree to which business and nonbusiness functional requirements can be traced into the architecture, design, and implementation of the system. Unless there are frameworks in place to measure this to test the ability to track sample sets of requirements into the design and implementation components, subject matter experts can be used to assess the degree to which the system supports requirements traceability encompassing software lines of code, configuration settings, rules engine rules, and complex event processing rules.

Resilience—is the degree to which an acceptable level of service can be maintained in the face of failures by minimizing the elapse times in which the system is unavailable to end users. For some systems, frequent outages are not a problem as the system bounces back quickly enough just causing a momentary delay where services were not available. Unless there are frameworks in place to measure this, subject matter experts can be used to assess resiliency of a system.

Resource consumption predictability—is the degree to which the resources consumed can be predicted through various workloads of the system. Unless there are successful frameworks and methodologies in place to measure this, subject matter experts can be used to assess resource consumption predictability of a system.

Resource constraint tolerance—is the degree to which the system can provide an acceptable level of service when various resources (e.g., CPU, memory, paging files, disk space, and network capacity) become constrained. This can be determined through the development of service-level agreements and testing.

Response time for support—is the rate at which levels 1, 2, and 3 issues reported to the helpdesk are resolved. Helpdesks typically have frameworks to report these metrics although there can be significant flaws in these metrics when incidents have to be reported repeatedly without linkages to their original ticket.

Reusability—must meet multiple criteria beginning with the ability to develop components that are highly reusable, once created are easily locatable, and once located are incorporated without customization affecting prior usage. Developing components that are highly reusable is often poorly understood causing repositories to house endless numbers of components that are not reusable, not easily locatable, and if found not usable without customization. This nonbusiness requirement category requires a highly competent subject matter expert with a strong foundation in both information and application architecture.

Robustness—refers to the degree to which abnormalities of inputs can be gracefully handled to avoid unexpected results or failures. This can be tested and measured with strong test planning of expected results involving a wide variety of use cases that provide handling of normal and abnormal data inputs.

Scalability—is the degree with which additional capacity can be supported through simple actions, such as the addition of commodity or proprietary servers/nodes, blades, and memory cards. This can be tested and measured by introducing additional work or data velocity and then addressing it with additional hardware.

Security—is the degree to which unauthorized access to services and/or data, including the ability to disseminate data, can be appropriately protected. Considerations for security must be provided for in test planning in systems that house sensitive data or that provide services that are necessarily restricted.

Self-serviceability of end users—refers to the degree to which the system supports self-service to end users in a manner that empowers end users to independently meet their own needs. This is an architectural framework that establishes that if IT must be engaged for a service, then that service is provided only once with the provision that it persists so that the same activities (e.g., data analysis, data sourcing, data cleansing, data standardization, data reformatting, data restructuring, and data integration) do not have to be performed again. Unless there are frameworks in place to measure this, subject matter experts can be used to assess self-serviceability of end users.

Software backward compatibility—is the degree to which older standards for interfaces can be supported with newer versions of the system. This can be tested as each new version of the system emerges.

Software forward compatibility—is the degree to which newer standards for interfaces can be supported with older versions of the system. This can be tested as each new interface standard emerges.

Stability—is the degree to which components of the system are stable over time from the perspective that they will not need to be changed to meet additional or modified requirements. This can be developed as an architectural style that emphasizes rules engine-driven system within each aspect of the system framework that would otherwise be susceptible to instability. Unless there are frameworks in place to measure this, subject matter experts familiar with modern architectural frameworks for systems can be used to assess system stability.

Staffing and skill availability—is the degree to which an ample number of resources with the appropriate experience are available for the periods and locations required. Personnel procurement can be conducted in such a way as to gather useful metrics on this topic, although a subject matter expert is generally required to identify and set up the appropriate frameworks.

Standards compliance—is the degree to which applicable standards are represented in standards and frameworks, and can be identified and complied with while incorporating traceability. Without traceability, standards compliance will become a fleeting concept. Unless there are successful frameworks in place to measure this, subject matter experts can be used to assess the degree to which standards compliance is delivered.

Supportability—is the degree to which internal or external resources are able to provide competent support for the system on a timely basis. Unless there are successful frameworks in place to measure this, subject matter experts can be used to assess the supportability of a system.

Testability—is the degree to which testing has been incorporated into the architecture, design, and implementation of the system to address expected and unexpected abnormalities in a controlled and traceable way. Unless there are successful frameworks in place to measure this, subject matter experts can be used to assess the testability of a system.

Total cost of ownership—related to affordability, total cost of ownership is the degree to which the various architectural areas of a system have undergone a thorough return on investment (ROI) analysis.

These include the costs, benefits, and risks associated with deploying:

- applications and decommissioning or reallocating existing applications
- infrastructure and decommissioning or reallocating existing infrastructure
- personnel and decommissioning or reallocating existing personnel
- hosting services and or setup as well as decommissioning existing hosting services
- operational procedures and decommissioning existing operational procedures
- business capabilities and decommissioning existing ones

Unless there are successful frameworks in place to measure this, subject matter experts can be used to determine the architectural ROI of a system from a comprehensive enterprise architecture perspective.

Traceability—is a synonym of requirements traceability.

Trainability—refers to the level of effort required to train various types of end users to use the system effectively for each type of use case associated with their respective role. Methods to enhance trainability include usage tips that can be built into the system to facilitate rapid learning or a refresh of training. Training subject matter experts can enhance and assess the trainability factors of a system.

Transaction velocity—is the degree to which the system can support bursts as well as sustained periods of increased loads of a system and its various components. Unless there are successful frameworks in place to measure this, thorough testing and/or subject matter experts can be used to assess the ability of the system to support bursts as well as sustained periods of increased loads of a system.

Usability—is the degree to which the system supports each type of end user using ideal human interfaces to communicate with the system including the ability to understand its user interface and outputs.

Verifiability—is the degree to which the outputs of the system can be independently confirmed as being accurate and timely.

8.1.2 NONSENSICAL BUZZWORDS

As with any taxonomy, there are bound to be terms that emerge that misrepresent information and mislead others; most of them are accidental from individuals that see one side of an issue, but lack the experience to have encountered the other sides of the issue that help put it in perspective. We see this in books and commonly on the Web.

While it is neither practical nor possible for that matter to identify them all, we will share one of our favorites.

My recommendation is to ask lots of questions to learn what any buzzword means. If you don't get an explanation that makes it crystal clear, keep asking questions. The others in the room probably have no idea what the buzzword means either.

8.1.2.1 Object Relational Impedance Mismatch

Entity relationship diagrams were in use nearly a decade before IBM announced their first relational database management system. Entity relationship diagrams were routinely used with:

- "hierarchical databases" (e.g., DL/I and IMS),
- "inverted list databases" (e.g., Adabas), and
- "network databases" (e.g., IDMS).

The point here is that entity relationship diagrams provide a basic method with which to depict collections of data points and the relationships that those collections have with one another.

It is therefore amusing how often one can find statements on the Web, including in Wikipedia, that state that entity relationship diagrams can only depict designs for relational databases. But that said, it gets even better.

Now that the reader is now knowledgeable in many of the differences between information systems and control systems, it is easy to understand how object-oriented paradigms originated with control systems, and then became adapted to information systems.

Yes, the architectural foundation between the two paradigms is different, but that's only because there are no tangible things that you can consistently touch in an information system.

Stable collections of data points within information systems are "objects" around which the application may be architected, as with collections of data that are identified within a logical data architecture. This goes down to the smallest collection of data points for which there are many synonyms, which include:

- record,
- tuple,
- entity,
- table, and
- object.

A conceptual or logical data model, as represented by an entity relationship diagram, is suited to model the data, regardless of what anyone decides to call the collections of data points. In other words, relational has nothing to do with it.

Now that there are a few generations of developers that only know object-oriented and relational, who have seen the differences between object-oriented control systems and relational database-oriented information systems, they have coined a new term called, "object relational impedance mismatch."

The following are examples of what has been used as justification for the existence of "object relational impedance mismatch."

Encapsulation: Object-oriented programming languages (e.g., Ada) use concepts to hide functionality and its associated data into the architecture of the application. *However, this reason speaks to application, not database architecture.*

Accessibility: Public data versus private data, as determined by the architecture of the application, are introduced as additional metadata, which are impertinent to data models.

Interfaces: Objects are said to have interfaces, which simply confuses interfaces that exist between modules of applications with data objects.

Data type differences: Object-oriented databases support the use of pointers, whereas relational does not. From the perspective of database management system architectures, the architectures that support pointers include hierarchical, network, and object oriented, whereas inverted list, relational, and columnar do not.

Structural and integrity differences: Objects can be composed of other objects. Entity relationship diagrams support this construct as well.

Transactional differences: The scope of a transaction as a unit of work varies greatly with that of relational transactions. *This is simply an observation of one of the differences between control systems and information systems. What does "transaction" even mean when you are flying a B2 Stealth bomber, and if the transaction rolls back, does that make the plane land backwards where it took off from?*

Okay, I can predict the e-mails that I am going to receive on this last one, but you have to inject a little fun into everything you do.

8.1.3   PRAGMATIC ENTERPRISE ARCHITECTURE

What makes enterprise architecture pragmatic?

First, it is important to know what enterprise architecture is. It is not solution architecture for the enterprise, where without frameworks one individual is supposed to provide specialized technology advice across business and IT any more than a physician is supposed to provide specialized medical advice across the townsfolk. Rule number one is that EA is not a GP practice, as that would rapidly lead to architectural malpractice.

Just as physicians who specialize in various highly technical areas and their specialized staff support a medical center, enterprise architects provide expertise and services to business leaders and solution architects, who in turn deliver care directly to the home of an application team, or set of application teams.

One of the most valuable aspects of having specialists co-located together in a medical center is that they are better able to collaborate. Similarly, once enterprise architects collaborate with other enterprise architects of different specialties, they discover the synergies that exist and recognize new ways of looking at issues and approaching them, perhaps with much greater effectiveness.

What may be most challenging is if the local tribe has never seen a medical center before, it is likely that they will not understand what a medical center is, what it does, how it works, and what its value proposition is. This issue is not that uncommon when it comes to growing organizations with an emerging need for an EA capability. To such an organization, the role of a true EA capability will sound theoretical, where it is action that they want as if action could be supported by one general practitioner given the role of "chief enterprise architect."

The less likely challenge is that the growing organization knows what an EA practice is, they realize that they need the services of a mature enterprise architecture practice, but don't have one yet and need to get one. Normally, the folks in small towns go to a nearby city to get the services and expertise they need as they need them. Hence, the city medical center supports the city plus all of its neighboring towns for any specialty services that a GP would not be able to address.

Similarly, enterprise architecture can be supported by a consulting firm that specializes in the various architectural disciplines that comprise EA, however few of these consulting firms presently exist, and few of those have the breadth of skills that would be tuned to meet the specific needs of the large organization. Enterprise architecture practices are tuned to the organization just as medical centers establish the skills most commonly needed by the population in their geographic area, whether that includes specialization for snake bites, tick bites, altitude sickness, or hypothermia.

Other important dimensions of what constitutes enterprise architecture are that as a technology medical center it provides a significant amount of preventive care. There are numerous known illnesses that culminate from certain inadvisable technology practices, and EA can help the organization establish the healthy behaviors that prevent these expensive and complex automation diseases.

Most importantly, however, pragmatic enterprise architecture is opportunistic. As issues arise across a large organization, or as awareness of issues emerges due to an insightful enterprise architect or senior manager, it presents an opportunity to establish an architectural discipline, its frameworks, and its assorted collateral to help guide solution architects going forward. As architectural disciplines get built out, their specialized personnel are either delivering a good ROI, or they are not. As in any business, you reduce overhead as you find ways of supporting the capabilities required using alternate means.

Pragmatic enterprise architecture as such is essentially a pragmatic medical center that provides services that reduce technology costs in personnel, software licenses, and computing hardware and infrastructure acquisition. Once an organization is mature and knows how to avoid unnecessary technology complexity and costs, then fewer or different enterprise architects can be considered.

8.1.4 SUMMARY

Some people actually believe that there are simply a finite number of jobs in the marketplace, and if one big company doesn't employ people, then lots of small companies will. This version of economic theory is not only wrong, but is reckless.

Companies, especially those that can count themselves as among the largest enterprises, are systems that employ tens of thousands of individuals on their payrolls, and additional tens of thousands more are gainfully employed due to the vast purchases of products, services, and equipment to make the company run. And then there are thousands more that are employed in government positions and thousands more that are assisted with foreign aid, not to mention the financial support upon which thousands of retired shareholders depend.

While few realize it, and fewer admit it, management and employees of all companies bear an important responsibility to the many families that rely upon the continued success of large enterprises for their livelihood. This is just the beginning of why success of large global conglomerates is so important, and as enterprise architects, you can make a meaningful difference to their continued success.

8.1.5 CONCLUSION

It was a pleasure writing this book; the first draft completed while vacationing at a friend's beach house on the Dutch side of Sint Maarten, overlooking calm blue waters of the Caribbean, while taking advantage of the unusually affordable French wine that is available on this vividly international island.

The process of putting thought to paper has caused me to become even more aware of the value of the conceptual EA framework that I have attempted to communicate. While no individual concept may be earth shattering, together they are like raindrops that can cause a flood of improvement across any large organization.

I definitely look forward to collaborating again on my next book. With luck this one is the first in a series as we build upon the material in this book.

Some people ask us, "What is our measure of success?"

One view is that the measure of success is whether we can fuel a trend for business and executive management to retake control of the enterprise, so that the many technologies are harnessed wisely instead of them taking on a life of their own.

It is truly our belief that the better executive management understands the issues that plague IT, that our largest organizations can sustain their part in expanding the world economy.

Why you might ask does anyone need to look out for the survival of large organizations? Don't they automatically grow and survive?

Well, if you were to look at the list of the companies in the Fortune 500 either domestically or globally say 50 years ago, and then look to see where they are now, we could not draw the conclusion that large companies survive and grow just from momentum.

This author is fairly certain that advisement of our largest enterprises cannot rest with vendors, research companies, or high-powered consulting companies. Instead, large organizations can only do well if they have great talents that make great decisions in every part of the organization.

"Take everyone's information, just not their advice."

Companies do not need to follow the pack, especially when to do so means that at best one can only achieve mediocrity. As with anything, understand the problem, understand how we got there, understand where the big vendors want to go, but understand where you should go based upon your business direction and competitive landscape, and then go there.

"Anyone who thinks talk is cheap never argued with a traffic cop."

It is good to debate many issues, but useless unless you have the right people in the room.

Appendix

A.1 Transaction Path Analysis (TAPA)

A.1.1 TAPA 01 SIGNIFICANT TRANSACTIONS

Many software applications contain a large variety of transactions, and usually, the majority of these transactions are incapable of having a noticeable impact upon the performance of the application. Since time and labor are valuable, it is best to focus only on the small number of transactions that are likely to impact the availability of shared resources.

A significant transaction would be an application function that is expected to have any of the following characteristics:

- Business criticality
  - The functionality of some business transactions is more business critical than others, and it is important for the business users to alert the database administrator as to which transactions are the most business critical.
- High volume
  - As computer processing power increases, the threshold that defines high volume continues to increase. In general, it is worth bringing it to the attention of your DBA when the frequency of the transaction is expected to exceed one hundred per minute, or when the number of concurrent users may exceed one hundred.
- Complex
  - A number of factors should be considered when determining whether a transaction is complex. The types of characteristics to be on the alert for are transactions that use the database and contain:
    - Lengthy calculations, either embedded or called externally
    - Intersystem and/or intra-session communication
    - SQL JOINS that exceed three tables
    - An excess of 20 SQL statements within the transaction
    - Multiple commits to the database

- Long running
  - A number of factors also should be considered when determining whether a transaction is long running. The types of characteristics that you may wish to alert the DBA to include transactions that contain:
    - CURSORS that may touch more than 500,000 rows before completing
    - Batch transactions that may process more than 100,000 input records
    - Conversational interaction (two-way communication) with an end-user
- Memory intensive
  - In general, it is worth bringing the transaction to the attention of the DBA when the transaction contains large arrays or data fields that exceed the typical 4 kB size, such as an XML tag or column that is defined with a large data type, such as CLOB, BLOB, TEXT, NTEXT, and VARCHAR(MAX), or a large return set exceeding a gigabyte.

In order to provide the DBA the opportunity to perform their responsibilities, the DBA will need to become familiar with the significant transactions. As a result, the DBA will be looking to the development team to provide the following information for their significant transactions:

- Transaction name
  - A database transaction is considered the component that has the most pertinent information that a DBA can learn about to perform physical design.
- Maximum transactions per minute
  - Transaction rates are usually stated in transactions per minute or transactions per second.
- Maximum number of concurrent users
  - The overall resources that are required to allow a database management system (DBMS) to keep up with new requests are often determined by the amount of concurrent user activity.
- Lengthy calculation(s)
  - Some calculations can prolong the length of time that locks are maintained on database tables.
- Intersystem and intra-session communication
  - Communication across the transaction boundary creates an interdependency that can prolong the length of time that locks are maintained on database tables.
- Maximum number of SQL tables in a join
  - Table joins that exceed three tables can severely prolong the length of time that locks are maintained on database tables.
- Number of SQL statements
  - A large volume of SQL statements in a transaction can severely prolong the length of time that locks are maintained on database tables.

- Multiple commits within a transaction
  - Although uncommon within online transactions, the presence of multiple commits is a signal to the DBA to consult with the development team to learn more about the factors creating a need for multiple commits.
- Maximum number of cursor rows
  - A large number of cursor rows can severely increase the number of update locks in a relational DBMS and may also prolong the length of time that locks are maintained on database tables.
- Batch versus online
  - Batch and online transactions usually demonstrate a significantly different performance profile from one another.
- Number of batch input records
  - A large volume of input records can significantly increase the execution time of a batch transaction, thus requiring the DBA to become aware of the commits and restart recovery capabilities of the transaction.
- Two-way user communication
  - Online transactions that employ a conversational design approach to communications can lock resources for prolonged time periods, as compared to a pseudo-conversational design approach.
- CLOBs or BLOBs or TEXT or NTEXT or VARCHAR(MAX)
  - Data columns that support large data sizes are an indication of transactions that may prolong the length of time that locks are maintained on database tables by incurring waits for large storage requests.

A.1.2   TAPA 02 SQL DATA SERVICES

Application programs may contain a variety of database I/O requests. The database optimizer is the database component that receives the database I/O request. What is most important is that the way in which the database I/O request is structured can often have a profound impact upon the way that the optimizer interprets and processes the request.

> *For example, some database I/O requests for data may be structured as one large JOIN statement, or a statement with one or more statements embedded within it, or as multiple individual statements that follow after one another.*

Since many database I/O requests can exhibit unexpected results, or may adopt inefficient access strategies when accessing the data, it is important to pass your SQL statements to the DBA so that the structure of the I/O request as well as the structure of the database's physical design can be adjusted to eliminate performance problems and programming errors that are easy for someone intimately familiar with the database's physical design, and the particular DBMS's physical design options, to avoid.

By presenting the application's database I/O requirements to the DBA, the interaction allows the DBA to add value by sharing their knowledge of the particular DBMS, including alternatives involving the use of database built-in functions, the applicability of unions, the correct use of cursors, or the use of carefully chosen options within the syntax of the database I/O request.

Aside from having the DBA participate as a valued member of the software development team, the SQL Data Services Workbook allows the DBA to determine and ensure the necessary SLA for database performance. In order to provide the DBA the opportunity to perform their responsibilities, the DBA will need to become familiar with every database I/O request in the application requiring the following information:

- Transaction name
    - A transaction is considered the source of all database I/O requests, and hence the first piece of information to identify the DBA is the transaction making the database I/O request.
- Average # times invoked in transaction
    - Transactions that are infrequently invoked can also be responsible for frequently invoking one or more database I/O requests, such as I/O requests that are repeated in a loop.
- Purpose of SQL statement
    - Only after the intent of the database I/O request is made known to the DBA will the DBA be able to determine whether the actual request will support the needs of the developer, and it will also make it easier for the DBA to recommend an alternate structure for the database I/O request.
- SQL statement
    - Paste the SQL statement here for the DBA to review its structure and to determine how the optimizer might better support the request by potentially altering the structure of the database I/O request or by altering various aspects of the physical database design.
- Suggestions, questions, concerns
    - A working knowledge of an application's components can provide the developer with a perspective that the DBA may not have considered, or it may simply be an opportunity for the developer to pose a question or concern.

As information is provided by the developers, the following pieces of information can be documented by their DBA:

- DBA notes
    - The DBA can record notes, such as the determination that the particular SQL statement is simple or infrequently invoked, thereby not requiring further analysis.

- Alternate SQL
  - After analyzing the purpose of the I/O request, the DBA can propose an alternate SQL statement to address accuracy/performance issues.
- Indexing and other design considerations
  - A wide variety of physical design decisions can result from understanding an application's database I/O requirements, potentially leading the DBA to partition tables, resize table spaces, reallocate tables to table spaces, or alter the use of indices. However, the most common use for an application's I/O requests is to determine the cost benefit for denormalization.
- Status
  - A status can help organize SQL data services into useful groups that help communicate which database I/O requests are pending, in progress, or approved.

A.1.3   TAPA 03 Significant Transaction DB Table Use

The primary flow of business transactions and their underlying activities tend to demonstrate a natural progression and sequence of data and information recorded and retrieved.

For example, let us focus momentarily on a set of business transactions common to a retail outlet.

We begin the business process by placing an initial order, where we should record the new product information, including its description, wholesale and retail price, and the order that we placed for the product, including its order date, price, quantity, vendor, and vendor contact information. If this is our first transaction with this vendor, we will provide the vendor with our company credit card information, our shipping instructions, and our business sales tax id so that we will not be invoiced for sales tax on top of the product cost, and shipping and handling.

When the shipment arrives, the second activity in the sequence will be to record the delivery information, including its delivery date, delivered quantity, invoice amount, invoice number, as well as updating the product inventory.

The third activity may be to read the product information to generate a barcode product labels for each unit containing the product price and product identifier, and to record the fact that each unit was placed in the retail area for sale, as opposed to being allocated for consumption by the business operation.

The fourth activity occurs when customers purchase the product, which would cause the sale to be recorded and the product inventory to be updated.

In the abovementioned example, we have a total of four business transactions: (1) order product, (2) accept delivery, (3) put product out for sale, and (4) sell product.

In our bookkeeping, we have seven separate types of records to house the data related to these business transactions, which include a place to record: (1) product information, (2) a delivery, (3) inventory line item increases, (4) expenses, (5) a product line item sale, (6) receipts from a sale, and (7) inventory line item reductions.

If we look at our definition of "significant transactions," our transactions for ordering product, accepting delivery, and putting product out for sale are not high volume, complex, long running, or memory intensive. Our highest volume transaction is selling product, which places update locks on a product line item sale entry, a receipt from a sale, and an inventory line item reduction. As additional business transactions of the application are identified, we will be on the alert for any other "significant transactions" that share any of the same data, and whether they use an access sequence that opposes the sequence of this transaction.

In order to provide the DBA the opportunity to perform their responsibilities, the DBA will need to become familiar with the significant transactions in this and every application. As a result, the DBA will be looking to the development team to provide the following information for their significant transactions:

- Transaction name
  - A transaction is considered the source of all database I/O requests, and hence the first piece of information to identify to the DBA is the transaction making the database I/O request.
- Table name
  - Each table name that is acted upon by the transaction.
- Control record
  - A control record would include one or few rows that centrally manage information, such as an application maintained sequence number, that has the probability of creating a single point of contention.
- CRUD (C, R, U, D)
  - The database operation that the table participates in, representing Create, Read, Update, Delete, and Cursor Select.
- Execution sequence
  - A number indicating the order in which the tables are acted upon within the transaction.
- Average number of rows
  - The average number of rows that are affected by the database operation.

As information is provided by the developers, the following pieces of information can be documented by their DBA.

- Lock type (S, X, U)
  - Shared lock types result from selects; exclusive lock types result from updates, inserts, and deletes; and update lock types result from cursor selects from schemas/users with other than read-only access.

- Number of indices affected
    - Deadlock contention occurs most frequently within the data structures of indices, as opposed to occurring on rows of the underlying target tables, and the probability of a problem increases proportionally with an increase in the number of indices updated.
- Number of columns per index
    - The probability of an index being updated generally increases as the number of columns participating in the index increases.
- Direction
    - When the sequence of tables having locks placed on them coincides with the sequence those tables are being updated by other transactions, then the direction is in "agreement"; however, when the sequence of tables having locks placed on them conflicts with the sequence of prior transactions by opposing their sequence, then the direction is in "conflict."
- Conflicts with transaction name(s)
    - When conflicts in sequence have been identified, the name(s) of the transaction with which a conflict exists is recorded.

A.1.4   TAPA 04 Database Tables

Database tables represent a significant portion of what a DBA works with for the bulk of their planning and administration. Database tables determine database size, each having their own growth rate, retention period, purge frequency, and archival requirements, and they represent the focal point of the access strategy for the optimizer of the DBMS.

In order to provide the DBA the opportunity to perform their responsibilities, the DBA will need to become familiar with the various tables and indices of the database. As a result, the DBA will be looking to the development team to provide the following information:

- Table name
    - A table will be strategically located within a table space, isolated, or among other tables and indices, sized to manage the growth rate needed to support the online retention period.
- Average row length
    - The columns of a table will vary in size, and they will be populated to various degrees, called sparseness, which together will determine the average length for a row of data.
- Initial volume
    - The database may contain an initial set of data that may be loaded from another file, database, or by manual entry.

- Annual rate of growth
    - This estimates the net rate of growth at which additional data is added to the table. Tables that have the same amount of growth each year as the initial year have an annual rate of growth of 100%.
- Distribution of growth
    - Depending upon the values of the columns that get added as rows, their position within the prime key may be placed at the beginning, end, at hot spots, or evenly distributed within the index. The distribution and rate of growth will help the DBA determine the desired frequency of database reorganizations and the amount of free space necessary to promote good access behavior.
- Percent column expansion
    - Depending upon the degree to which NULL values will be populated in subsequent, the DBA will want to appreciate how much FREESPACE to allocate on the database pages to allow for expansion without causing splits and pointers to distant database pages.
- Online retention period
    - Availability requirements for data online will determine the retention period. Many databases hold their data indefinitely, although they may only have a business requirement that spans a specified number of years for historical and analytical purposes. Please note that online data retention should not be confused with archival requirements, which are governed by more than regulatory requirements (see "Archival requirements" below).
- Purge frequency
    - Depending upon the rate at which data is accumulated for archival, data from the online database may be offloaded and purged at a higher or lower frequency.
- Archival requirements
    - Once data is offloaded and purged from online storage, archives can be retained both internally and externally for various periods of time. The determination of archival requirements, however, does not stem solely from laws and regulations, as senior management needs to determine how best to deal with lawsuits and discovery requests.

Hence, when considering laws such as Sarbanes-Oxley, which specifies, in section 103, that firms retain records relevant to audit and financial review for 7 years, and the Securities and Exchange Commission, which specifies, in SEC rule 17a-4, that records pertaining to certain parties be retained for specified periods of time, the most valuable criteria overall to consider may be the statute of limitations for various legal actions that the company may need to protect itself from.

The issues are:

- Laws and regulations
- Lawsuits and discovery requests

- Ability to access and support the necessary search capabilities
- Data security of both data archived in-house and externally
- Balancing the cost to the business of both providing and not providing various search capabilities for performing discovery
- Encryption
  - The implementation of encryption is such that it should be limited in use to database columns that are considered to be moderately sensitive or higher (see Section A.1.4.2).
- Number of indices
  - Tables should have a minimum of one index which would be associated with the primary key columns; however, a number of additional indices may provide a worthwhile benefit to read performance at the expense of update and insert performance.
- Index key size(s)
  - Each index is built upon one or more columns, each having an average length. In order to calculate the variable portion of the space needed to support each index, the average length of the columns that comprise an index must be added together. The average length of columns that are in multiple indices must be included in the size for each index they participate in.
- Triggers/stored procedures
  - As an alert to the DBA, if there is an expectation that application components will be developed as either a trigger or a stored procedure, then the DBA can prepare for compiling their source code.

As information is provided by the developers, the following pieces of information can be documented by their DBA:

- Projected number of gigabytes required
  - The DBA can calculate the sum of the space needed for any initial data, one year's growth for tables and indices, free space, and an initial margin of 30%.
- Originating versus passed
  - The DBA can document whether the data in this table originates in this database, or is passed from another database, or contains data that both originates in this database as well as data that is passed from another database.
- Data quality
  - See Section A.1.4.1.
- Data sensitivity
  - See Section A.1.4.2.
- Status
  - The DBA can designate the status of this table's analysis as pending, in progress, or approved.

A.1.4.1 Data Quality

Data quality is ultimately a rating that communicates the level of which one can reasonably rely upon the accuracy of each data field within that database. The process of assigning a data quality level of a data field should be limited to database fields that originate at the database, as nonoriginating fields should have their respective data quality rating established at their point of origin. The levels of data quality assigned a field should be defined in business terms addressing how sparsely populated the data is when a value can exist, and how accurate the data values are when they are populated:

High data quality should be assigned to fields that are fully populated with a non-null value on each and every row of data, and whose values are considered to be completely accurate and fully reliable. These are typically required fields with comprehensive edits to ensure reliability.

Moderate data quality should be assigned to fields that are populated a majority (90%) of the time when a value was known, and whose values are considered to have a majority of accurate (90%) data and may hence be considered to be reasonably reliable. These are typically nonrequired fields usually populated when their value was known, having edits that minimally guarantee format. To ensure against the possibility that the value contained within these fields has not been systematically populated with inaccurate data of the correct format, one or more statistical analyses may be performed.

No data quality should be assigned to fields that are either sparely populated with a value, or when populated with a value the accuracy is not reasonably reliable in either value or format. These are typically nonrequired fields with no edits to ensure reliability or correct data format.

This initiative should begin by analyzing the (a) root causes of the various data qualities, (b) extent of data quality issues within various databases, and (c) identification of procedural and organizational approaches for addressing data quality, so that the requirements and planning for addressing our data quality needs may be determined.

The assignment of database data quality should begin with those databases that originate the majority of their data so that downstream databases can benefit by inheriting the data quality associated with those fields that are passed on down to them.

A.1.4.2 Data Sensitivity

Data sensitivity should be assigned to a database, as derived by identifying the data field(s) with the highest sensitivity within that database. The process of assigning a data sensitivity level of a data field should be limited to database fields that originate at the database, as nonoriginating fields should have their respective sensitivity rating established at their point of origin. The levels of data sensitivity assigned a field should be defined in business terms:

Highest level of sensitivity assigned to fields that should only be disclosed on a strict need to know basis within the enterprise in that disclosure to nonauthorized individuals poses a legal and/or financial risk to the enterprise, including anything that can be used to adversely affect its credit rating or stock price, or severely diminish any aspect of the public's perception of the enterprise, the value of the enterprise, or its ability to secure private information.

Moderate level of sensitivity should only be disclosed on a need to know basis within the enterprise in that disclosure to nonauthorized individuals may pose a near certain competitive risk to the enterprise if the data fell into the hands of a competitor, including anything that can be used to moderately diminish any aspect of the public's perception of the enterprise, the value of the enterprise, or its ability to secure private information.

Low level of sensitivity should be disclosed to a limited set of individuals that have been trusted to work with particular sets of data in that disclosure to nonauthorized individuals may pose some level of competitive risk to the enterprise if the data fell into the hands of a competitor, including anything that can be used to slightly diminish any aspect of the public's perception of the enterprise, the value of the enterprise, or its ability to secure private information.

Nonsensitive data, usually limited to externally acquired data, should be disclosed to a limited set of individuals that have been trusted to work with particular sets of data in that disclosure to nonauthorized individuals would not be usable to determine anything about the enterprise, or its practices.

The assignment of database data sensitivity should begin with those databases that originate the majority of their data so that downstream databases can benefit by inheriting the data sensitivities associated with those fields that are passed on down to them.

A.1.5 TAPA 05 DATABASE USER AVAILABILITY

At a high level, the profile of database availability is useful to help determine which databases can coexist from an availability perspective, which will facilitate system maintenance to the server and the various components within its configuration.

At a more detailed level, database user availability communicates to the DBA when they will be able to schedule database maintenance, including regular maintenance, such as database backups and reorganizations, as well as any extraordinary maintenance, such as design changes or the application of database software patches.

Hence, in order to provide the DBA the opportunity to perform their responsibilities, the DBA will need to know the availability profile of the online business users and business batch processing. As such, the following information needs to be provided:

- Time of day/day of week availability
    - Two fields exist for each 1-hour time period of the day, where the application's availability for online and batch processing can be recorded.
- User business holidays
    - The commonly observed business holidays for the business users need to be recorded for both domestic and international users.

As an example, if Thanksgiving is observed in the USA, but not observed among international users, then the system should be available for international users on Thanksgiving Day.

A.1.6 TAPA 06 DATABASE PROCESSING VOLUME PROFILE

The profile of database processing volume is useful to help determine which databases can coexist from the perspective of system resources. If the sum of the processing volume profiles of various databases remains within acceptable levels across the entire time period, then they can coexist. If, however, peak processing volume periods coincide with one another, then the maximum capacity of the server may be exceeded, rendering those databases incompatible with one another.

In order to provide the DBA the opportunity to safely determine database compatibility, the DBA will need to know the processing volume of online business users and batch processes. As such, the following information needs to be provided:

- Daily transaction volume profile by hour
    - The most useful estimate of transaction volume is simply to designate the magnitude of the volume by each hour, as opposed to an exact number. A single-digit number representing the range of volume will make it easy for the DBA to work with. As the TAPA diagram indicates, the volume will be represented as a range of up to 10, up to 100, up to 1000, and so on, where the only number that needs to be captured is the number of trailing zeros. Hence, the selection for "up to 10,000," or using scientific notation $= 1 \times 10^4$, is simply the number "4," which is just the exponent on the 10.
- Monthly transaction volume profile by week

The primary use of this volume profile is to communicate cyclical peak processing periods that occur during particular times of the year, as would be the situation for quarterly reporting or year-end processing. Applications that do not have cyclical peak processing periods will assume a consistent value each week of each month, which is equivalent to the sum of the volume for the week.

A.1.7   TAPA 07 Database Performance SLA

The service-level agreement (SLA) for database response time is useful to help determine the physical design objectives of the database and the corresponding hardware configuration needed to support the application. It is important to note that the majority of transaction response time is often determined by transaction design and the total amount of time that transactions spend in performing their non-database activities. Even though this may be the situation, the importance of estimating the database portion of a transaction's overall response time cannot be overstated.

At the most technical level, every random and every sequential access to the database is determined by the specifications of the hardware components that participate in servicing each I/O request. When accuracy is absolutely critical for an application, a DBA will determine the number of random and sequential I/Os for each transaction type, and referencing the manufacturer's specifications for the device, and then total up the milliseconds to determine the response time.

When the actual response time varies unexpectedly from the projected response time, it is almost always due to expected behavior within either the application transaction or the number and type of I/Os that the DBMS is performing. Using the proper performance analysis tools, a DBA can readily determine the source of the unexpected result.

In order for the DBA to focus their attention appropriately, the following information needs to be provided:

- Geographic locations of users
  - Locations may be identified in terms of whatever is most useful to describe where the users are located. This can be an address housing company offices, a city, state, country, or even continent. Communicating the location is still important even if the application is Internet based, as many countries and regions have various degrees of Internet infrastructure in place. The geographic variety of the users can also help explain an application's availability profile to the DBA.
- Communications
  - The application may be communicating through the Internet, Intranet, or the company network. Depending upon the communication mechanism and the location of the application, the database should be located within the zone that affords the appropriate level of firewall protection.
- Number of users per location
  - The SLA for various geographic regions will likely differ from another, and the number of users can determine the relative priority that performance tuning should be assigned.

- Number of concurrent users per location
  - The number of concurrent users can have a significant impact upon the performance profile of the database server, and testing should incorporate as many of the real world constraints as is reasonably required to support Production.
- Maximum acceptable average response time in seconds
  - It is important that the SLA stated for the maximum acceptable average response time be realistic for two reasons.

    First, the maximum acceptable average response is not the same as the ideal response time desired; otherwise, it would be called that. It is intended to communicate what the users realistically can tolerate as a maximum average response time in order to conduct their business activities without causing harm to the users' ability to actually conduct business.

    Second, unnecessarily identifying a more stringent SLA will unnecessarily increase the demand upon the limited resources of the company, thereby causing expenses to escalate. If, however, performance is critical to the business function, such as with certain program trading systems, then a more stringent SLA would be appropriate.
- Application environment
  - Applications are most frequently based on one or more application servers, which may support connectivity with "end-users" through an Internet, an Intranet, or a company network. When application servers are involved, database performance analysis can focus upon the requests received directly from the application server.
  - Applications that run local on the user's workstation are far less common, as they are more expensive to maintain than application server-based environments.
  - Applications that are colocated on the database server are the least common type of application environment, as they are usually not permissible because they pose the greatest degree of risk to the database and everything that is dependent upon the database server.

    In contrast, it is far more convenient for an application server to fail, while the database rapidly recovers from any in-flight updates from the failed application server, remaining available for the return of the application server. When a database server fails, the overall recovery process for the databases supported by the particular server is far more complex and far more time consuming.

    When applications are permitted to run on a database server, the company's support expenses are usually higher due to the fact that the environment is typically dedicated exclusively to the application in order to avoid introducing unnecessary risk to other systems.

A.1.8 TAPA 08 DATABASE INSTANCES

Database instance information provides an opportunity to identify additional requirements of the production database as well as the application team's development process.

In order for the DBA to focus their attention appropriately, the following information needs to be provided:

- DBMS
  - Although the choice of DBMS is determined by EDM in accordance with the EDM Database Strategy, the application development team is afforded the opportunity to communicate their preference. If there is sufficient justification, such as a major business or technical requirement for features that would otherwise be unavailable, then the project team may wish to request a variance.

    There are multiple economic and technical demands that motivate the enterprise to standardize the use of DBMS platforms to DB2 and SQL Server, which both strictly adhere to the ANSI standard. Developers having a preference or familiarity with one brand over another would not be able to use that to provide sufficient justification to vary from the EDM Database Strategy. Since all relational databases use SQL, developers that need to know SQL should not be hindered with the deployment of one brand over another.

    To name two examples, most developers are unaware of the fact that Oracle does not comply with the ANSI standards, and both developers and DBAs are often completely unaware of the resulting technical, financial, and business implications.

- DBMS version
  - The choice of version is also determined by EDM in accordance with EDM Standards. In general, the version to be deployed is the highest version that EDM has validated as being stable and reliable. Newer versions may sometimes be requested by a development team usually to take advantage of a new or enhanced feature only available in the newer version, and depending upon the business and/or technical requirements, EDM may grant a variance to allow the use of DBMS software that data engineering has not yet verified as production ready.

- Backup window
  - The backup window refers to a standard start and end time each day that database can be successfully backed up by momentarily preventing business activity.

- Environment and relative database sizing in gigabytes
  - The standard number of database environments for supporting the entire SDLC is generally five, usually consisting of a Unit Test, Integration Test,

User Acceptance Test, Production, and Production Maintenance environment. Since the names and uses of some of these environments may vary, the names can be changed.

- The relative size of each database environment is identified to allow varying database sizes, such as a much smaller unit test environment, or a much larger integration test environment for testing higher than expected system capacity.
- Applications requiring access and access type
  - Certain databases will contain data that may meet the informational needs of more than a single application. As they become known, these applications should be identified along with the type of access (i.e., update or read-only) they require.
- Database use
  - The possible uses for the database are OLTP/transactional, operational data store (ODS)/operational data store, OLAP/multidimensional, DW/data warehouse, or a combination of purposes. When the database captures data that originates here, then it is a transactional database (OLTP). If it captures a subset of data from across multiple other databases, then it is an ODS. If it calculates aggregates of data from detail data, then it is a multidimensional database (OLAP). If it generally consolidates all detail data from across many databases, then it is a data warehouse (DW). If it does some combination of the above, then it is a combination of database types.
- Inter-database dependencies
  - Rather than replicating data that is not entirely stable in multiple locations, databases will occasionally provide views of data that is managed centrally in another database. This dependency may extend to or from other databases.
- Production failover and hot backup requirements
  - Business critical applications need to identify their requirements for recovery.
- Firewall requirements
  - Database servers must be accessible from the various ports supporting communications, and hence, it is important to note where the various interfacing applications and databases reside within our security architecture.
- Security requirements
  - Databases can vary substantially in their security requirements, such as requiring access to encryption key files on other servers when using data encryption.
- Comments
  - Additional notes or comments may be pertinent to the database instance, particularly when advanced business intelligence and analysis capabilities need to be incorporated into the database environment as add-ons.

▌ A.2   Bibliography

[1]This is an architectural style that divides a larger processing task into a sequence of smaller, independent processing steps, referred to as "filters," which are connected by channels, referred to as "pipes." Each filter exposes a very simple interface receiving inbound messages from an inbound pipe, then processes the data, and then generates a message on an outbound pipe. The pipe connects one filter to the next, until the processing is complete.

There are a number of architectural subpatterns based on pipeline patterns, such as the aggregator subpattern, which is a special filter that receives a stream of messages and correlates the ones that are related, aggregates information from them, and generates an outbound message with the aggregated information. In contrast, a splitter subpattern is a special filter that separates messages into subsets that can be routed to distinct outbound pipes.

---

[1]For a more complete list of messaging patterns and subpatterns of architectural subtypes, refer to *Enterprise Integration Patterns: Designing, Building, and Deploying Messaging Solutions* by Gregor Hohpe and Bobby Woolf, 2004, published by Addison-Wesley, ISBN: 0-321-20068-3.

Index

Note: Page numbers followed by *f* indicate figures.